Lecture Notes in Computer Science 6647

Commenced Publication in 1973
Founding and Former Series Editors:
Gerhard Goos, Juris Hartmanis, and Jan van Leeuwen

Jurriaan Hage   Marco T. Morazán (Eds.)

Implementation and Application of Functional Languages

22nd International Symposium, IFL 2010
Alphen aan den Rijn, The Netherlands
September 1-3, 2010
Revised Selected Papers

 Springer

Volume Editors

Jurriaan Hage
Utrecht University
Department of Information and Computing Sciences
3584 CC Utrecht, The Netherlands
E-mail: jur@cs.uu.nl

Marco T. Morazán
Seton Hall University
Department of Mathematics and Computer Science
South Orange, NJ 07079, USA
E-mail: marco.morazan@shu.edu

ISSN 0302-9743   e-ISSN 1611-3349
ISBN 978-3-642-24275-5   e-ISBN 978-3-642-24276-2
DOI 10.1007/978-3-642-24276-2

Springer Heidelberg Dordrecht London New York

Library of Congress Control Number: 2011936540

CR Subject Classification (1998): F.3, D.3, D.2, F.4.1, D.1, D.2.4

LNCS Sublibrary: SL 1 – Theoretical Computer Science and General Issues

Typesetting: Camera-ready by author, data conversion by Scientific Publishing Services, Chennai, India

Printed on acid-free paper

Springer is part of Springer Science+Business Media (www.springer.com)

Preface

This volume contains the selected peer-reviewed revised articles that were presented at the 22nd International Symposium on Implementation and Application of Functional Languages (IFL 2010). IFL 2010 was held September 1–3, 2010 at Avifauna in Alphen aan den Rijn, The Netherlands. It was hosted by the Software Technology group of Utrecht University.

The IFL symposia bring together researchers and practitioners that are actively engaged in the implementation and the use of functional and function-based programming languages. This year, IFL was attended by 65 participants from Belgium, Bolivia, Brazil, Denmark, Estonia, France, Germany, Greece, Hungary, The Netherlands, Poland, Spain, Sweden, the UK, and the USA. Every year IFL provides a venue for the presentation and discussion of new ideas and concepts, of work in progress, and of publication-ripe results. Participants are invited to submit either a draft paper or an extended abstract describing work to be presented at the symposium. These submissions are screened by the Program Committee Chair to make sure they are within the scope of IFL. The submissions accepted for presentation appear in the *draft* proceedings distributed at the symposium. IFL 2010 featured a total of 39 submitted presentations.

Submissions appearing in the draft proceedings are not peer-reviewed publications. After the symposium, authors were given the opportunity to consider the feedback received from discussions at the symposium and were invited to submit full revised articles to the formal review process. In total, 31 full papers were submitted. The revised submissions were reviewed by the Program Committee using prevailing academic standards (four reviews per paper) and after plenty of discussion, 13 submissions were chosen to appear in the formal proceedings that are contained in this volume.

Johan Nordlander was the IFL 2010 guest speaker from Luleå University. He is the main designer and developer of the Timber language. In his talk he discussed the craft of building applications with Timber, a programming language that claims to be purely functional, classically object-oriented and inherently concurrent at the same time, while also fostering a purely reactive model of interaction that naturally lets its real-time behavior be controlled by declaration.

Following the IFL tradition, IFL 2010 provided participants with an opportunity to get to know each other and to talk outside the formal setting of presentations with a social event on the second day of the symposium. Participants traveled to the city of Utrecht to visit the Dom tower and the Speelklokkenmuseum. The latter is a museum that displays a large range of old programmable musical instruments. After this visit, we returned to Alphen aan den Rijn and embarked for a boat trip over the Dutch lakes. The sun setting over the lakes was one of the high points of IFL 2010.

Shortly before the previous edition of IFL, Peter J. Landin passed away. IFL has honored Peter since 2003 by awarding each year the *Peter J. Landin Award* to the best article presented at the symposium. The recipients of the award for IFL 2010 were George Giorgidze, Torsten Grust, Tom Schreiber, and Jeroen Weijers from the Eberhard Karls Universität Tübingen in Germany for their contribution entitled "Haskell Boards the Ferry: Database-Supported Program Execution for Haskell."

Many people contributed to the success of IFL 2010. A debt of gratitude for addressing every need that came up during the symposium is owed to Sean Leather, José Pedro Magalhães, and Jan Rochel. From the Department of Information and Computing Sciences, we are grateful for the help provided by Doaitse Swierstra, Wilke Schram, Marinus Veldhorst, Edith Stap, Frans Wiering, Geraldine Leebeek, Martijn Dekker, and Corine Jolles. We were fortunate to use the portal of the UU Summer Schools for registration; we thank in particular Marc Gebuis and Roos Nieuwenhuizen for their continuing support. The people at Avifauna, in particular Marit van der Louw, Suzanne Oldenburg, and Victor Galjé, helped us with the local planning. We thank the people at Springer for their willingness to answer questions regarding the construction of this volume. We thank all the members of the Program Committee for their advice, time, and thoughtful reviews. Finally, we thank the authors for submitting their articles and trusting that we would do our best to positively showcase their work.

IFL 2010 was made possible by the generous support provided by Microsoft Research, Cambridge, the Department of Information and Computing Sciences of Utrecht University, and the Koninklijke Nederlandse Academie van Wetenschappen (KNAW).

In closing, we hope that the readers of this volume will find its contents engaging and inspire them to start or continue their work on the implementation and the use of functional languages. Make sure to join us at a future version of IFL!

June 2011   Jurriaan Hage
                                                        Marco T. Morazán

Organization

Program Committee

Jost Berthold	University of Copenhagen, Denmark
Olaf Chitil	University of Kent, UK
John Clements	California Polytechnic State University, USA
Matthew Fluet	Rochester Institute of Technology, USA
Andy Gill	Kansas University, USA
Jurriaan Hage (Chair)	University of Utrecht, The Netherlands
Bastiaan Heeren	Open University of The Netherlands, The Netherlands
Ralf Hinze	University of Oxford, UK
John Hughes	Chalmers University of Technology, Sweden
Yukiyoshi Kameyama	University of Tsukuba, Japan
Gabriele Keller	University of New South Wales, Australia
Pieter Koopman	Radboud University Nijmegen, The Netherlands
Luc Maranget	INRIA, France
Simon Marlow	Microsoft Research, UK
Marco T. Morazán	Seton Hall University, USA
Rex Page	University of Oklahoma, USA
Ricardo Peña	Universidad Complutense de Madrid, Spain
Sven-Bodo Scholz	University of Hertfordshire, UK
Tom Schrijvers	Catholic University of Leuven, Belgium
Don Stewart	Galois, USA
Wouter Swierstra	Vector Fabrics, The Netherlands
Don Syme	Microsoft, UK
Peter Thiemann	University of Freiburg, Germany
Phil Trinder	Heriott-Watt University, UK
Janis Voigtländer	University of Bonn, Germany
Viktória Zsók	Eötvös Loránd University, Hungary

Additional Reviewers

Sebastian Fischer	Manuel Montenegro	Yolanda Ortega-Mallén
Thomas Harper	Matt Naylor	Frank Penczek
Graham Hutton	Lasse R.H. Nielsen	Fernando Rubio
Daniel James	Susumu Nishimura	David Sabel
Wolfgang Jeltsch	Thomas van Noort	Olha Shkaravska
Manfred Minimair	Atsushi Ohori	

Local Organizing Committee

Jurriaan Hage (Chair)
Sean Leather
José Pedro Magalhães
Jan Rochel

Sponsoring Institutions

Microsoft Research, Cambridge, UK
Koninklijke Nederlandse Academie van Wetenschappen (KNAW),
    The Netherlands
Department of Information and Computing Sciences, Utrecht University,
    The Netherlands

Table of Contents

Haskell Boards the Ferry
Database-Supported Program Execution for Haskell

George Giorgidze, Torsten Grust, Tom Schreiber, and Jeroen Weijers

Wilhelm-Schickard-Institut für Informatik,
Eberhard Karls Universität Tübingen
{george.giorgidze,torsten.grust,
tom.schreiber,jeroen.weijers}@uni-tuebingen.de

Abstract. Relational database management systems can be used as a *coprocessor* for general-purpose programming languages, especially for those program fragments that carry out *data-intensive* and *data-parallel* computations. In this paper we present a Haskell library for database-supported program execution. Data-intensive and data-parallel computations are expressed using familiar combinators from the standard list prelude and are entirely executed on the database coprocessor. Programming with the expressive list comprehension notation is also supported. The library, in addition to queries of basic types, supports computations over arbitrarily nested tuples and lists. The implementation avoids unnecessary data transfer and context switching between the database coprocessor and the programming language runtime by ensuring that the number of generated relational queries is only determined by the program fragment's type and not by the database size.

1 Introduction

Relational database management systems (RDBMSs) provide well-understood and carefully engineered query processing capabilities. However, RDBMSs are often operated as plain stores that do little more than reproduce stored data items for further processing outside the database host, in the general-purpose programming language heap. One reason for this is that the query processing capabilities of RDBMSs require mastering of advanced features of specialised query languages, such as SQL, in addition to the general-purpose language the application is programmed in. Moreover, query languages are often inadequately integrated into host programming languages.

An application that is programmed in the aforementioned manner may perform substantial data transfers even when the final result of the computation is very small. Instead, it may be much more efficient (and sometimes the only option when dealing with data that can not be fitted in the heap) to transfer a part of the program to the database and then let the database perform the computation. Database kernels are optimised for intra-query parallel execution and can thus very efficiently carry out *data-intensive* and *data-parallel* computations.

J. Hage, M.T. Morazán (Eds.): IFL 2010, LNCS 6647, pp. 1–18, 2011.
© Springer-Verlag Berlin Heidelberg 2011

A number of approaches have been proposed providing for better integration of database query languages into programming languages. Well-known examples include: Kleisli [18], LINQ [21] and Links [8]. Although very successful (e.g., LINQ is distributed with the Microsoft .NET framework and is widely adopted), current language-integrated approaches have a number of limitations. For example, Links only permits the database-supported execution of program fragments that compute a flat result (i.e., a list of tuples of basic types), while Kleisli and LINQ support data nesting but may compile the fragment into queries whose number is proportional to the size of the queried data (i.e., they do not possess the so-called *avalanche-safety* property). In addition, LINQ's standard query operators do not maintain list order and thus may fail to preserve the host programming language's semantics.

Recently, in order to solve the aforementioned problems with the current language-integrated approaches, and more generally, to investigate to what extent one can push the idea of RDBMSs that directly and seamlessly participate in program evaluation, the Ferry language has been proposed [12]. Ferry is a functional programming language that is designed to be entirely executed on RDBMSs. So far, the most notable feature of Ferry has been its compilation technique that supports database execution of programs of nested types, maintains list order and provides avalanche-safety guarantees [13].

Although the Haskell programming language [23] has inspired a number of language-integrated query facilities (most notably LINQ which is based on monad comprehensions) so far no such system has been proposed or implemented for Haskell. With *Database-Supported Haskell* (DSH) we provide a library that executes parts of a Haskell program on an RDBMS. The library is available online [2]. The design and implementation of the library is influenced by Ferry and it can be considered as a Haskell-embedded implementation of Ferry.

The library is based on Haskell's list comprehensions and the underlying list-processing combinators and provides a convenient query integration into the host language. The library, just like the Ferry language, in addition to queries of basic types, supports computations over arbitrarily nested tuples and lists. The implementation minimises unnecessary data transfer and context switching between the database *coprocessor* and the programming language runtime. Specifically, in DSH, the number of queries is only dependent on the number of list type constructors in the result type of the computation and does not depend on the size of the queried data.

Our contribution with this paper is the first proposal and implementation of a library for database-supported program execution in Haskell.

2   DSH by Example

Consider the database table facilities in Figure 1 which lists a sample of contemporary facilities (query languages, APIs, *etc.*) that are used to query database-resident data. We have attempted to categorise these facilities (see column cat of table facilities): query language (QLA), library (LIB), application programming interface (`API`), host language integration (`LIN`), and object-relational mapping (`ORM`). Furthermore, each of these facilities has particular features (table features). A verbose description of these features is given by the table meanings.

facilities

fac	cat
SQL	QLA
ODBC	API
LINQ	LIN
Links	LIN
Rails	ORM
DSH	LIB
ADO.NET	ORM
Kleisli	QLA
HaskellDB	LIB

features

fac	feature
SQL	aval
SQL	type
SQL	SQL!
LINQ	nest
LINQ	comp
LINQ	type
Links	comp
Links	type
Links	SQL!
Rails	nest
Rails	maps
DSH	list
DSH	nest
DSH	comp
DSH	aval
DSH	type
DSH	SQL!
ADO.NET	maps
ADO.NET	comp
ADO.NET	type
Kleisli	list
Kleisli	nest
Kleisli	comp
Kleisli	type
HaskellDB	comp
HaskellDB	type
HaskellDB	SQL!

meanings

feature	meaning
list	respects list order
nest	supports data nesting
aval	avoids query avalanches
type	is statically type-checked
SQL!	guarantees translation to SQL
maps	admits user-defined object mappings
comp	has compositional syntax and semantics

Fig. 1. Database-resident input tables for example program

Given this base data, an interesting question would be: what are the features characteristic for the various query facility categories (column `cat`) introduced above? Interpreting a table as a list of tuples, this question can be answered with the following list-based Haskell program:

$$descrFacility :: String \rightarrow [String]$$
$$descrFacility\ f = [\,mean \mid (feat, mean) \leftarrow meanings,$$
$$(fac, feat') \quad \leftarrow features,$$
$$feat \equiv feat' \wedge fac \equiv f\,]$$
$$query :: [(String, [String])]$$
$$query = [\,(the\ cat, nub\ (concatMap\ descrFacility\ fac))$$
$$\mid (fac, cat) \leftarrow facilities, \mathbf{then}\ group\ by\ cat\,]$$

The program consists of the actual query and the helper function *descrFacility*. Function *descrFacility*, given a query facility f, returns a list of descriptions of its features. We deliberately use a combination of list comprehension notation and list-processing combinators in this example program to demonstrate the breadth of DSH. Evaluating this program results in a nested list like:

```
[("API",[]),
 ("LIB",["respects list order",...]),
```

```
("LIN",["supports data nesting",...]),
("ORM",["supports data nesting",...]),
("QLA",["avoids query avalanches",...])]
```

As the example program processes database-resident data, it would be most efficient to perform the computation close to the data and let the database query engine itself execute the program. With DSH, this is exactly what we propose and provide. The program is translated into two SQL queries (see Appendix). These queries fully represent the program and can be completely executed on the database.

In order to execute the program on the database we have to apply a few modest changes to the example program. These changes turn the program into a DSH program. We will discuss these changes in the remainder of this section. The adapted program will be our running example in the remainder of this paper.

First, consider the function *descrFacility*. There are three modest changes to this function related to its type signature, the comprehension notation and a new combinator named *table*. The new function looks as follows:

$$descrFacility :: Q\ String \to Q\ [String]$$
$$descrFacility\ f = [\,qc \mid mean \mid (feat, mean) \leftarrow table\ \texttt{"meanings"},$$
$$(fac, feat') \quad \leftarrow table\ \texttt{"features"},$$
$$feat \equiv feat' \wedge fac \equiv f\,|]$$

The slight change of the list comprehension syntax is due to *quasi-quotes* [19], namely $[\,qc \mid$ and $|]$. Otherwise, the syntax and semantics of quasiquoted comprehensions match those of regular Haskell list comprehensions with the only exception that, instead of having type $[a]$, a quasiquoted comprehension has type $Q\ [a]$ (to be read as "*a query that returns a value of type* $[a]$"). This explains the change in the type signature of function *descrFacility*. The last change that has to be made is to direct the program to use database-resident data instead of heap data. This is achieved by using the *table* combinator that introduces the name of the queried table.

Finally, let us consider the main function, *query*. With DSH, we support most of the Haskell list prelude functions, modified to work with queries that return lists. Once the changes are applied, the code looks as follows:

$$query :: IO\ [(String, [String])]$$
$$query = fromQ\ connection$$
$$[\,qc \mid (the\ cat, nub\ (concatMap\ descrFacility\ fac))$$
$$\mid (cat, fac) \leftarrow table\ \texttt{"facilities"}, \textbf{then}\ group\ by\ cat\,|]$$

The list comprehension in this function is adapted as in the *descrFacility* function. Function *fromQ*, when provided with a connection parameter, executes its query argument on the database and returns the result as a regular Haskell value. This value is wrapped inside the *IO* monad as database updates may alter the queried data between two invocations of *fromQ* (i.e., this is not a referentially transparent computation).

The following section describes how DSH programs are compiled and executed by effectively using RDBMSs as coprocessors supporting the Haskell runtime.

3   Internals

The execution model of DSH is presented in Figure 2. By using the quasi-quoter that implements the well-known desugaring approach [16], list comprehensions are translated into list-processing combinators at Haskell compile-time (①, Figure 2). With a translation technique coined *loop-lifting* [13], these list-processing combinators are compiled into an intermediate representation called *table algebra*, a simple variant of relational algebra (②, Figure 2). Through Pathfinder [10, 11], a table algebra optimiser and code generation facility, the intermediate representation is optimised and compiled into relational queries (③, Figure 2). Pathfinder supports a number of relational back-end languages (e.g., SQL:1999 and the MonetDB Interpreter Language (MIL) [5]). The resulting relational queries can then be executed on off-the-shelf relational database systems (④, Figure 2). The tabular query results are transferred back into the heap and then transformed into vanilla Haskell values (⑤ and ⑥, Figure 2). In the remainder of this section we describe the aforementioned steps in further detail.

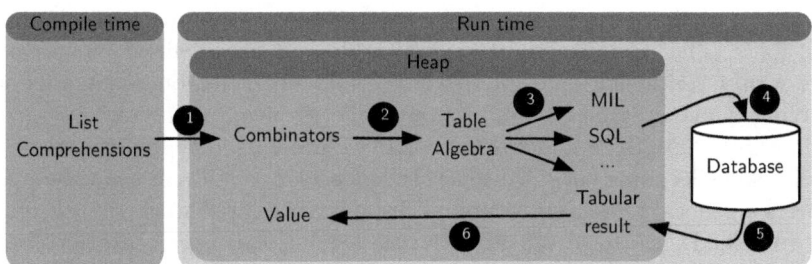

Fig. 2. Code Motion in DSH

3.1   Haskell Front-End

The following provides an incomplete lineup of the supported Haskell list combinators along with their types:

$$
\begin{aligned}
map &:: (QA\ a, QA\ b) & \Rightarrow (Q\ a \to Q\ b) \to Q\ [a] \to Q\ [b] \\
filter &:: (QA\ a) & \Rightarrow (Q\ a \to Q\ Bool) \to Q\ [a] \to Q\ [a] \\
concat &:: (QA\ a) & \Rightarrow Q\ [[a]] \to Q\ [a] \\
groupWith &:: (Ord\ b, QA\ a, QA\ b) & \Rightarrow (Q\ a \to Q\ b) \to Q\ [a] \to Q\ [[a]] \\
sortWith &:: (Ord\ b, QA\ a, QA\ b) & \Rightarrow (Q\ a \to Q\ b) \to Q\ [a] \to Q\ [a] \\
the &:: (Eq\ a, QA\ a) & \Rightarrow Q\ [a] \to Q\ a \\
nub &:: (Eq\ a, QA\ a) & \Rightarrow Q\ [a] \to Q\ [a] \\
table &:: (TA\ a) & \Rightarrow String \to Q\ [a]
\end{aligned}
$$

These combinators behave as their namesakes in the Haskell list prelude, but instead of operating on regular lists and values they work on *queryable lists and values*. This is reflected in their type signatures. It is easy to arrive at the type signature of a DSH combinator starting from the type signature of its namesake in the Haskell list prelude: (1) the Q type constructor needs to be applied to all types except function types, and (2) the QA type class constraint (read: *queryable*) needs to be applied to all type variables in the signature.

In order to restrict the combinators to only work with the data types that we are able to represent relationally, the QA type class is used:

class QA a **where**
    toQ $:: a \rightarrow Q$ a
    $fromQ :: Connection \rightarrow Q$ $a \rightarrow IO$ a

DSH provides QA instances for the basic types (i.e., Boolean, character, integer, real, text, date and time types), as well as arbitrarily nested lists and tuples of these basic types. In addition, by leveraging metaprogramming capabilities of Template Haskell [25], we provide for automatic derivation of QA instances for *any* user-defined product type (including Haskell records) and automatic generation of Haskell records from database schemas. The relational representation of the supported Haskell types is given in Section 3.2.

The current implementation of DSH does not support general folds (e.g., *foldr* and *foldl*). All other functions from the list prelude are supported, including the special folds. The compilation of general folds and user-defined recursive definitions would yield relational queries that build on recursion constructs of the underlying query language (e.g., recursive queries using common table expressions in SQL:1999). This is something that we are currently investigating.

DSH also lacks sum types. However, this is easier to address than the missing support for general folds and recursion. In fact, in related work (which remains to be published), we have already devised a relational representation for sum types and compilation rules for functions on sum types. The aforementioned related work addresses the shortcomings of Links that are outlined in Section 1 by leveraging and extending the compilation technology developed for the Ferry language.

The QA type class provides functions to convert Haskell values into queries (i.e, the toQ function) and vice versa ($fromQ$). The latter function triggers the compilation of queries, communicates with the database, submits the generated relational queries to the database, fetches the results and converts them into Haskell values. These values can be used in the program for further in-heap processing as well as for the generation of new database-executable program fragments. Thus, DSH supports iterative staging of embedded programs [9, 20] by allowing for runtime code generation, compilation, and execution of database-executable programs.

The combinator *table* deserves special attention. As can be seen in the lineup of combinators, its type features a type class constraint TA a. The constraint restricts the type variable a, which represents the table rows, to the basic types and flat tuples of the basic types. Use of the *table* combinator does not result in I/O, as it does not initiate communication with the database: it just references the database-resident table by its unique name. In the case that the table has multiple columns, these columns are gathered in a flat tuple whose components are ordered alphabetically by column name. With the current DSH implementation, it is the user's responsibility to make sure that the referenced table does exist in the database and that type *a* indeed matches the table's row type—otherwise, an error is thrown at runtime.

The DSH combinators, in the tradition of deep embeddings, construct an internal data representation of the embedded program fragment they represent. The subsequent optimisation and compilation into relational queries is based on this representation. The following presents the data type that is used to represent the DSH combinators internally:

```
data Exp = BoolE     Bool      Type
         | IntegerE  Integer   Type    -- ... and other basic types
         | TupleE    [Exp]     Type
         | ListE     [Exp]     Type
         | VarE      String    Type
         | TableE    String    Type
         | LamE      String Exp Type
         | AppE      Exp   Exp Type
```

The type annotations are used to map the DSH-supported data types to their relational encodings (see Section 3.2). The *Exp* data type features type annotations at the value-level, represented by elements of the algebraic datatype *Type*. As a direct result of this, the internal representation is not guaranteed to represent a type-correct expression. However, this data type is not exposed to the user of the library and extra care has been taken to make sure that the combinators map to a consistent underlying representation.

The DSH combinators are typed using a technique called *phantom typing* [17, 24]. In particular, the *Q* data type is defined as **data** *Q a = Q Exp* featuring the type variable *a* that does not occur in the type definition. Instead, as shown above, this type variable is used to give the required Haskell types to the DSH combinators. Thus, we obviate the need for type-checking the internal representation by delegating this task to the host language type-checker.

The abstract data type *Q a* and its representation is not exposed to the user. As a consequence, direct pattern matching on values of type *Q a* is not possible. However, we do provide a limited form of pattern matching on queries of product types using *view patterns*, a syntactic extension of the Glasgow Haskell Compiler (GHC) [3]. To illustrate, the following expression that contains a view pattern $\lambda(view \rightarrow pat) \rightarrow expr$ is desugared to $\lambda x \rightarrow$ **case** $view\ x$ **of** $pat \rightarrow expr$. A view pattern can match on values of an abstract type if it is given a *view* function that maps between the abstract type and a matchable data type. In order to support multiple types with the same *view* function, we introduce a type class *View* as follows:

class *View a b* | *a → b* **where**
    view :: *a → b*

Instead of projecting all data types onto the same matchable type, we use a type variable *b* that is uniquely determined by the type *a*. The signature of the *View* instance for pairs, for example, reads:

instance $(QA\ a, QA\ b) \Rightarrow View\ (Q\ (a, b))\ (Q\ a, Q\ b)$

DSH provides for automatic derivation of *View* instances for *any* user-defined product type.

Regular Haskell list comprehensions only support generators, guards and local bindings [23, Section 3.11]. List comprehensions extended with SQL-inspired *order by* and *group by* constructs were added as a language extension to improve the expressiveness of the list comprehensions notation [16]. Further, parallel list comprehensions are supported by GHC as an extension. DSH supports standard list comprehensions as well as both extensions through quasi-quoting machinery [19, 25]. This results only in a slight syntactic overhead. A DSH list comprehension is thus written as:

[*qc* | *expr* | *quals* |]

where *qc* (read: *query comprehension*) is a quasi-quoter that desugars list comprehensions into DSH list-processing combinators.

3.2   Turning Haskell into SQL

After building the type-annotated abstract syntax tree (AST) of a DSH program, we use a syntax-directed and compositional translation technique called loop-lifting to compile this AST into table algebra plan(s) [13]. This intermediate representation has been designed to reflect the query capabilities of modern off-the-shelf relational database engines.

Loop-lifting implements DSH computations over arbitrarily nested data using a flat data-parallel evaluation strategy (see Section 4.2) executable by any relational database system. Specific database engines are targeted by code generators that derive tailored back-end queries from the generic table algebra plans. A SQL:1999 code generator allows us to target any standards-compliant RDBMS [11], a MIL back-end enables DSH to target the MonetDB database system [5] .

All data types and operations supported by DSH are turned into relational representations that *faithfully* preserve the DSH semantics on a relational back-end. We will discuss this relational encoding in the following.

Atomic values and (nested) tuples. DSH values of atomic types are directly mapped into values of a corresponding table column type. An *n*-tuple $(v_1, ..., v_n)$, $n \geqslant 1$, of such values maps into a table row of width *n*. A singleton tuple (v) and value *v* are treated alike. A nested tuple $((v_1, ..., v_n), ..., (v_{n+k}, ..., v_m))$ is represented like its flat variant $(v_1, ..., v_n, ..., v_{n+k}, ..., v_m)$.

Ordered lists. Relational back-ends normally cannot provide ordering guarantees for rows of a table. We therefore let the compiler create a *runtime-accessible encoding of row order*. A list value $[x_1, x_2, ..., x_l]$—where x_i denotes the n-tuple $(v_{i1}, ..., v_{in})$—is mapped into a table of width $1 + n$ as shown in Figure 3(a). Again, a singleton list $[x]$ and its element x are represented alike. A dedicated column pos is used to encode the order of a list's elements.

Nested lists. Relational tables are flat data structures and special consideration is given to the representation of nested lists. If a DSH program produces the list $[[x_{11}, x_{12}, ..., x_{1m_1}], ..., [x_{k1}, x_{k2}, ..., x_{km_k}]]$ (with $m_i, k \geqslant 0$) which exhibits a nesting depth of two, the compiler will translate the program into a *bundle* of two separate relational queries, say Q_1 and Q_2. Figure 3(b) shows the resulting tabular encodings produced by the relational query bundle:

Q_1, a query that computes the relational encoding of the outer list $[@_1, ..., @_k]$ in which all inner lists (including empty lists) are represented by *surrogate keys* $@_i$, and

Q_2, a query that produces the encodings of *all* inner lists—assembled into a single table. If the ith inner list is empty, its surrogate $@_i$ will not appear in the nest column of this second table.

pos	item_1	···	item_n
1	v_{11}	···	v_{1n}
2	v_{21}	···	v_{2n}
⋮		⋮	
ℓ	$v_{\ell 1}$	···	$v_{\ell n}$

(a) Encoding a flat ordered list

Q_1

pos	item_1
1	$@_1$
⋮	⋮
k	$@_k$

Q_2

nest	pos	item_1 ··· item_n
$@_1$	1	x_{11}
⋮	⋮	⋮
$@_1$	m_1	x_{1m_1}
⋮	⋮	⋮
$@_k$	1	x_{k1}
⋮	⋮	⋮
$@_k$	m_k	x_{km_k}

(b) Encoding a nested list (Q_1: outer list, Q_2: all inner lists)

Fig. 3. Relational encoding of order and nesting on the database backend

This use of the surrogates $@_i$ resembles Van den Bussche's simulation of the nested algebra via the flat relational algebra [27]. In effect, our compiler uses a non-parametric representation for list elements [15] in which the element *types* determine their efficient relational representation: either in-line (for tuples of atomic items) or surrogate-based (for lists)—we come back to this in Section 4.2. In [13], we describe a compile-time analysis phase—coined *(un)boxing*—that infers the correct non-parametric representation for all subexpressions of a DSH program.

The most important consequence of this design is that it is exclusively the *number of list constructors* $[\cdot]$ *in the program's result type* that determines the number of queries contained in the emitted relational query bundle. We refer to this crucial property as *avalanche safety*.

For the example program from Section 2 with type $[(String, [String])]$, the bundle size thus is two. This is radically different from related approaches like LINQ [21] or HaskellDB [17] which may yield sequences of SQL statements whose size is dependent on the *size of the queried database instance* (see Section 4.1). The two SQL queries that are generated by the SQL:1999 code generator for the example program are given in the Appendix.

Operations. Relational query processors are specialists in *bulk-oriented evaluation*: in this mode of evaluation, the system applies an operation to *all* rows in a given table. In absence of inter-row dependencies, the system may process the individual rows in any order or even in parallel. Our compiler makes sure that the parallelism inherent to most of DSH's list combinators (see Section 3.1) is indeed turned into queries that the relational back-end can process in its data-parallel evaluation mode. Consider this application of *map*,

$$map \ (\lambda x \rightarrow e) \ [v_1, ..., v_n] = [e \, [v_1/x] \, , ..., e \, [v_n/x]]$$

which performs n *independent* evaluations of expression e under different bindings of x ($e \, [v/x]$ denotes the consistent replacement of free occurrences of x in e by v). Loop lifting exploits this semantics and compiles *map* into an algebraic plan that evaluates $e \, [v_i/x]$ ($i = 1, ..., n$) in a data-parallel fashion: all n bindings for x are supplied in a single table and the database system is free to consider these bindings and the corresponding evaluations of e in any order it sees fit (or in parallel). Loop-lifting thus fully realises the independence of the iterated evaluations and enables the relational query engine to take advantage of its bulk-oriented processing paradigm. A detailed account of the loop-lifting of operations is given in [13].

4   Related Work

Embedding database query capabilities into a functional programming language is not a new idea. The most notable examples include Kleisli [18], Links [8], LINQ [21, 26] and HaskellDB [17].

Kleisli [18] is a data integration system mainly used to query bioinformatics data. The system features the Collection Programming Language (CPL) for specifying queries. This language supports a rich data model with arbitrarily nested sets, bags, lists, tuples, records and variants. CPL queries can be formulated using comprehension notation for the supported collection types. However, the Kleisli system does not provide for avalanche safety, the feature that DSH inherits from the Ferry language. The Kleisli system supports querying of disparate data that resides in different databases—this is something we have not yet considered in the design and implementation of DSH.

Links [8] is a web programming language that provides for tier-less web development. That is, a Links program is compiled into client-side, server-side and database-executable fragments. The Links system only supports database execution of program fragments that deal with flat data.

LINQ seamlessly embeds a declarative query language facility into Microsoft's .NET language framework [21, 26]. Similar to DSH, a LINQ query against database-resident relational tables is compiled into a sequence of SQL statements, but without DSH's avalanche safety guarantee. Also, LINQ does not provide any relational encoding of order. As a consequence, in LINQ, particular order-sensitive operations are either flagged as being unsupported or are mapped into database queries that return list elements in some arbitrary order [13].

HaskellDB [17] is a combinator library for Haskell that enables the construction of SQL queries in a type-safe and declarative fashion. As HaskellDB is a well-known system in the Haskell community that is related to DSH's approach of letting developers use the Haskell programming language itself to formulate (type-safe) queries against database-resident data, we will compare DSH to HaskellDB in more detail in the following.

4.1 HaskellDB

As with DSH, a HaskellDB [17] query is formulated completely within Haskell without having to resort to SQL syntax. Let us highlight two significant differences between HaskellDB and DSH.

Query Avalanches. DSH provides a guarantee that the *number of SQL queries issued* to implement a given program is exclusively *determined by the program's static type*: each occurrence of a list type constructor $[t]$ accounts for exactly one SQL query. Our running example from Section 2 with its result type of shape $[[\cdot]]$ thus led to the bundle of two SQL queries shown in Appendix. This marks a significant deviation from HaskellDB: in this system, the length of the SQL statement sequence may depend on the *database instance size*, resulting in an avalanche of queries.

To make this concrete, we reformulated the example program in HaskellDB (Figure 4). Table 1 shows the number of SQL queries emitted by HaskellDB and DSH in dependence of the number of distinct categories in column cat of table facilities. Table 1 also gives the overall runtimes of both programs for the different category counts. To measure these times we ran both programs on the same 2.8 GHz Intel Core 2 Duo computer (running Mac OS X 10.6.6) with 8 GB of RAM. PostgreSQL 9.0.2-1 was used as the database back-end. We executed each program ten times. Table 1 lists the average runtimes for the two programs along with upper and lower bounds with 95% confidence interval, as calculated by the criterion library [1].

For HaskellDB, the query avalanche effect is clearly visible: the number of queries generated depends on the population of column cat and the relational database back-end is easily overwhelmed by the resulting query workload. With DSH, the number of queries issued remains constant significantly reducing the overall runtime.

List Order Preservation. List element order is inherent to the Haskell data model. DSH relationally encodes list order (column pos) and carefully translates operations such that this order encoding is preserved (see Section 3.2).

In contrast, HaskellDB does not provide any relational encoding of order. As a consequence, HaskellDB does not support order-sensitive operations.

$getCats :: Query\ (Rel\ (RecCons\ Cat\ (Expr\ String)\ RecNil))$
$getCats = \textbf{do}$
$\qquad facs \leftarrow table\ facilities$
$\qquad cats \leftarrow project\ (cat << facs\ !\ cat)$
$\qquad unique$
$\qquad return\ cats$

$getCatFeatures :: String \rightarrow Query\ (Rel\ (RecCons\ Meaning\ (Expr\ String)\ RecNil))$
$getCatFeatures\ cat = \textbf{do}$
$\qquad\qquad facs\quad \leftarrow table\ facilities$
$\qquad\qquad feats\quad \leftarrow table\ features$
$\qquad\qquad means \leftarrow table\ meanings$
$\qquad\qquad restrict\ \$\ feats\ !\ feature\ .==.\ means\ !\ feature\ .\&\&.$
$\qquad\qquad\qquad facs\ !\ cat\qquad .==.\ constant\ cat\ .\&\&.$
$\qquad\qquad\qquad facs\ !\ fac\qquad .==.\ feats\ !\ fac$
$\qquad\qquad m \leftarrow project\ (meaning << means\ !\ meaning)$
$\qquad\qquad unique$
$\qquad\qquad return\ m$

$query :: IO\ [(Record\ (RecCons\ Cat\ String\ RecNil)$
$\qquad\qquad ,[Record\ (RecCons\ Meaning\ String\ RecNil)])]$
$query = \textbf{do}$
$\qquad cs \leftarrow doQuery\ getCats$
$\qquad sequence\ \$\ map\ (\lambda c \rightarrow \textbf{do}$
$\qquad\qquad\qquad m \leftarrow doQuery\ \$\ getCatFeatures\ \$\ c\ !\ cat$
$\qquad\qquad\qquad return\ (c, m))\ cs$

Fig. 4. HaskellDB version of running example

4.2   Data Parallel Haskell

RDBMSs are carefully tuned and highly efficient table processors. A look under the hood reveals that, indeed, database query engines provide a sophisticated *flat data-parallel* execution environment: most of the engine's primitives—typically a variant of the relational algebra—apply a single operation, e.g., relational selection, projection and join, to all rows of an input table.

In this sense, DSH is a close relative of Data Parallel Haskell (DPH) [6, 7, 15]: both accept very similar comprehension-centric Haskell fragments, both yield code that is amenable for execution on flat data-parallel backends (relational query engines or contemporary multi-core CPUs). We shed light on a few striking similarities here.

Parallel arrays *vs.* tables. DPH programs operate over so-called parallel arrays of type $[:a:]$, the primary abstraction of a vector of values that is subject to bulk computation. Positional indexing into these arrays (via !:) is ubiquitous. Parallel arrays are strict: evaluating one array element evaluates the entire array.

Table 1. Number of SQL queries emitted and observed overall program execution times in dependence of the population of column cat for the HaskellDB and DSH implementations of the running example (DNF: did not finish within hours)

	HaskellDB		DSH	
# categories	# queries	⏱ (sec)	# queries	⏱ (sec)
1 000	1 001	$11.712^{+0.2\%}_{-0.2\%}$	2	$0.604^{+1.1\%}_{-0.3\%}$
10 000	10 001	$291.369^{+3.2\%}_{-2.4\%}$	2	$6.419^{+1.5\%}_{-2.0\%}$
100 000	100 001	DNF	2	$74.709^{+0.5\%}_{-0.3\%}$

```
type Vector = [: Float :]
type SparseVector = [: (Int, Float) :]
sumP :: Num a ⇒ [: a :] → a
(!:)   :: [: a :] → Int → a
dotp :: SparseVector → Vector → Float
dotp sv v = sumP[: x * (v !: i) | (i, x) ← sv :]
```

Fig. 5. DPH example: sparse vector multiplication (taken from [7])

In comparison, the DSH-generated database primitives operate over (unordered) tables in which a dedicated column pos explicitly encodes element indexes (see Section 3.2). Primitive operations are always applied to all rows of their input tables.

Non-parametric data representation. In DPH, arrays of tuples $[: (a, b) :]$ are represented as tuples of arrays $([: a :], [: b :])$ of identical length. The representation of a nested array $[: [: a :] :]$ has two components: (1) an array of (*offset*, *length*) descriptors, and (2) a flat data array $[: a :]$ holding the actual elements.

In DSH, the fields of a tuple live in adjacent columns of the same table. A nested list is represented in terms of two tables: (1) a table of surrogate keys, each of which identifies a nested list, and (2) a table of data elements, each accompanied by a foreign surrogate key to encode list membership.

This foreign-key-based representation of nesting can readily benefit from relational indexes that map any data element x to the surrogate key of its containing list. A direct adoption of DPH's (*offset*, *length*) descriptor-based representation, instead, would ultimately lead to range queries of the form x.pos **BETWEEN** *offset* **AND** *offset* + *length*— a workable but less efficient alternative on off-the-shelf relational database back-ends.

Note that it is crucial, though, that DPH's as well as DSH's representation preserve the locality of the actual elements held in nested data structures.

Lifting operations. In DPH, operations of type $a → b$ are lifted to apply to entire arrays of values: $[: a :] → [: b :]$. Consider a DPH variant of sparse vector multiplication (Figure 5). The comprehension defines an iterative computation to be applied to each element of sparse vector sv: project onto the components i and x, perform positional array access into v ($!$:), multiply. With *vectorisation*, Data Parallel Haskell trades comprehension notation for data-parallel combinators (*e.g.*, $fst\hat{\ }$, $*\hat{\ }$, $bpermuteP$), all operating over entire arrays (Figure 6, left).

DSH's translation strategy, loop-lifting, compiles a family of Haskell list combinators into algebraic primitives, all of which operate over entire tables (*i.e.*, the relational engine performs lifted application by definition) [13]. Intermediate code produced by DPH and DSH indeed exhibits structural similarities. To illustrate, we have identified the database primitives that implement the sparse vector multiplication program of Figure 5 in Figure 6 (right): $bpermuteP$, which performs bulk indexed array lookup, turns into a relational equi-join over column pos, for example.

A study of the exact relationship between DPH and DSH still lies ahead. We conjecture that DSH's loop-lifting compilation strategy does have an equivalent formulation in terms of vectorisation or Blelloch's flattening transformation [4].

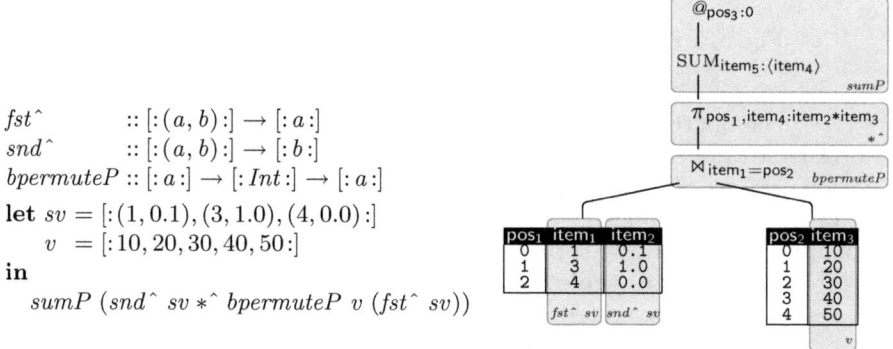

Fig. 6. Intermediate code generated for the sparse vector multiplication example of Fig. 5: DPH (left) *vs.* DSH (right)

4.3   Embedding Approaches

The DSH implementation is realised through a combination of a number of established language embedding techniques. In the tradition of deep embeddings [14] DSH's list processing combinators construct data representation of embedded queries allowing for domain-specific optimisation and code generation. Haskell's template meta-programming and quasiquoting facilities are used to provide convenient syntactic sugar (i.e., the list comprehension notation with extensions) for the list-processing combinators. Type correctness of the embedded queries is ensured by phantom typing [17, 24]. View patterns [28] provide for pattern matching on otherwise abstract data representation of embedded queries.

5 Future Work and Conclusions

In this paper we presented Database Supported Haskell (DSH), a library that allows the use of a relational database management system (RDBMS) as a co-processor for the Haskell runtime. Thus, DSH is capable of processing large scale data, that would otherwise exceed heap capacity. Database-executable program fragments are written in a style that has been designed to imitate the syntax, types and semantics of typical Haskell functions over lists. The expressive list comprehension notation is supported with only slight syntactic overhead (due to our use of quasi-quoting).

Overall, as a host language, Haskell served our needs well in the process of DSH design and implementation. However, there is room for improvements. In particular, if the comprehension notation would have been supported not only for lists but for any monad [29], as was the case in Haskell 1.4 [22], we could define DSH combinators as monadic combinators and reuse monad comprehension notation instead of implementing our own quasi-quoter. This would save the implementation effort, eliminate the syntactic overhead and lead to better error messages referring to the original source code instead of the generated code.

We think that monadic **do** notation is a poor fit for DSH and, more generally, for list-based libraries and Domain Specific Languages (DSLs). Thus, we are bringing back monad comprehensions to Haskell, and are currently working on an implementation as an extension for the Glasgow Haskell Compiler [3]. We are also generalising the recently proposed extensions of the list comprehension notation [16] to monads so that those extensions could also be used in the monad comprehension notation. Although we think that list-based libraries and DSLs would benefit most, this extension could have other interesting applications.

DSH uses compilation technology developed for the Ferry language. Thus, we support nested lists, preserve list order and guarantee that the number of generated relational queries only depends on the static type of the query result and remains unaffected by the database instance size. We expect to continue work on DSH and Ferry in the following directions:

- support for functions as first-class citizens (so that the result of a sub-query can also be a function),
- support for sum types,
- support for general folds and recursion,
- the application of DSH to large-scale data analysis problems, and
- an exploration of DSH's relationship to Data Parallel Haskell.

Acknowledgements. Tom and Jeroen have been supported by the German Research Foundation (DFG), Grant GR 2036/3-1. George has received support from the ScienceCampus Tübingen: Informational Environments. We would also like to acknowledge Alexander Ulrich, Jan Rittinger and the anonymous reviewers for their helpful comments and feedback.

References

[1] Criterion, http://hackage.haskell.org/package/criterion
[2] Database Supported Haskell, http://hackage.haskell.org/package/DSH
[3] The Glasgow Haskell Compiler, http://www.haskell.org/ghc/
[4] Blelloch, G.E., Sabot, G.W.: Compiling Collection-Oriented Languages onto Massively Parallel Computers. Journal of Parallel and Distributed Computing 8, 119–134 (1990)
[5] Boncz, P.A., Kersten, M.L.: MIL primitives for querying a fragmented world. The VLDB Journal 8, 101–119 (1999)
[6] Chakravarty, M.M.T., Keller, G.: More Types for Nested Data Parallel Programming. In: Proceedings of the Fifth ACM SIGPLAN International Conference on Functional Programming (ICFP), Montreal, Canada, pp. 94–105. ACM, New York (2000)
[7] Chakravarty, M.M.T., Leshchinskiy, R., Jones, S.P., Keller, G., Marlow, S.: Data Parallel Haskell: a status report. In: Proceedings of the 2007 Workshop on Declarative Aspects of Multicore Programming (DAMP), Nice, France, pp. 10–18. ACM, New York (2007)
[8] Cooper, E., Lindley, S., Wadler, P., Yallop, J.: Links: Web programming without tiers. In: de Boer, F.S., Bonsangue, M.M., Graf, S., de Roever, W.-P. (eds.) FMCO 2006. LNCS, vol. 4709, pp. 266–296. Springer, Heidelberg (2007)
[9] Giorgidze, G., Nilsson, H.: Mixed-level Embedding and JIT Compilation for an Iteratively Staged DSL. In: Mariño, J. (ed.) WFLP 2010. LNCS, vol. 6559, pp. 48–65. Springer, Heidelberg (2011)
[10] Grust, T., Mayr, M., Rittinger, J.: Let SQL Drive the XQuery Workhorse (XQuery Join Graph Isolation). In: Proceedings of the 13th International Conference on Extending Database Technology (EDBT), Lausanne, Switzerland, pp. 147–158. ACM, New York (2010)
[11] Grust, T., Mayr, M., Rittinger, J., Sakr, S., Teubner, J.: A SQL: 1999 Code Generator for the Pathfinder XQuery Compiler. In: Proceedings of the 2007 ACM SIGMOD International Conference on Management of Data (SIGMOD), Beijing, China, pp. 1162–1164. ACM, New York (2007)
[12] Grust, T., Mayr, M., Rittinger, J., Schreiber, T.: FERRY: Database-Supported Program Execution. In: Proceedings of the 35th SIGMOD International Conference on Management of Data (SIGMOD), Providence, RI, USA, pp. 1063–1066. ACM, New York (2009)
[13] Grust, T., Rittinger, J., Schreiber, T.: Avalanche-Safe LINQ Compilation. In: Proceedings of the 36th International Conference on Very Large Databases (VLDB), Singapore, pp. 162–172. VLDB Endowment (September 2010)
[14] Hudak, P.: Modular Domain Specific Languages and Tools. In: Proceedings of Fifth International Conference on Software Reuse (ICSR), pp. 134–142 (June 1998)
[15] Jones, S.P., Leshchinskiy, R., Keller, G., Chakravarty, M.M.T.: Harnessing the Multicores: Nested Data Parallelism in Haskell. In: IARCS Annual Conference on Foundations of Software Technology and Theoretical Computer Science (FSTTCS), Bangalore, India, vol. 2, pp. 383–414 (2008) Schloss Dagstuhl–Leibniz-Zentrum fuer Informatik
[16] Jones, S.P., Wadler, P.: Comprehensive Comprehensions. In: Proceedings of the ACM SIGPLAN Workshop on Haskell, Freiburg, Germany, pp. 61–72. ACM, New York (2007)

[17] Leijen, D., Meijer, E.: Domain Specific Embedded Compilers. In: Proceedings of the 2nd Conference on Domain-Specific Languages (DSL), Austin, Texas, United States, pp. 109–122. ACM, New York (1999)

[18] Limsoon, W.: Kleisli, a functional query system. Journal of Functional Programming 10, 19–56 (2000)

[19] Mainland, G.: Why It's Nice to be Quoted: Quasiquoting for Haskell. In: Proceedings of the ACM SIGPLAN Workshop on Haskell, Freiburg, Germany, pp. 73–82. ACM, New York (2007)

[20] Mainland, G., Morrisett, G.: Nikola: Embedding Compiled GPU Functions in Haskell. In: Proceedings of the Third ACM Haskell Symposium on Haskell, Baltimore, Maryland, USA, pp. 67–78. ACM, New York (2010)

[21] Meijer, E., Beckman, B., Bierman, G.: LINQ: Reconciling Objects, Relations and XML in the NET Framework. In: Proceedings of the 2006 ACM SIGMOD International Conference on Management of Data (SIGMOD), Chicago, IL, USA, pp. 706–706. ACM, New York (2006)

[22] Peterson, J., Hammond, K.: Haskell 1.4: A Non-strict, Purely Functional Language. Technical Report YALEU/DCS/RR-1106, Department of Computer Science. Yale University (1997)

[23] Jones, S.P. (ed.): Haskell 98 Language and Libraries – The Revised Report. Cambridge University Press, Cambridge (2003)

[24] Rhiger, M.: A Foundation for Embedded Languages. ACM Transactions on Programming Languages and Systems (TOPLAS) 25, 291–315 (2003)

[25] Sheard, T., Jones, S.P.: Template Meta-programming for Haskell. In: Proceedings of the ACM SIGPLAN Workshop on Haskell, Pittsburgh, PA, USA, pp. 1–16. ACM, New York (October 2002)

[26] Syme, D.: Leveraging.NET Meta-programming Components from F#: Integrated Queries and Interoperable Heterogeneous Execution. In: Proceedings of the 2006 Workshop on ML, Portland, Oregon, USA, pp. 43–54. ACM, New York (2006)

[27] Van den Bussche, J.: Simulation of the nested relational algebra by the flat relational algebra, with an application to the complexity of evaluating powerset algebra expressions. Theoretical Computer Science 254, 363–377 (2001)

[28] Wadler, P.: Views: A way for pattern matching to cohabit with data abstraction. In: Proceedings of the 14th ACM SIGACT-SIGPLAN Symposium on Principles of Programming Languages (POPL), Munich, West Germany, pp. 307–313. ACM, New York (1987)

[29] Wadler, P.: Comprehending monads. In: Proceedings of the 1990 ACM Conference on LISP and Functional Programming (LFP), Nice, France, pp. 61–78. ACM, New York (1990)

Appendix

DSH's SQL:1999 code generator emits the following bundle of two SQL queries for the Haskell example program of Section 2:

```
WITH
  -- binding due to duplicate elimination
  t0000 (item1_str) AS
    (SELECT DISTINCT a0000.categorie AS item1_str
      FROM facilities AS a0000)
SELECT
  DENSE_RANK () OVER
    (ORDER BY a0001.item1_str ASC) AS item4_nat,
  1 AS iter3_nat, a0001.item1_str
FROM t0000 AS a0001
ORDER BY a0001.item1_str ASC;


WITH
  -- binding due to rank operator
  t0000 (item9_str, item10_str, item37_nat) AS
    (SELECT a0000.categorie AS item9_str, a0000.facility AS item10_str,
        DENSE_RANK () OVER
          (ORDER BY a0000.categorie ASC) AS item37_nat
      FROM facilities AS a0000),

  -- binding due to rank operator
  t0001 (item9_str, item10_str, item37_nat, item3_str, item4_str,
    item1_str, item2_str, item38_nat) AS
    (SELECT a0001.item9_str, a0001.item10_str, a0001.item37_nat,
        a0002.feature AS item3_str, a0002.meaning AS item4_str,
        a0003.facility AS item1_str, a0003.feature AS item2_str,
        DENSE_RANK () OVER
        (ORDER BY a0001.item9_str ASC, a0001.item10_str ASC,
          a0002.feature ASC, a0002.meaning ASC,
          a0003.facility ASC, a0003.feature ASC) AS item38_nat
      FROM t0000 AS a0001,
        meanings AS a0002,
        features AS a0003
      WHERE a0002.feature = a0003.feature
        AND a0001.item10_str = a0003.facility),

  -- binding due to aggregate
  t0002 (pos29_nat, iter30_nat, item31_str) AS
    (SELECT MIN (a0004.item38_nat) AS pos29_nat,
        a0004.item37_nat AS iter30_nat,
        a0004.item4_str AS item31_str
      FROM t0001 AS a0004
      GROUP BY a0004.item37_nat, a0004.item4_str)
SELECT a0005.item31_str, a0005.iter30_nat
  FROM t0002 AS a0005
  ORDER BY a0005.iter30_nat ASC, a0005.pos29_nat ASC;
```

Theory and Practice of Fusion

Ralf Hinze, Thomas Harper, and Daniel W.H. James

Computing Laboratory, University of Oxford
Wolfson Building, Parks Road, Oxford, OX1 3QD, England
{ralf.hinze,tom.harper,daniel.james}@comlab.ox.ac.uk

Abstract. There are a number of approaches for eliminating intermediate data structures in functional programs—this elimination is commonly known as *fusion*. Existing fusion strategies are built upon various, but related, recursion schemes, such as folds and unfolds. We use the concept of *recursive coalgebras* as a unifying theoretical and notational framework to explore the foundations of these fusion techniques. We first introduce the calculational properties of recursive coalgebras and demonstrate their use with proofs and derivations in a calculational style, then provide an overview of fusion techniques by bringing them together in this setting. We also showcase these developments with examples in Haskell.

1 Introduction

Functional programmers love modular programs. It is easy for them to create clear, concise, and reusable code by composing functions. Consider the following Haskell program as an example:

$$f \ : \ (Integer, Integer) \to Integer$$
$$f = sum \cdot map\ sq \cdot filter\ odd \cdot between \ .$$

The program takes a pair of integers representing an interval and returns the sum of the squared odd integers in this interval. We have expressed this a composition of four functions: *between* generates an enumeration between two natural numbers as a list, *filter odd* removes any even numbers, *map sq* squares the remaining (odd) numbers, and *sum* adds them together. Unfortunately, the clarity of this program comes at a cost. The constituent functions of this program communicate with each other using intermediate data structures, the production and immediate consumption of which carries an obvious performance penalty. Yet, because these definitions are recursive, eliminating the need for these transient structures is beyond the reach of a typical compiler.

Nonetheless, such a transformation is possible. We can manually construct a program that is equivalent to f, but without the intermediate data structures

$$f'\,(m, n) = go\ m$$
$$\textbf{where}\ go\ m \mid m > n \quad = 0$$
$$\mid otherwise = go\,(m + 1) + \textbf{if}\ odd\ m\ \textbf{then}\ sq\ m\ \textbf{else}\,0 \ .$$

J. Hage, M.T. Morazán (Eds.): IFL 2010, LNCS 6647, pp. 19–37, 2011.

This new program has lost the desirable qualities of the original—our concise, modular and declarative code has been hammered into a long, opaque and specialised function. In doing so, however, we have accomplished our goal of removing the intermediate data structures by transforming the numerous recursive traversals into a single one. This process is called *fusion*.

Fusing programs by hand quickly becomes infeasible for those of non-trivial length. Furthermore, it can be difficult to manually pinpoint all the opportunities for fusion. Instead, such a transformation should be performed automatically. Difficulties arise, however, in automatically fusing functions defined using general recursion. Specifically, such transformations often have proof obligations that cannot be discharged by the compiler.

One remedy is to standardise the way data structures are produced or consumed by encapsulating the recursion scheme in a higher-order function. The arguments to these functions are the non-recursive 'steps'. Simple syntactic transformations can then fuse many recursive traversals into a single one, and then non-recursive steps can be optimised using conventional methods. This approach is known as *shortcut fusion*. Different incarnations of this technique utilise different recursion schemes, e.g. *folds* for consumers or *unfolds* for producers. The steps of such a scheme are known as algebras or coalgebras, respectively.

The implementation of these fusion techniques is usually described syntactically, by giving a definition of the production and consumption combinators and accompanying rewrite rules. This alone does not really explain the underlying fusion mechanism. Furthermore, it is difficult to construct correctness proofs, or relate various fusion approaches to one another, despite the fact that such close relations exist. In this paper, we move fusion to a clearer setting, where the syntactic details of fusion fall away.

Category theory provides the tools we need to tackle the semantics of the recursion schemes. While some fusion techniques have been individually given this treatment before, our focus is to bring them all under one roof. In this paper, we propose using *recursive coalgebras* as that roof. We will show how recursive coalgebras enable us to explain the fusion rules underlying the various fusion techniques and give short, simple proofs of correctness.

Some proofs and source code examples have been elided from this paper. Any reader who desires further material should consult the associated technical report [10].

2   Background: Algebras and Coalgebras

The category theory concept of an *initial algebra* is key in the theory of functional programming languages, specifically for giving a semantics to recursive datatypes [15]. The remainder of this section will refresh the salient details. For the more functional-programming-minded reader, we will parallel these developments with examples in Haskell, where possible.

Let $F : \mathbb{C} \to \mathbb{C}$ be a functor. An F-*algebra* is a pair $\langle a, A \rangle$ consisting of an object $A : \mathbb{C}$ and an arrow $a : F\,A \to A : \mathbb{C}$. An F-*algebra homomorphism* between algebras $\langle a, A \rangle$ and $\langle b, B \rangle$ is an arrow $h : A \rightarrow B : \mathbb{C}$ such that $h \cdot a = b \cdot \mathsf{F} h$. The fact that functors preserve identity and composition entails that identity is a homomorphism and that homomorphisms compose. Consequently, F-algebras and their homomorphisms form a category, called $\mathbf{Alg}(\mathsf{F})$. We abbreviate a homomorphism, $h : \langle a, A \rangle \rightarrow \langle b, B \rangle : \mathbf{Alg}(\mathsf{F})$, by $h : a \rightarrow b : \mathbf{Alg}(\mathsf{F})$ if the objects are obvious from the context, or simply by $h : a \rightarrow b$ if the functor F is also obvious.

In Haskell, we model a functor as a datatype whose constructors describe its action on data (i.e. objects). Its action on arrows is defined by making that data type an instance of the *Functor* typeclass

> **class** *Functor f* **where**
> $\quad fmap : (a \rightarrow b) \rightarrow (f\, a \rightarrow f\, b)$.

We can then simply treat the concept of an F-algebra as a function, where F is a datatype that is an instance of the *Functor* class. The F-algebra $\langle a, A \rangle$ is simply a function $a : \mathsf{F}\, A \rightarrow A$. An F-algebra homomorphism between a and $b : \mathsf{F}\, B \rightarrow B$ is a function $h : A \rightarrow B$ that satisfies the side condition $h \cdot a = b \cdot fmap\, h$. This property cannot, however, be deduced from the type and must be checked by the programmer.

If the category $\mathbf{Alg}(\mathsf{F})$ has an initial object, then we call it $\langle in, \mu\mathsf{F} \rangle$. Initiality means that there is a *unique* arrow from $\langle in, \mu\mathsf{F} \rangle$ to any other F-algebra $\langle a, A \rangle$. This arrow, called *fold*, is written $(\!|a|\!) : in \rightarrow a$. We construct elements of $\mu\mathsf{F}$ using in and deconstruct them using $(\!|a|\!)$. We can think of $(\!|a|\!) : in \rightarrow a$ as replacing constructors by functions, represented by the algebras in and a, respectively. Initiality is captured by the *uniqueness property* of folds:[1]

$$h = (\!|a|\!) \quad \Longleftrightarrow \quad h : in \rightarrow a \quad \Longleftrightarrow \quad h \cdot in = a \cdot \mathsf{F}\, h \ . \tag{1}$$

It is important to note that we have omitted the quantification of the names that appear in property (1); we have done so for presentational succinctness and we will continue in this manner. In this case we will spell out implicit quantification: the uniqueness property holds for all functors F, where the category $\mathbf{Alg}(\mathsf{F})$ has an initial object named $\langle in, \mu\mathsf{F} \rangle$, and for all F-algebras $\langle a, A \rangle$, and for all F-algebra homomorphisms $h : in \rightarrow a$.

This property provides us with a general definition of $(\!|-|\!)$ in Haskell. First, we define the μ datatype, which takes a functor to its least fixed point:

> **data** $\mu f = in\, \{\, out : f\, (\mu f)\, \}$

The constructor in allows us to construct a structure of type μf out of something of type $f\, (\mu f)$ and out deconstructs it. The relationship between in and out in our setting is discussed further in Sections 3 and 4.

---

[1] The formula $P \Longleftrightarrow Q \Longleftrightarrow R$ has to be read *conjunctively* as $P \Longleftrightarrow Q \wedge Q \Longleftrightarrow R$. Likewise, $P \Longleftarrow Q \Longleftrightarrow R$ is shorthand for $P \Longleftarrow Q \wedge Q \Longleftrightarrow R$.

We can define $(\!-\!)$ as a higher-order function that takes an algebra $f\,a \to a$ and returns a function $\mu f \to a$, according to the uniqueness property:

$$(\!-\!) : (Functor\,f) \Rightarrow (f\,a \to a) \to (\mu f \to a)$$
$$(\!a\!) = a \cdot fmap\,(\!a\!) \cdot out$$

By allowing us to substitute $(\!a\!)$ for h, we see that the uniqueness property provides us with a definition of $(\!-\!)$ that recursively replaces occurrences of in by some algebra a. The placement of the recursive call for a given structure μf is determined by the definition $fmap$.

We will not employ the uniqueness property in an example proof just yet. In fact the uniqueness property is rarely used in its raw form; instead, there are a number of specific forms that we will introduce now.

If we set h to the identity id and a to the initial algebra in, then we obtain the *reflection law*: $(\!in\!) = id$. If we substitute the left-hand side into the right-hand side, then we obtain the *computation law*: $(\!a\!) : in \to a$, or expressed in terms of the base category, $(\!a\!) \cdot in = a \cdot \mathsf{F}\,(\!a\!)$.

The most important consequence of the uniqueness property is the *fusion law* for fusing an arrow with a fold to form a new fold.

$$h \cdot (\!a\!) = (\!b\!) \quad \Longleftarrow \quad h : a \to b \quad \Longleftrightarrow \quad h \cdot a = b \cdot \mathsf{F}\,h \qquad (2)$$

As its name would suggest, the fusion law is closely related to the program transformation techniques described in the introduction. It allows a fold to absorb a function on its left, thereby producing a single fold. The law also shows the difficulty of mechanising this process; in order to produce the fused program, we must invent a new algebra b that satisfies the precondition.

Folds enjoy an additional fusion law. Whereas fusion allows us to absorb an additional function on the left, the *functor fusion law* allows us to absorb a function on the right. In order to formulate it, we have to turn μ into a higher-order functor of type $\mathbb{C}^{\mathbb{C}} \to \mathbb{C}$. The object part of this functor maps a functor to its initial algebra. (This is only well-defined for functors that have an initial algebra.) The arrow part maps a natural transformation $\alpha : \mathsf{F} \overset{\cdot}{\to} \mathsf{G}$ to an arrow $\mu\alpha : \mu\mathsf{F} \to \mu\mathsf{G} : \mathbb{C}$. It is defined as $\mu\alpha = (\!in \cdot \alpha\,(\mu\mathsf{F})\!)$. To reduce clutter, we will henceforth omit the argument of the natural transformation α. From these definitions we obtain the *functor fusion law* (we have annotated $(\!-\!)$ with the underlying functors):

$$(\!b\!)_{\mathsf{G}} \cdot \mu\alpha = (\!b \cdot \alpha\!)_{\mathsf{F}} . \qquad (3)$$

It states that a fold after a map can be fused into a single fold — the map $\mu\alpha$ can be seen as a "base changer".

We can also provide a Haskell definition of μ as a functor. The action on data is given by its datatype declaration. The action on functions is given by:

$$\mu- : (Functor\,f) \Rightarrow (\forall\,a\,.\,f\,a \to g\,a) \to (\mu f \to \mu g)$$
$$\mu\alpha = (\!in \cdot \alpha\!)$$

Note that we use a rank-2 polymorphic type to express the idea that μ maps a natural transformation from f to g to a function between their fixpoints.

Finally, the initial algebra $\mu\mathsf{F}$ is the least fixed point of F — this is known as Lambek's Lemma [13]. One direction of the isomorphism $\mathsf{F}\,(\mu\mathsf{F}) \cong \mu\mathsf{F}$ is given by in, its inverse is $in^\circ = (\!|\mathsf{F}\,in|\!)$. Lambek's Lemma is the key to giving a semantics to recursively defined datatypes. To illustrate this, the recursive definition of lists of natural numbers

$\quad$ **data** List $=$ *Nil* $\mid$ *Cons* $(\mathbb{N}, \mathsf{List})$

implicitly defines an underlying functor $\mathsf{L}\,X = 1 + \mathbb{N} \times X$, the so-called base functor of List. (This notation is a categorical rendering of sum-of-products algebraic datatypes, and defines a functor L with an argument X, where 1 denotes the terminal object of the underlying category.) Since the initial object $\mu\mathsf{L}$ satisfies the equation $X \cong \mathsf{L}\,X$, we can use it to assign meaning to the recursive datatype definition. (As an aside, the fold of the List datatype is a specialisation of Haskell's library function *foldr*.)

The initial F-algebra is the least solution of the equation $X \cong \mathsf{F}\,X$. If we dualise the development above, we obtain another canonical solution, namely the greatest one. In category theory, dualisation is denoted by the prefix "co-".

An F-*coalgebra* is a pair $\langle C, c \rangle$ consisting of an object $C : \mathbb{C}$ and an arrow $c : C \to \mathsf{F}\,C : \mathbb{C}$. An F-*coalgebra homomorphism* between coalgebras $\langle C, c \rangle$ and $\langle D, d \rangle$ is an arrow $h : C \to D : \mathbb{C}$ such that $\mathsf{F}\,h \cdot c = d \cdot h$. Coalgebras and coalgebra homomorphisms also form a category, called **Coalg**(F). The dual of the initial algebra is the final coalgebra, whose carrier $\nu\mathsf{F}$ is the greatest fixed point of F. Finality means that, for any other coalgebra, there is a unique arrow from it to the final coalgebra. Whereas a fold consumes a data structure, an unfold produces some data structure from a given seed.

Unfortunately, least and greatest fixed points are different beasts in general. In the category **Set** of sets and total functions, $\mu\mathsf{L}$ is the set of finite lists, whereas $\nu\mathsf{L}$ also contains infinite lists. This means that folds and unfolds are incompatible, in general. In the following section, we will focus on a restricted species of coalgebras, enabling us to work with folds and unfolds under the same roof.

3 Recursive Coalgebras

In this section we will introduce *recursive* coalgebras. We follow the work of Capretta et al. [2], who motivate the use of hylomorphisms based on recursive coalgebras as a structured recursion scheme. We shall continue to parallel our developments with examples in Haskell.

A coalgebra $\langle C, c \rangle$ is called *recursive* if for *every* algebra $\langle a, A \rangle$ the equation in the unknown $h : A \leftarrow C$,

$$h = a \cdot \mathsf{F}\,h \cdot c , \tag{4}$$

has a *unique* solution. The equation captures *divide-and-conquer*: a problem is divided into sub-problems (c), the sub-problems are solved recursively ($\mathsf{F}\,h$), and finally the sub-solutions are combined into a single solution (a). The uniquely defined function h is called a *hylomorphism* or *hylo* for short and is written $(\!| a \leftarrow c |\!)_\mathsf{F} : A \leftarrow C$. The notation is meant to suggest that h takes a coalgebra to an algebra. We omit the subscripted functor name if it is obvious from the context. Uniqueness of h is captured by the following property.

$$h = (\!| a \leftarrow c |\!) \quad \Longleftrightarrow \quad h = a \cdot \mathsf{F}\, h \cdot c \tag{5}$$

In Haskell, $(\!|- \leftarrow -|\!)$ becomes a function that takes an algebra and a recursive coalgebra (which, dual to algebras, is a function of type $c \to f\, c$) as arguments and returns the resulting hylo according to the definition in the universal property:

$$(\!|- \leftarrow -|\!) : (\mathit{Functor}\, f) \Rightarrow (f\, a \to a) \to (c \to f\, c) \to (c \to a)$$
$$(\!| a \leftarrow c |\!) = a \cdot \mathit{fmap}\, (\!| a \leftarrow c |\!) \cdot c \ .$$

This function takes an algebra and a recursive coalgebra, yielding a hylo. Note that the type of this function does not guarantee that c is a *recursive* coalgebra and therefore does not guarantee that the resulting hylo has a unique solution; the programmer needs to discharge this obligation by some other means.

The category of recursive coalgebras and coalgebra homomorphisms forms a full subcategory of $\mathbf{Coalg}(\mathsf{F})$, called $\mathbf{Rec}(\mathsf{F})$. If the latter category has a final object $\langle F, \mathit{out} \rangle$, then there is a unique arrow from any other *recursive* coalgebra $\langle C, c \rangle$ to $\langle F, \mathit{out} \rangle$. This arrow, called *unfold*, is written $[\![c]\!] : c \to \mathit{out}$. Finality is captured by the following uniqueness property.

$$h = [\![c]\!] \quad \Longleftrightarrow \quad h : c \to \mathit{out} \quad \Longleftrightarrow \quad \mathsf{F}\, h \cdot c = \mathit{out} \cdot h \tag{6}$$

This is the usual property of unfolds, except that we are working in the category $\mathbf{Rec}(\mathsf{F})$, *not* $\mathbf{Coalg}(\mathsf{F})$. As with folds, we can draw out a Haskell definition of unfolds from the uniqueness property:

$$[\![-]\!] : (\mathit{Functor}\, f) \Rightarrow (c \to f\, c) \to (c \to \mu f)$$
$$[\![c]\!] = \mathit{in} \cdot \mathit{fmap}\, [\![c]\!] \cdot c \ .$$

In contrast to folds, we are *creating* a structure of type μf from a seed value. The recursion, similarly, is determined by the form of the underlying functor f through the use of *fmap*. The uniqueness property for unfolds, like the one for folds, implies the *reflection law*, $[\![\mathit{out}]\!] = \mathit{id}$, the *computation law*, $\mathsf{F}[\![c]\!] \cdot c = \mathit{out} \cdot [\![c]\!]$, and the *fusion law*:

$$[\![c]\!] = [\![d]\!] \cdot h \quad \Longleftarrow \quad h : c \to d \quad \Longleftrightarrow \quad \mathsf{F}\, h \cdot c = d \cdot h \ . \tag{7}$$

The definition of a hylomorphism does not assume that the initial F-algebra exists. The powerset functor, for instance, admits no fixed points. However, if the initial algebra exists, then it coincides with the final recursive coalgebra and, furthermore, folds and unfolds emerge as special cases of hylos. We can state this more formally:

Theorem 1. *Initial F-algebras and final recursive F-coalgebras coincide: (1) If*
$\langle C, out \rangle$ *is the final recursive F-coalgebra, then* $\langle out^\circ, C \rangle$ *is the initial F-algebra.*
Furthermore, $(\!| a |\!) = (\!| a \leftarrow out |\!)$. *(2) If* $\langle in, A \rangle$ *is the initial F-algebra, then*
$\langle A, in^\circ \rangle$ *is the final recursive F-coalgebra. Furthermore,* $[\![c]\!] = (\!| in \leftarrow c |\!)$.

Theorem 1 allows us to treat folds and unfolds in the same setting—note that
an unfold produces an element of an initial algebra! An alternative is to work in
a setting where μF and νF coincide; an *algebraically compact* category is such
a setting [8]. Haskell's ambient category $\mathbf{Cpo}_\perp$ serves as the standard example.
This is the usual approach [7], however, the downside is that the hylo equation (4)
only has a canonical, least solution, not a unique solution, so (5) does not hold.

4   Calculational Properties

In this section we will cover the calculational properties of our hylomorphisms.
In a similar fashion to folds and unfolds, hylomorphisms have an identity law and
a computation law, and they follow similarly from the uniqueness property (5).

Identity law. Setting $h := id$, we obtain the *identity law*

$$(\!| a \leftarrow c |\!) = id \quad \Longleftrightarrow \quad a \cdot c = id \ . \tag{8}$$

Computation law. Substituting the left-hand side into the right-hand side
gives the *computation law*:

$$(\!| a \leftarrow c |\!) \ = \ a \cdot F (\!| a \leftarrow c |\!) \cdot c \ . \tag{9}$$

For hylomorphisms, we have *three* fusion laws: algebra fusion, coalgebra fusion,
and composition.

Algebra fusion. An algebra homomorphism after a hylo can be fused to form
a single hylo.[2]

$$h \cdot (\!| a \leftarrow c |\!) = (\!| b \leftarrow c |\!) \quad \Longleftarrow \quad h : a \to b \quad \Longleftrightarrow \quad h \cdot a = b \cdot F h \tag{10}$$

For the proof we appeal to the uniqueness property and show that $h \cdot (\!| a \leftarrow c |\!)$
satisfies the recursion equation of $(\!| b \leftarrow c |\!)$. The obligation is discharged as
follows:

$$\begin{aligned}
& h \cdot (\!| a \leftarrow c |\!) \\
= \ & \{ \text{ hylo computation (9) } \} \\
& h \cdot a \cdot F (\!| a \leftarrow c |\!) \cdot c \\
= \ & \{ \text{ assumption: } h : a \to b \} \\
& b \cdot F h \cdot F (\!| a \leftarrow c |\!) \cdot c \\
= \ & \{ \text{ F functor } \} \\
& b \cdot F (h \cdot (\!| a \leftarrow c |\!)) \cdot c \ .
\end{aligned}$$

---

[2] Note that h appears as both an algebra homomorphism in $\mathbf{Alg}(F)$ and as the underlying arrow in the underlying category.

Coalgebra fusion. Dually, we can fuse a coalgebra homomorphism before a hylo to form a single hylo.

$$(a \leftarrow c) = (a \leftarrow d) \cdot h \quad \Longleftarrow \quad h : c \to d \quad \Longleftrightarrow \quad \mathsf{F}\, h \cdot c = d \cdot h \qquad (11)$$

Like the law, the proof is the dual of that for algebra fusion.

Composition law. A composition of hylos can be merged into a single one if the coalgebra of the hylo on the left inverts the algebra of the right hylo.

$$(a \leftarrow c) \cdot (b \leftarrow d) = (a \leftarrow d) \quad \Longleftarrow \quad c \cdot b = id \qquad (12)$$

Composition is, in fact, a simple consequence of algebra fusion as the hylomorphism $(a \leftarrow c) : b \to a$ is simultaneously an F-algebra homomorphism.

$$(a \leftarrow c) \cdot b$$
$$=\quad \{ \text{ hylo computation (9) } \}$$
$$a \cdot \mathsf{F}\, (a \leftarrow c) \cdot c \cdot b$$
$$=\quad \{ \text{ assumption: } c \cdot b = id \}$$
$$a \cdot \mathsf{F}\, (a \leftarrow c)$$

Alternatively, we can derive the composition law from coalgebra fusion by showing that $(b \leftarrow d) : d \to c$ is an F-coalgebra homomorphism. The composition law, together with the next law, generalises the functor fusion law of folds.

Hylo shift law or base change law. If we have a natural transformation $\alpha : \mathsf{G} \overset{.}{\to} \mathsf{F}$, then

$$(a \cdot \alpha\, A \leftarrow c)_\mathsf{G} \;=\; (a \leftarrow \alpha\, C \cdot c)_\mathsf{F} \; . \qquad (13)$$

In fact, the statement can be strengthened: if c is recursive, then $\alpha\, C \cdot c$ is recursive, as well.

$$h = a \cdot \mathsf{F}\, h \cdot \alpha\, C \cdot c$$
$$\Longleftrightarrow \quad \{ \alpha \text{ natural } \}$$
$$h = a \cdot \alpha\, A \cdot \mathsf{G}\, h \cdot c$$
$$\Longleftrightarrow \quad \{ \text{ uniqueness property of hylos (5) } \}$$
$$h = (a \cdot \alpha\, A \leftarrow c)_\mathsf{G}$$

It is worth pointing out that the laws stated thus far are independent of the existence of initial algebras. Only the following law makes this assumption.

Fold/unfold law. A fold after an unfold is a hylo.

$$(a) \cdot [\![c]\!] \;=\; (a \leftarrow c) \qquad (14)$$

From left to right we are performing fusion and thus deforesting an intermediate data structure. From right to left we are turning a control structure into a data structure. The *fold/unfold law* is a direct consequence of Theorem 1 and any of the fusion laws.

5   Fusion

In the previous sections we have introduced the fusion laws that we will now use to help us explain a collection of specific fusion techniques. We collectively brand these techniques *shortcut fusion*, as they share the common characteristic of standardising the way data structures are recursively consumed and produced. Where shortcut fusion techniques differ is in their choice of recursion scheme. By using recursive coalgebras, we can clearly lay out and compare these approaches within the *same* framework.[3] This allows us to examine the relationships among these fusion approaches which are not readily apparent when examining their individual implementations.

5.1   Warm-Up: Type Functors

We have seen in Section 2 that μ is a functor, whose action on arrows is defined $\mu\alpha = (\!| in \cdot \alpha |\!)$. Using Theorem 1 and the hylo shift law (13) we can actually express $\mu\alpha$ as a fold, an unfold or a hylo.

$$\mu\alpha \;=\; (\!| in \cdot \alpha |\!) \;=\; (\!| in \cdot \alpha \leftarrow out |\!) \;=\; (\!| in \leftarrow \alpha \cdot out |\!) \;=\; [\![\alpha \cdot out]\!] \ .$$

In Section 5.5 we shall see a key use of μ for stream fusion. For now, let us show a use of μ with the base functor of parametrized List

> **data** L $a\, b = Nil \mid Cons\,(a, b)$.

This is a higher-order functor of type $\mathsf{L} : \mathbb{C} \to \mathbb{C}^{\mathbb{C}}$ that takes objects to functors and arrows to natural transformations. In Haskell, we can make this datatype an instance of the *Functor* class:

> **instance** *Functor* (L a) **where**
>   *fmap f Nil* $= Nil$
>   *fmap f* ($Cons\,(a, b)$) $= Cons\,(a, f\, b)$.

We define this instance for the functor obtained by applying L to some type a. Haskell allows us to define this polymorphically for all a. The list datatype defined in terms of its base functor is List $A = \mu(\mathsf{L}\,A)$. The parametric type List is itself a functor, a so-called type functor, whose action on arrows is Haskell's *map* function, defined in this setting by List $f = \mu(\mathsf{L}\,f)$. Note that μ expects a natural transformation and that L delivers one.

5.2   Generalised *Foldr/Build* Fusion

We now move on to the main target of our new setting: shortcut fusion. The original shortcut fusion technique is a fold-centric approach called *foldr/build* fusion [9]. As its name would suggest, its original intention was to provide fusion

---

[3] Previously these recursion schemes were only compatible for analysis by restricting the working category to one that is algebraically compact, such as $\mathbf{Cpo}_{\perp}$.

for list functions written in terms of *foldr* and an additional combinator *build*. In this section, we will explore the foundations of this technique.

The mother of all fusion rules is algebra fusion (10). It allows us to fuse a hylo followed by an algebra homomorphism into a single hylo. It is similar to fold fusion in the sense that to use this law, we must construct a new algebra that satisfies a pre-condition. To illustrate this, the pipeline $sum \cdot filter\ odd$ can be expressed as a composition of two folds: $(\!|\mathfrak{s}|\!) \cdot (\!|\mathfrak{f}|\!)$. The algebras $\mathfrak{s}$ and $\mathfrak{f}$ are given by

$$\mathfrak{f} : \mathsf{L}\,\mathbb{N}\,(\mu(\mathsf{L}\,\mathbb{N})) \rightarrow \mu(\mathsf{L}\,\mathbb{N})$$
$$\mathfrak{f}\,Nil = in\,Nil$$
$$\mathfrak{f}\,(Cons\,(x,y)) = \textbf{if } odd\,x \qquad \mathfrak{s} : \mathsf{L}\,\mathbb{N}\,\mathbb{N} \rightarrow \mathbb{N}$$
$$\textbf{then } in\,(Cons\,(x,y)) \qquad \mathfrak{s}\,Nil = 0$$
$$\textbf{else } y \qquad\qquad \mathfrak{s}\,(Cons\,(x,y)) = x+y \ .$$

To be able to apply algebra fusion (10), we have to show that $(\!|\mathfrak{s}|\!)$ is an algebra homomorphism from $\mathfrak{f}$ to some unknown algebra $\mathfrak{sf}$. By hand, it is not hard to derive $\mathfrak{sf}$ so that $(\!|\mathfrak{s}|\!) \cdot \mathfrak{f} = \mathfrak{sf} \cdot \mathsf{F}\,(\!|\mathfrak{s}|\!)$.

$$\mathfrak{sf} : \mathsf{L}\,\mathbb{N}\,\mathbb{N} \rightarrow \mathbb{N}$$
$$\mathfrak{sf}\,Nil = \mathfrak{s}\,Nil$$
$$\mathfrak{sf}\,(Cons\,(x,y)) = \textbf{if } odd\,x \textbf{ then } \mathfrak{s}\,(Cons\,(x,y)) \textbf{ else } y$$

Since $(\!|\mathfrak{s}|\!)$ replaces *in* by $\mathfrak{s}$, we simply have to replace the occurrences of *in* in $\mathfrak{f}$ by $\mathfrak{s}$. While this is an easy task to perform by hand, it is potentially difficult to mechanise as it requires analysis of the body of $\mathfrak{f}$; within it, the constructor *in* could easily have any name and conversely any function could be named *in*. Also, $\mathfrak{f}$ could contain unrelated occurrences of *in*. This transformation is therefore not purely syntactic, but also involves some further analysis of the source program; this is not an approach we wish to pursue.

The central idea of *foldr/build* fusion is to expose *in* so that replacing it by the algebra a is simple to implement. Consider fold fusion (2) again.

$$h \cdot (\!|a|\!) = (\!|b|\!) \quad \Longleftarrow \quad h : a \rightarrow b$$

A fold $(\!|-|\!)$ is a transformation that takes an algebra to a homomorphism. Assume that we have another such transformation, say, β that satisfies

$$h \cdot \beta\,a = \beta\,b \quad \Longleftarrow \quad h : a \rightarrow b \ . \tag{15}$$

The generalisation of *foldr/build* from lists to arbitrary datatypes, the so-called *acid rain rule* [19], is then

$$(\!|a|\!) \cdot \beta\,in = \beta\,a \ . \tag{16}$$

Using β we expose *in* so that replacing *in* by a is achieved through a simple function application. Instead of building a structure and then folding over it, we eliminate the *in* and pass a directly to β. The proof of correctness is painless.

$$(\!| a |\!) \cdot \beta \, in = \beta \, a$$
$$\Longleftarrow \quad \{ \text{ assumption (15) } \}$$
$$(\!| a |\!) : in \to a$$

But, have we made any progress? After all, before we can apply (16), we have to prove (15). Fold satisfies this property, but this instance of (16) is trivial: $(\!| a |\!) \cdot (\!| in |\!) = (\!| a |\!)$. Now, it turns out that in a *relationally parametric* programming language [16], the proof obligation (15) amounts to the *free theorem* [21] of the polymorphic type

$$\beta : \forall A \,.\, (\mathsf{F}\, A \to A) \to (B \to A) \;, \tag{17}$$

where B is some fixed type. In other words, in such a language the proof obligation can be discharged by the type checker.

Returning to our example, we redefine *filter odd* as $(\lambda\, a \,.\, (\!| \phi\, a |\!))\, in$ where

$$\phi : (\mathsf{L}\, \mathbb{N}\, b \to b) \to (\mathsf{L}\, \mathbb{N}\, b \to b)$$
$$\phi\, a\, Nil \qquad\qquad = a\, Nil$$
$$\phi\, a\, (Cons\, (x, y)) = \textbf{if } odd\, x \textbf{ then } a\, (Cons\, (x, y)) \textbf{ else } y \;\;.$$

We derived ϕ from the algebra f by abstracting away from in. The reader should convince herself that $\lambda\, a \,.\, (\!| \phi\, a |\!)$ has indeed the desired polymorphic type (17). We can then invoke the acid rain rule (16) to obtain

$$(\!| \mathsf{s} |\!) \cdot (\lambda\, a \,.\, (\!| \phi\, a |\!))\, in = (\lambda\, a \,.\, (\!| \phi\, a |\!))\, \mathsf{s} = (\!| \phi\, \mathsf{s} |\!) \;\;.$$

The example also shows that the *acid rain* rule is somewhat unstructured in that a hylo is hidden inside the abstraction $\lambda\, a$. Without performing an additional beta-reduction, we can apply the rule only once. We obtain a more structured rule if we shift the abstraction to the algebra and achieve *cata-hylo fusion:* If τ is a transformation that takes F-algebras to G-algebras satisfying

$$h : \tau\, a \to \tau\, b : \textbf{Alg}(\mathsf{G}) \qquad \Longleftarrow \qquad h : a \to b : \textbf{Alg}(\mathsf{F}) \;, \tag{18}$$

then

$$(\!| a |\!)_{\mathsf{F}} \cdot (\!| \tau\, in \leftarrow c |\!)_{\mathsf{G}} \;=\; (\!| \tau\, a \leftarrow c |\!)_{\mathsf{G}} \;\;. \tag{19}$$

If τ is $\lambda\, a \,.\, a$, then this is just the fold/unfold law (14). For $\tau\, a = a \cdot \alpha$, this is essentially functor fusion (3). The proof of correctness is straightforward.

$$(\!| a |\!)_{\mathsf{F}} \cdot (\!| \tau\, in \leftarrow c |\!)_{\mathsf{G}} = (\!| \tau\, a \leftarrow c |\!)_{\mathsf{G}}$$
$$= \quad \{ \text{ algebra fusion (10) } \}$$
$$(\!| a |\!)_{\mathsf{F}} : \tau\, in \to \tau\, a : \textbf{Alg}(\mathsf{G})$$
$$= \quad \{ \text{ assumption (18) } \}$$
$$(\!| a |\!)_{\mathsf{F}} : in \to a : \textbf{Alg}(\mathsf{F})$$

The proof obligation (18) once again amounts to a theorem for free, this time of the polymorphic type

$$\tau : \forall A \, . \, (F\, A \to A) \to (G\, A \to A) \ .$$

Using cata-hylo fusion, the running example simplifies to

$$(\!(\mathsf{s})\!) \cdot (\!(\phi \, in)\!) = (\!(\phi \, \mathsf{s})\!) \ .$$

We can now also fuse a composition of folds:

$$(\!(a)\!) \cdot (\!(\tau_1 \, in)\!) \cdot \ldots \cdot (\!(\tau_n \, in)\!) \cdot [\![c]\!] = (\!((\tau_n \cdot \ldots \cdot \tau_1) \, a \leftarrow c)\!) \ .$$

This demonstrates how the rewrite rule is able to achieve fusion over an entire pipeline of functions.

5.3   Generalised *Destroy/Unfoldr* Fusion

The *foldr/build* brand of shortcut fusion, and its generalisation to algebraic datatypes, is *fold-centric*. This limits the kind of functions that we can fuse, simply because some functions such as *zip* or *take* are not folds, or are not naturally written as folds. We can dualise *foldr/build* fusion to achieve an *unfold-centric* approach, called *destroy/unfoldr* [18]. To illustrate, consider the simple pipeline *take* 5 · *between*, where *take n* takes n elements (if available) from a list. It can be written as an unfold after an initialisation step: *take n* $= [\![\mathsf{t}]\!] \cdot start \, n$, where *start n* $= (\lambda \, l \, . \, (n, l))$, and where the coalgebra t is given by

type State $a = (\mathbb{N}, a)$
t : State $(\mu(\mathsf{L}\, a)) \to \mathsf{L}\, a \, (\text{State} \, (\mu(\mathsf{L}\, a)))$
t $(0, x)$ $= Nil$
t $(n + 1, x) = $ **case** *out x* **of** $Nil \to Nil$; $Cons \, (a, y) \to Cons \, (a, (n, y))$.

Here we make explicit the notion that an unfold models the steps of a stateful computation. The coalgebra takes a state as an argument and uses it to produce a value and a new state. In this example, the state type pairs the input list with a natural number, enabling us to track the overall number of values produced. The number of elements to take, paired with the list where the values are to be taken from, forms the initial state.

   We can dualise the *acid rain rule* to fuse the pipeline. If β is a transformation that satisfies

$$\beta \, c = \beta \, d \cdot h \quad \Longleftarrow \quad h : c \to d \ , \tag{20}$$

then

$$\beta \, c \ = \ \beta \, out \cdot [\![c]\!] \ . \tag{21}$$

Previously we exposed *in*, now we expose *out*. To apply the dual of acid rain we redefine *take n* as $(\lambda\, c\,.\, [\![\gamma\, c]\!] \cdot start\, n)\, out$, where

$$\gamma : (c \to \mathsf{L}\, a\, c) \to (\mathsf{State}\, c \to \mathsf{L}\, a\, (\mathsf{State}\, c))$$
$$\gamma\, c\, (0, x) = Nil$$
$$\gamma\, c\, (n, x) = \mathbf{case}\ c\, x\ \mathbf{of}\ Nil \to Nil;\ Cons\, (a, y) \to Cons\, (a, (n-1, y))\ .$$

The transformation γ is derived from t by abstracting away from *out*. We can now tackle our example:

$$(\lambda\, c\,.\, [\![\gamma\, c]\!] \cdot start\, 5)\, out \cdot [\![\mathfrak{b}]\!] = (\lambda\, c\,.\, [\![\gamma\, c]\!] \cdot start\, 5)\, \mathfrak{b} = [\![\gamma\, \mathfrak{b}]\!] \cdot start\, 5\ .$$

The proof obligation (20) corresponds to the free theorem of

$$\beta : \forall C\,.\, (C \to \mathsf{F}\, C) \to (C \to D)\ , \tag{22}$$

where D is fixed. And, indeed, $\lambda\, c\,.\, [\![\gamma\, c]\!] \cdot start\, 5$ has the required type.

Similarly, we can dualise our more structured *cata-hylo fusion* to achieve *hylo-ana fusion*: If τ is a transformation that takes recursive F-coalgebras to recursive G-coalgebras satisfying

$$h : \tau\, c \to \tau\, d : \mathbf{Rec}(\mathsf{G}) \quad\Longleftarrow\quad h : c \to d : \mathbf{Rec}(\mathsf{F})\ , \tag{23}$$

then

$$(\![a \leftarrow \tau\, c]\!)_\mathsf{G} = (\![a \leftarrow \tau\, out]\!)_\mathsf{G} \cdot [\![c]\!]_\mathsf{F}\ . \tag{24}$$

This time the proof obligation (23) cannot be discharged by the type checker alone as τ has to transform a *recursive* coalgebra into a *recursive* coalgebra! As an aside, the new rule cannot handle our running example as the two unfolds are separated by the initialisation function *start*.

Our example has focused on fusing the list parameter of *take*, yet if we admit to the fact that natural numbers are an inductive datatype, then *take* is really a function that consumes *two* data structures. The aforementioned *zip* is another function that consumes two data structures, and therefore has the potential to be fused with both of these inputs. Let us employ the expression $zip \cdot (between \times between)$ as another example that can be written in terms of unfolds: $[\![\mathfrak{z}]\!] \cdot ([\![\mathfrak{b}]\!] \times [\![\mathfrak{b}]\!])$. The algebra $\mathfrak{z}$ is given by

$$\mathfrak{z} : (\mu(\mathsf{L}\, a_1), \mu(\mathsf{L}\, a_2)) \to \mathsf{L}\, (a_1, a_2)\, (\mu(\mathsf{L}\, a_1), \mu(\mathsf{L}\, a_2))$$
$$\mathfrak{z}\, (x_1, x_2) = \mathbf{case}\, (out\, x_1,\, out\, x_2)\, \mathbf{of}$$
$$\qquad (Cons\, (a_1, b_1),\, Cons\, (a_2, b_2)) \to Cons\, ((a_1, a_2), (b_1, b_2))$$
$$\qquad otherwise \qquad\qquad\qquad \to Nil\ .$$

Our rules (21) and (24) are not applicable as we have *two* producers to the right of *zip*. Now, to fuse such a function, we need to employ *parallel hylo-ana fusion*: If τ satisfies,

$$h_1 \times h_2 : \tau\, (c_1, c_2) \to \tau\, (d_1, d_2) : \mathbf{Rec}(\mathsf{G})$$
$$\Longleftarrow \quad h_1 : c_1 \to d_1 : \mathbf{Rec}(\mathsf{F}_1) \wedge h_2 : c_2 \to d_2 : \mathbf{Rec}(\mathsf{F}_2)\ , \tag{25}$$

then

$$(a \leftarrow \tau \, (c_1, c_2))_{\mathsf{G}} \;=\; (a \leftarrow \tau \, (out, out))_{\mathsf{G}} \cdot ([\![c_1]\!]_{\mathsf{F}_1} \times [\![c_2]\!]_{\mathsf{F}_2}) \; . \tag{26}$$

Using this rule, we are now able to fuse the *zip* example:

$$[\![\zeta \, (out, out)]\!] \cdot ([\![\flat]\!] \times [\![\flat]\!]) = [\![\zeta \, (\flat, \flat)]\!] \; ,$$

where the transformation ζ is defined

$$\zeta : (b_1 \to \mathsf{L} \, a_1 \, b_1, b_2 \to \mathsf{L} \, a_2 \, b_2) \to (b_1, b_2) \to \mathsf{L} \, (a_1, a_2) \, (b_1, b_2)$$
$$\zeta \, (c_1, c_2) \, (x_1, x_2) = \textbf{case} \, (c_1 \, x_1, c_2 \, x_2) \, \textbf{of}$$
$$(\mathit{Cons} \, (a_1, b_1), \mathit{Cons} \, (a_2, b_2)) \to \mathit{Cons} \, ((a_1, a_2), (b_1, b_2))$$
$$\mathit{otherwise} \qquad\qquad\qquad \to \mathit{Nil} \; .$$

The proofs of correctness for (parallel) hylo-ana fusion are contained in an extended version of this paper.

5.4   Church and Co-church Encodings

In the two previous sections we have studied generalisations of *foldr/build* and *destroy/unfoldr* fusion. We have noted that $(\!-\!)$ generalises the list function *foldr*, and, likewise, $[\![-]\!]$ generalises *unfoldr*. We have been silent, however, about their counterparts *build* and *destroy*. It is time to break that silence, and in the process, provide a fresh perspective on recursive datatypes. For simplicity, we assume that we are working in **Set**.[4]

Consider again the polymorphic type of β (17) repeated below.

$$\forall A \, . \, (\mathsf{F} \, A \to A) \to (B \to A) \;\cong\; B \to (\forall A \, . \, (\mathsf{F} \, A \to A) \to A)$$

We have slightly massaged the type to bring B to the front. The universally quantified type on the right is known as the *Church encoding* of $\mu\mathsf{F}$ [4]. The type is quite remarkable as it encodes a recursive type without using recursion. One part of the isomorphism $\mu\mathsf{F} \cong \forall A \, . \, (\mathsf{F} \, A \to A) \to A$ is given by the acid rain rule (16). The following derivation, which infers the isomorphisms, makes this explicit—the initial equation is (16) with the arguments of β swapped.

$$\forall a \, . \, (\!a\!) \, (\beta \, b \, in) = \beta \, b \, a$$
$$\Leftrightarrow \quad \{ \text{ change of variables } \beta \, b = \gamma \, \}$$
$$\forall a \, . \, (\!a\!) \, (\gamma \, in) = \gamma \, a$$
$$\Leftrightarrow \quad \{ \text{ extensionality } \}$$
$$\lambda a \, . \, (\!a\!) \, (\gamma \, in) = \gamma$$
$$\Leftrightarrow \quad \{ \text{ define } \mathit{toChurch} \, x = \lambda a \, . \, (\!a\!) \, x \, \}$$
$$\mathit{toChurch} \, (\gamma \, in) = \gamma$$
$$\Leftrightarrow \quad \{ \text{ define } \mathit{fromChurch} \, \gamma = \gamma \, in \, \}$$
$$\mathit{toChurch} \, (\mathit{fromChurch} \, \gamma) = \gamma$$

---

[4] The development can be generalised using ends and coends [14].

The isomorphism *toChurch*, creates a function whose argument is an algebra and which folds that algebra over the given data structure. Its converse *fromChurch*, commonly called *build*, applies this function to the *in* algebra. Going back and forth, we get back the original structure: *fromChurch* (*toChurch s*) = *s*. This is the other part of the isomorphism, which follows directly from fold reflection.

As to be expected, everything nicely dualises. The polymorphic type (22) gives rise to the *co-Church encoding*.

$$\forall\, C \,.\, (C \to \mathsf{F}\, C) \to (C \to D) \;\cong\; (\exists\, C \,.\, (C \to \mathsf{F}\, C) \times C) \to D$$

Think of the co-Church encoding $\exists\, C \,.\, (C \to \mathsf{F}\, C) \times C$ as the type of state machines encapsulating a transition function $C \to \mathsf{F}\, C$ and the current state C.

The conversion to (co-)Church-encoding types are central to the concept of shortcut fusion. By changing representations to one with the recursion "built-in", we can write our transformations as non-recursively-defined (co-)algebras. Unlike recursive programs, compositions of these (co-)algebras can be optimised by the compiler to remove any intermediate allocations. All that remains is for the programmer to instruct the compiler to remove any unnecessary conversions, i.e. cases of *toChurch · fromChurch*. Removing these transformations preserves the semantics of the program because we can prove the isomorphism between these representations. More importantly, however, prevents us from producing a data structure only to immediately consume it. The co-Church encoding also underlies the original formulation of stream fusion, which we consider next.

5.5 Stream Fusion

The *foldr/build* flavour of fusion is fold-centric, in that it requires all functions that are intended to be fusible to be written as folds; similarly, *destroy/unfoldr* is unfold-centric. The boundaries of these world views are fuzzy. A *zip* can be written as a fold, the snag is that only one of the two inputs can be fused [9, §9]. Along a similar vein, a *filter* for the odd natural numbers, which we wrote before as a fold, can also be written as an unfold: $⟦f⟧$ where

$f : \mu(\mathsf{L}\, \mathbb{N}) \to \mathsf{L}\, \mathbb{N}\, (\mu(\mathsf{L}\, \mathbb{N}))$
$f\, x = \mathbf{case}\ out\ x\ \mathbf{of}\ Nil \to Nil;\ Cons\,(x, y) \to \mathbf{if}\ odd\ x\ \mathbf{then}\ Cons\,(x, y)\ \mathbf{else}\ f\, y$.

The coalgebra f is recursive and thus theoretically fine, but it is also recursive in its definition and this is a practical problem. A coalgebra must be non-recursively defined for it to be fused with others. We have two definitions and are caught between two worlds; is it possible to free ourselves?

Perhaps surprisingly, the answer is yes. Let us first try to eliminate the recursion from the definition above—the rest will then fall out. The idea is to use a different base functor, one that allows us to skip list elements. We draw inspiration from stream fusion [5] here:

data S a b = $Done$ | $Yield$ (a, b) | $Skip$ b .

instance $Functor$ (S a) **where**
    $fmap\,f\ Done$ = $Done$
    $fmap\,f\ (Skip\ b)$ = $Skip\ (f\ b)$
    $fmap\,f\ (Yield\ (a, b))$ = $Yield\ (a, f\ b)$

The *filter* coalgebra can now be written as a composition of *out* with

$f : S\,\mathbb{N}\,b \rightarrow S\,\mathbb{N}\,b$
$f\ Done$ = $Done$
$f\ (Skip\ y)$ = $Skip\ y$
$f\ (Yield\ (x, y))$ = **if** $odd\ x$ **then** $Yield\ (x, y)$ **else** $Skip\ y$.

So, *filter* = $[\![f \cdot out]\!]$. Something interesting has happened: since f is a natural transformation, we also have *filter* = $(\![in \cdot f]\!)$. We are unstuck; *filter* is both a fold and an unfold. Moreover, it is an application of a mapping function: *filter* = μf.

In general, consumers are folds, transformers are maps, and producers are unfolds. An entire pipeline of these an be fused into a single hylo:

$$(\![a]\!) \cdot \mu\alpha_1 \cdot \cdots \cdot \mu\alpha_n \cdot [\![c]\!] = (\![a \cdot \alpha_1 \cdot \cdots \cdot \alpha_n \leftarrow c]\!) .$$

Inspecting the types, the rule is clear:

$$A \xleftarrow{\ (\![a]\!)\ } \mu F_0 \xleftarrow{\ \mu\alpha_1\ } \mu F_1 \quad \cdots \quad \mu F_{n-1} \xleftarrow{\ \mu\alpha_n\ } \mu F_n \xleftarrow{\ [\![c]\!]\ } C .$$

In a sense, the introduction of *Skip* keeps the recursion in sync. Each transformation consumes a token and produces a token. Before, *filter* possibly consumed several tokens before producing one. We are finally in a position to deal with the example from the introduction, written in terms of the combinators we have

$$(\![s]\!) \cdot \mu(m\ sq) \cdot \mu(f\ odd) \cdot [\![b]\!] = (\![s \cdot m\ sq \cdot f\ odd \leftarrow b]\!) .$$

Utilising streams in this fashion is an instance of data abstraction; although we wish to present the List type using $\mu(L\ a)$, we intend to do all the work using $\mu(S\ a)$. We have functions $\rightarrow$S and $\leftarrow$S to convert to and from streams, respectively. They are defined as an algebra and a coalgebra that allow us to consume streams using a fold and produce them using an unfold:

$\leftarrow$S : S a $(\mu(L\ a)) \rightarrow (\mu(L\ a))$
$\leftarrow$S $Done$ = $in\ Nil$
$\leftarrow$S $(Skip\ xs)$ = xs
$\leftarrow$S $(Yield\ (x, xs))$ = $in\ (Cons\ (x, xs))$
$\rightarrow$S : $\mu(L\ a) \rightarrow$ S a $(\mu(L\ a))$
$\rightarrow$S $(in\ Nil)$ = $Done$
$\rightarrow$S $(in\ (Cons\ (x, xs)))$ = $Yield\ (x, xs)$.

We must prove that our stream implementations, together with the conversion functions, fulfil the same specification as the analogous functions over $\mu(L\ a)$ (*cf.*

Lemma 1 and Theorem 3 in [23]). This is called the *data abstraction property*. In our framework, this obligation is expressed as a simple equality between a conventional list function definition and its associated stream version composed with our conversion functions. For example, for *filter* we must prove

$$filter = (\!|\!\leftarrow\!\mathsf{S}|\!) \cdot \mu\mathfrak{f} \cdot [\![\rightarrow\!\mathsf{S}]\!] \ .$$

Because we can phrase these functions as folds, unfolds, and natural transformations, the proof is straightforward, using the laws we have set out in previous sections. We leave it as an exercise to the reader.

Just as for lists, every datatype can be extended with a *Skip*. Although stream fusion is the first to make use of this augmentation, we note its relation to Capretta's representation of general recursion in type theory [1], which proposes adding a "computation step" constructor to coinductive types.

6   Related Work

Wadler first introduced the idea of simplifying the fusion problem with his deforestation algorithm [22]. This was limited to so-called *treeless* programs, a subset of first-order programs. The fusion transformation proposed by Chin [3] generalises Wadler's deforestation. It uses a program annotation scheme to recognise the terms that can be fused and skip the terms that cannot. Sheard and Fegaras focus on the use of folds over algebraic types as a recursion scheme [17]. Their algorithm for normalising the nested application of folds is based on the fold fusion law. Their recursion schemes are suitably general to handle functions such as *zip* that recurse over multiple data structures simultaneously [6].

Gill et al. first introduced the notion of shortcut fusion with *foldr*/*build* fusion [9] for Haskell. This allowed programs written as folds to be fused. It was subsequently introduced into the List library for Haskell in GHC. Takano and Meijer [19] provided a calculational view of fusion and generalised it to arbitrary data structures. It generalised the fusion law by using hylomorphisms and also noted the possibility of dualising *foldr*/*build* fusion. They worked in the setting of **Cpo**, however, where hylomorphisms do not have unique solutions, only canonical ones. Takano and Meijer claimed that, even when restricted to lists, their method is more powerful than that of Gill et al. as theirs could fuse both parameters of *zip*. This was incorrect, and the need for an additional parallel rule for *zip* was pointed out later by Hu et al. [11]. Their extension is what we present as the parallel hylo-ana rule.

Svenningson provided an actual implementation of *destroy*/*unfoldr* fusion [18], where he showed how *filter*-like functions could be expressed as unfolds. Svenningson did not, however, solve the issue of recursion in the coalgebras of such functions, which could therefore not be fused even though they could be written as unfolds. This was addressed by Coutts et al., who presented stream fusion [5], which introduced the *Skip* constructor as a way to encode non-productive computation steps, similar to Capretta's work on encoding general recursion in type theory [1].

The correctness and generalisation of fusion has been explored in many different settings. In addition to the work of Takano and Meier, Ghani et al. generalised *foldr/build* to work with datatypes "induced by inductive monads". Johann and Ghani further showed how to apply initial algebra semantics, and thus *foldr/build* fusion, to nested datatypes [12]. Voigtländer has also used free theorems to show correctness, specifically of the *destroy/build* rule [20].

7   Conclusions

We have presented a framework that has allowed us to bring three fusion techniques into the same setting. We have exploited recursive coalgebras and hylomorphisms as 'the rug that ties the room together'. This enabled us to formally describe and reason about these fusion techniques. In doing so, we have exposed their underlying foundations, including the importance of Church and co-Church encodings. The fact that our hylomorphisms have unique solutions plays a central rôle. The knock-on effect is that we gain clear, short proofs thanks to the calculational properties available to us.

References

1. Capretta, V.: General recursion via coinductive types. Logical Methods in Computer Science 1(2), 1–28 (2005)
2. Capretta, V., Uustalu, T., Vene, V.: Recursive coalgebras from comonads. Information and Computation 204(4), 437–468 (2006)
3. Chin, W.N.: Safe Fusion of Functional Expressions. In: LISP and functional programming, pp. 11–20 (1992)
4. Church, A.: The calculi of lambda-conversion. Annals of Mathematics Studies, vol. 6. Princeton University Press, Princeton (1941)
5. Coutts, D., Leshchinskiy, R., Stewart, D.: Stream Fusion: From Lists to Streams to Nothing At All. In: ICFP 2007, pp. 315–326 (2007)
6. Fegaras, L., Sheard, T., Zhou, T.: Improving Programs which Recurse over Multiple Inductive Structures. In: PEPM 1994 (June 1994)
7. Fokkinga, M.M., Meijer, E.: Program calculation properties of continuous algebras. Technical Report CS-R9104. CWI, Amsterdam (January 1991)
8. Freyd, P.J.: Remarks on algebraically compact categories. In: Fourman, M.P., Johnstone, P.T., Pitts, A.M. (eds.) Applications of Categories in Computer Science. LMS Lecture Note Series, vol. 177, pp. 95–106. Cambridge University Press, Cambridge (1992)
9. Gill, A., Launchbury, J., Peyton Jones, S.L.: A Short Cut to Deforestation. Functional programming languages and computer architecture, 223–232 (1993)
10. Hinze, R., Harper, T., James, D.W.H.: Theory and Practice of Fusion. Tech. Rep. CS-RR-11-01. Oxford University Computing Laboratory (2011)
11. Hu, Z., Iwasaki, H., Takeichi, M.: An Extension of The Acid Rain Theorem. Functional and Logic Programming, 91–105 (1996)
12. Johann, P., Ghani, N.: Initial algebra semantics is enough! In: Della Rocca, S.R. (ed.) TLCA 2007. LNCS, vol. 4583, pp. 207–222. Springer, Heidelberg (2007)

13. Lambek, J.: A fixpoint theorem for complete categories. Math. Zeitschr. 103, 151–161 (1968)
14. Mac Lane, S.: Categories for the Working Mathematician, 2nd edn. Graduate Texts in Mathematics. Springer, Berlin (1998)
15. Meijer, E., Fokkinga, M., Paterson, R.: Functional programming with bananas, lenses, envelopes and barbed wire. In: Hughes, J. (ed.) FPCA 1991. LNCS, vol. 523, pp. 124–144. Springer, Heidelberg (1991)
16. Reynolds, J.C.: Types, abstraction and parametric polymorphism. In: Mason, R.E.A. (ed.) Information Processing 1983, pp. 513–523. North-Holland, Amsterdam (1983)
17. Sheard, T., Fegaras, L.: A Fold for All Seasons. Functional programming languages and computer architecture, 233–242 (1993)
18. Svenningsson, J.: Shortcut fusion for Accumulating Parameters & Zip-like Functions. In: ICFP 2002, pp. 124–132 (2002)
19. Takano, A., Meijer, E.: Shortcut deforestation in calculational form. Functional programming languages and computer architecture, 306–313 (1995)
20. Voigtländer, J.: Proving correctness via free theorems: the case of the destroy/-build-rule. Partial Eval. and Semantics-Based Prog. Manip. 13–20 (2008)
21. Wadler, P.: Theorems for free! In: FPCA, pp. 347–359 (1989)
22. Wadler, P.: Deforestation: transforming programs to eliminate trees. Theoretical Computer Science 73(2), 231–248 (1990)
23. Wang, M., Gibbons, J., Matsuda, K., Hu, Z.: Gradual refinement: Blending pattern matching with data abstraction. In: Bolduc, C., Desharnais, J., Ktari, B. (eds.) MPC 2010. LNCS, vol. 6120, pp. 397–425. Springer, Heidelberg (2010)

Orthogonal Serialisation for Haskell

Jost Berthold

Department of Computer Science
University of Copenhagen
berthold@diku.dk

Abstract. Data serialisation is a crucial feature of real-world programming languages, often provided by standard libraries or even built-in to the language. However, a number of questions arise when the language in question uses demand-driven evaluation and supports higher-order functions, as is the case for the lazy functional language Haskell. To date, solutions to serialisation for Haskell generally do not support higher-order functions and introduce additional strictness.

This paper investigates a novel approach to serialisation of Haskell data structures with a high degree of flexibility, based on runtime support for parallel Haskell on distributed memory platforms. This serialisation has highly desirable and so-far unrivalled properties: it is truly orthogonal to evaluation and also does not require any type class mechanisms. Especially, (almost) any kind of value can be serialised, including functions and IO actions. We outline the runtime support on which our serialisation is based, and present an API of Haskell functions and types which ensure dynamic type safety of the serialisation process. Furthermore, we explore and exemplify potential application areas for orthogonal serialisation.

1 Introduction

Serialisation of data is a crucial feature of real-world programming systems. Being able to write out and read in data structures without complications provides a simple and straightforward way of saving and restoring an application's configuration, and generally enables a program's state to persist between runs. Mainstream and scripting languages like Java, Ruby, Perl and Python provide powerful libraries for this purpose by default, concentrating on ease of use (consider e.g. Python's pickle interface or the omnipresent JSON format for object-oriented web programming). There is considerable interest and demand for general serialisation features in Haskell. In the past year, we have come across related requests on mailing lists or talked about it in personal discussion at several opportunities [1,12,14,13]. For the functional world, the characteristic equal treatment of a program (functions) and its (heap) data poses additional challenges to the design and implementation of serialisation features. Functions (in particular *higher-order functions*) are first-class citizens and should be serialisable as other data. Another complication is added if the language in question uses demand-driven evaluation: how should serialisation treat *unevaluated data?*

J. Hage, M.T. Morazán (Eds.): IFL 2010, LNCS 6647, pp. 38–53, 2011.

The lazy purely functional language Haskell [9] has both properties, yet existing serialisation approaches for Haskell do not preserve either of them.

To overcome this deficiency, this paper proposes and explores a new approach to serialisation of Haskell data structures, based on runtime support for parallel Haskell. Implementations of parallel Haskell variants for distributed memory systems obviously require transferring data from one heap to another. This transfer is based on breadth-first packing and unpacking of graph structures from the Haskell heap, which can represent Haskell data structures of various kind, independent of the evaluation state. In other words, the parallel runtime includes an internal built-in serialisation mechanism with novel and interesting properties. In this paper, we explore the potential and technical limits of using the parallel Haskell graph packing routines to serialise data in Haskell:

- In Section 3, we propose a serialisation mechanism based on runtime support, which is orthogonal in two ways:
    + Orthogonal to evaluation. That is, both normal form and non-normal form data can be serialised.
    + Orthogonal to type. That is, values of any data type can be serialised, no type class mechanisms are required. The notable exceptions are special concurrency types (MVar and transactional variables), serialisation of which is not supported by the runtime system.
- We show how to re-establish dynamic type safety for this type orthogonal serialisation support of the runtime system using suitable Haskell wrapper code.
- In Section 4, we propose and exemplify application areas for our approach which cannot be realised using other serialisation approaches.

2   Related Work

As already mentioned in the beginning, serialisation is a common standard feature present in many programming languages. We put the focus of our discussion on approaches specific to lazy functional languages and consider mechanisms for serialisation and persistence.

A very simple, yet unsatisfying, serialisation (and, thereby, data persistence) is to use the Show and Read class instances. Data types which define instances for these classes can simply be written to a string (`show`) and parsed back in (`read`). Efficiency can be drastically improved by using binary I/O (various libraries have been proposed), and integrated approaches like [25], which uses additional type classes to offer more programming comfort. More recently, we also see efforts to improve efficiency by reproducing the original sharing structure when reading in data [6].

However, all these approaches require the complete evaluation of the data which is to be serialised, and serialisation of infinite or cyclic data structures will send the program into an infinite loop[1]. The real challenge in combining

---

[1] In the Haskell wiki [11], we have found allusions to a library SerTH that allegedly supports cyclic data structures and uses template haskell. The provided links are however not accessible any more. This library seems to have perished (including all substantial information about its implementation techniques).

serialisation and laziness is to serialise only partially evaluated values. Only if data evaluation and data serialisation are truly orthogonal, a library for persistence can be established where previous evaluations are reused later. Efforts have been made in the past to join lazy functional languages and persistence in an orthogonal way.

McNally [19,18] has pioneered these questions with Staple, a programming system with a purely functional interpreter interface, related to Miranda and the then-upcoming Haskell. In an integrated whole-system approach, Staple supports two concepts of persistence: a store of persistent modules which evolve to more and more evaluated state transparently, and interactive stream persistence which allows the user to explicitly create, retrieve and update persistent values in the store. Stream I/O instead of monads and the simplistic interpreter interface characterise Staple as early pioneering work in the field. To our knowledge, no existing system is similar to the Staple persistent store, but it has set directions for several successors.

One such strand of work is Persistent Haskell [24, and earlier: [7]], which describes concepts for adding persistence to the GHC runtime, based on the GUM [26] runtime support for packing which we are using subsequently as well. As in GUM, special closures with fetch semantics are used for retrieving persistent data, which is stored in an external generic persistent object store. While these mechanisms remain completely transparent, the programming interface to the system requires to explicitly open a store and retrieve and store values. The approach of the authors is based on the same runtime system features as ours, yet the paper does not go beyond a high-level design and does not present working solutions to the inherent problems (some of which are nevertheless discussed). One essential advantage is, however, that their design will preserve sharing across several serialised values.

The system which comes closest to what we outline here is the way Clean provides lazy dynamics [27]. Clean dynamics both solve the problem of runtime typing and retain the laziness of stored data, while allowing to transfer data between different applications. However, this transfer feature for unevaluated data requires an integrated systemic design around an "application repository" which contains all functions referenced by persistent data (we will see why this is necessary in the technical main part).

Very limited support for dynamics is included in the Haskell base library [10] as well, in `Data.Dynamic`. We mention it here because we are going to use the underlying `Data.Typeable` to solve typing problems in our approach. Based on the module `Data.Typeable` which provides runtime type reification and guarded type casts, data can be converted to a `Dynamic` and back to its original type (failing at runtime if the type is wrong). Haskell Dynamics are very limited, since a Dynamic can only be used in the same *run* of the same program (binary). In practice, this limits their use to up and downcasting elements for a uniform container type.

3   Implementation

3.1   Runtime System Support

Our implementation of heap data serialisation is based on the functionality needed for the Eden [17] and GUM [26] parallel variants of Haskell, namely graph packing. The runtime system (RTS) for Eden and GUM contains methods to traverse and pack a computation graph in the heap in breadth-first manner, and the respective counterpart for unpacking. This is by far the most crucial and error-prone part of the parallel Haskell implementations Eden and GUM [17,4,26]. At the same time, it needs to be an integrated part of the RTS. Outsourcing its functionality into a library appears to require rather specialised and complex supporting runtime features (which we investigated in [3] and [2]).

Heap closures in GHC are laid out in memory as a header section containing metadata, followed by all pointers to other graph nodes, and then by all non-pointers[2]. The essential and first header field is the *info pointer*, which points to information such as the number of pointers and non-pointers in the particular heap closure, and the entry code.

When packing data, the respective computation graph structure is traversed and serialised. During the traversal, unevaluated data (thunks) are packed as the function to apply and its arguments, so they can be evaluated on the receiver side. Newly met closures are packed as their header data and non-pointer data. Pointers will be reestablished from the global packet structure when unpacking. Cyclic graph structures are broken up by using back references into the previous data. That is, when a closure is met again, the routine will not pack the actual closure data again, but will pack a special marker (REF) for a back reference and the relative position of the previously packed closure in the packet. As this requires a starting marker field, normal closures will start by another marker (CLO). A third type of marker indicates static closures (constant applicative forms).

Figure 1 shows an example packet (on the left) which serialises a subgraph of five nodes (depicted on the right), with a line of explanatory comments below the packet data. For simplicity, header data is assumed to be just one word (the info pointer). The graph traversal is breadth-first from left to right. As indicated, closures 2 and 4 appear twice in the packet, the second time only as references. All pointer fields are left out in the packet; they will be filled with references to the subsequent closures upon unpacking using a closure queue.

As the reader might already have noticed from the description, this packing routine relies on the closure layout information and info pointers being pre-shared between the sender and receiver. The packing algorithm in its current form also uses static memory addresses of the program's (and libraries') functions. In consequence, the algorithm assumes that the exact same binary is receiving the data. This limitation is discussed at the end of this section. Furthermore, packing may currently fail because a graph structure in the heap is bigger than

---

[2] There are some heap closures which use a *bitmap layout*, mixing pointers and non-pointers. We only describe the common case with standard layout here.

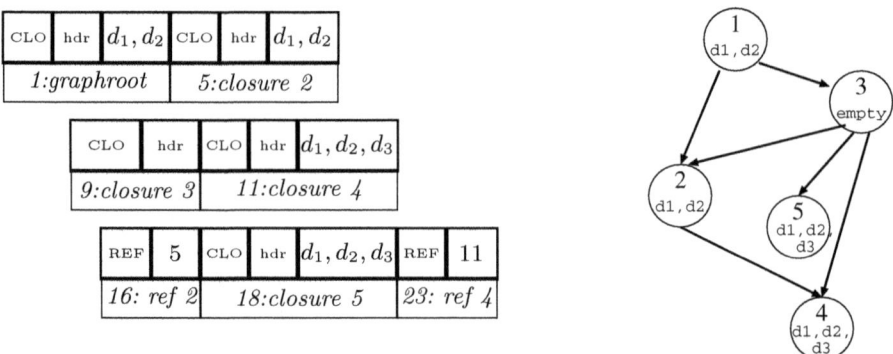

Fig. 1. Example serialisation packet for a computation graph

a configurable maximum buffer size. The RTS could reallocate a bigger buffer in this case, but this is not implemented yet.

On the plus side, graph packing works on most closure types in GHC and is therefore to a large extent independent of the data type to be packed. The notable exception are primitive data structures for synchronisation, mutable variables (MVars), and transactional variables, which cannot be packed. Typically, packing and transfering data structures which contain MVars does not make sense, since they imply and store external system state. Examples include IO file handles, as well as semaphores and other synchronisation structures. Apart from this restriction, serialisation is completely orthogonal to the Haskell type system.

3.2   Heap to Array: Unsafe Dynamics

As the first step towards our Haskell serialisation, we define a primitive operation which, instead of sending a serialised graph over the wire, returns the data in a Haskell byte array. A byte array is a primitive data type in GHC which provides a chunk of heap for unboxed non-pointer values. This type is the basis of every higher-level array which contains unboxed values (raw data, as opposed to "boxed" values which are stored in pointer arrays).

```
———————————————— Primitives and IO-monadic wrapper ————————————

serialize#   :: a -> State# s -> (# State# s, ByteArray# #)
deserialize# :: ByteArray# -> State# s -> (# State# s, a #)

heapToArray   :: a -> IO (UArray Int Word)
heapFromArray :: UArray Int Word -> IO a
```

Shown here are the types of the primitive operations and two small wrapper functions which provide an IO-monadic version and lift the result type to an unboxed array (`UArray`) of `Word`s. These two functions `heapToArray` and `heapFromArray` provide the minimum wrapper around the primitive operation: the functions return a regular Haskell data structure in the IO monad.

When used in a disciplined manner, these functions can already prove useful, for they contain all the necessary data to reconstruct the serialised structure in its current evaluation state. However, no type safety is provided: any type of value can be serialised and later, after unpacking, can be used as any other data type, interpreting the raw data in the heap closures in an incorrect way. A programmer might well be aware of this problem, but make wrong assumptions on the type inference defaults in the compiler, as the following example illustrates.

─────────────────── *An unintended type cast* ───────────────────

```
lucky = do let list = map (2^) [30..40]          -- defaults to [Integer]
           pack <- heapToArray list
           ...
           copy <- heapFromArray pack            -- type of copy??
           putStrLn (show (length copy : copy))  -- fixes copy :: [Int]
                                                 -- (length :: [a] -> Int)
```

In our example, a list of whole numbers is packed (its default type is a large (GMP-based) [Integer]), and most list elements will exceed 32bit in size. When unpacking the data, explicit type annotations or the type context of the copy (here, the added length copy) might lead to interpreting it as [Int] instead. Only the first number in the list retains its correct value 2^{30}, and only because Integers are handled by machine instructions and stored in a format similar to Int when they are small enough. For the following (larger) numbers, the data structures in the Haskell heap are GMP-specific. Their addresses are misinterpreted as 32bit Int values, leading to the following wrong program output:

─────────────────── *Output when running* lucky: ───────────────────

```
[11,1073741824,28788544,45565760,45565760,45565760,45565760,45565761,...]
```

Unpacking a serialised value into a value of the wrong type can lead to all kinds of runtime errors. The subsequent code makes false assumptions about its heap representation and enters the data structure at the wrong point. In the best case, the two types have a "similar" underlying heap representation, but might still be misinterpreted, as in our example above. Other cases might lead to complete failure.

3.3   Phantom Types: Type-Safe Dynamics in One Program Run

In order to provide more type safety, we wrap the array containing the serialised data inside a structure which uses a phantom type:

─────────────── *Serialisation data structure for type safety* ───────────────

```
data Serialized a = Serialized { packetSize :: Int
                               , packetData :: ByteArray#}
serialize   :: a -> IO (Serialized a)
deserialize :: Serialized a -> IO a
```

Passing the original type to a `Serialized` type constructor in this way ensures that the type checker refuses ill-typed programs with a meaningful error message. The type is not arbitrary any more, but included in the data structure passed to the deserialisation function (as a *phantom type*, at compile time). Data can be restored in a typesafe manner within the same program run now. In our example, the type `[Int]` inferred from concatenating the unpacked list to an `Int` propagates up to the original (exposing the `Int` overflow one can expect).

```
──────────────────── Type propagating up ────────────────────
works = do let list = map (2^) [30..40]      -- inferred: [Int]
           pack <- serialize list            -- inferred: Serialized [Int]
           ...
           copy <- deserialize pack
           putStrLn (show (length copy : copy)) -- fixes the type: [Int]
                                                -- (length :: [a] -> Int)
-- output: [11,1073741824,-2147483648,0,0,0,0,0,0,0,0,0,0]
```

3.4   Type-Safe Persistence

With the previously presented code in place, an obvious idea is to store and later retrieve the array which represents the serialised data. Essentially this is what we need in order to realise *persistence*, i.e., keeping partially evaluated data in an external store and loading it into a program. Using `Show` and `Read` instances with `read . show == id` for the `Serialized a` type allows one to write a representation to a file as a string and parse it. Much more space efficient, yet conceptually equivalent, the `Binary` interface can be used. Two problems become apparent when doing so, only one of which can be solved easily.

Dynamic Type Checks. The *first problem* is again one of typing: when reading `Serialized a` from a file and deserializing the represented data, the type a of these data has got to be accurate, either given by the programmer or inferred. Since a user can (attempt to) read from any arbitrary file, this type check needs to happen at runtime. Figure 2 shows how to realise this dynamic type check using the runtime type reification provided by `Data.Typeable`,

First, the `Serialized` data structure now needs to include type information.

```
data Serialized a = Serialized { packetSize :: Int
                               , packetType :: TypeRep
                               , packetData :: ByteArray#}
```

Second, the represented type has got to be established and checked when reading in and deserialising data. With the phantom type, the right place to do this type check is inside the `Read` instance for `Serialized`, requiring a `Typeable` context (instances can be automatically derived with GHC). Data loaded into the running program must have the appropriate type, or the program will halt with a runtime error and report the type mismatch.

```
instance Typeable a => Show (Serialized a)
  where ... -- showing packet in human-readable and parsable format.

parseP :: ReadS (Int,String,[Word]) -- Parser matching the Show format
parseP = ... -- not shown. Returns packet size, type string, values.

instance Typeable a => Read (Serialized a)
    where readsPrec _ input
          = case parseP input of
            [((size,tp,dat),r)] ->
                let !(UArray _ _ _ arr# ) = listArray (0,size-1) dat
                    t = typeOf (undefined::a)
                in if show t == tp
                      then [(Serialized size t arr# , r)]
                      else error ("Type error during parse: "
                                  ++ show t ++ " vs. " ++ tp)
            other -> error "No parse"
```

Fig. 2. Serialisation structure, `Read` instance

```
instance Typeable a => Binary (Serialized a) where
    put (Serialized sz tp bArr#)
        = do let typeStr = show tp
                 arr     = UArray 0 (sz-1) sz bArr# :: UArray Int Word
             put typeStr
             put arr
    get = do typeStr <- get :: Get String
             uarr    <- get :: Get (UArray Int Word)
             let !(UArray _ _ sz bArr#) = uarr
                 tp = typeOf (undefined :: a) -- for type check
             if (show tp == typeStr)
                  then return ( Serialized sz tp bArr# )
                  else error ("Type error during parse:\n\tExpected "
                              ++ show tp ++ ", found " ++ typeStr ++ ".")

encodeToFile :: Typeable a => FilePath -> a -> IO ()
encodeToFile path x = serialize x >>= encodeFile path

decodeFromFile :: Typeable a => FilePath -> IO a
decodeFromFile path = decodeFile path >>= deserialize
```

Fig. 3. Serialisation structure, `Binary` instances

Figure 3 shows the definition of a binary instance for type `Serialized`, using the same type check mechanism, and file interface functions `encodeToFile` and `decodeFromFile`, in analogy to `encodeFile` and `decodeFile` provided by the Binary module itself.

Using `Typeable` in our implementation now restricts the serialisation to monomorphic types. Furthermore, the check compares not the `TypeRep` itself, but its string representation–`TypeRep` is just an ID that changes from run to run. Both limitations are introduced by the GHC implementation of `Data.Typeable`.

Please note that the place of our type check is essentially different to dynamics in Clean [27], where a pattern match on types is performed at the time of unpacking a value from dynamic (corresponding to `deserialize`). Clean's approach is more liberal and even allows to "try" several different type matches in one function, as well as polymorphism through the dynamic apply function.

References to Raw Memory Addresses. The *second*, more serious, *limitation* of the approach is the use of static information and memory addresses (info pointers and static functions) in the packing code. The packing algorithm in its current form directly uses the memory addresses of functions in the program and in libraries which it uses, as well as static layout information. The latter could be easily fixed by duplicating this layout information in the packet. However, directly using code addresses in memory assumes that the exact same binary is receiving the data and that no code relocation takes place.

Dynamic assignment of code addresses (relocatable code) can be dealt with by packing offsets to a known reference point (as also mentioned in [24]). Another possibility is to inspect the application at runtime using binary utilities like `nm`. However, if an application is recompiled after making changes to its code, the addresses of static data and the compiler-generated names will necessarily change, thereby invalidating previously produced packet data without a chance of correction for the new binary.

Well-understood, the ability to store and retrieve only partially evaluated data is the main advantage of our proposal, and this property *conceptually requires* to keep references to a program's functions if they are needed in the serialised computation. Clean [27] achieves this by a system-wide application store which contains all code referenced from a saved dynamic, requiring special tools for its maintenance (transfer to other machines, deletion, garbage collection of the application store). We consider this a slightly too system-invasive and demanding solution[3]. It would be better to achieve a compromise design where serialisation packets stay independent and self-contained (at the price of higher failure potential at runtime).

To enable data transfer between several applications (and there is no fundamental difference between this and data exchange between different versions of one application), big changes to the packing format will be necessary. Not only does the code need to replace static addresses by relative references, the packet needs to include the static data itself, metadata as well as chunks of code for functions of the program which have to be dynamically linked at runtime. On the other hand, it is easy to make the system produce an understandable runtime error message when loading data with the wrong version. This can be achieved

---

[3] In a personal conversation [23], the author came to know that in practice, Clean uses a "reduced" version of Dynamics without application store which poses similar problems.

```
checkpoint :: Typeable a => FilePath -> IO a -> IO a
checkpoint name actions = encodeToFile name actions >> actions

recover :: Typeable a => FilePath -> IO a
recover name = doesFileExist name >>= \b ->
               if b then decodeFromFile name >>= id
                    else error ("No checkpoint file " ++ name)
```

Fig. 4. Basic checkpointing constructs

by including a hash value of the program code into the `Serialized` data and checking that value while parsing as an additional dynamic consistency check. All this can be realised purely at the Haskell level.

4   Potential Applications

4.1   Checkpointing Long-Running Applications

Checkpointing is the process of storing a snapshot of an application's current state during runtime.This allows the application to be restarted in the same state after interruptions.

With the presented serialisation approach, we can realise a simple checkpointing mechanisms to recover long-running Haskell applications from external failures and interruptions by serialising suitable parts of the running program (as a sequence of IO actions) and storing them for a potential recovery.

Figure 4 shows two utility functions which we propose for this purpose. The first function `checkpoint` serializes the given sequence of IO `actions` (which might be the whole remainder of a program at a certain stage of program execution) and executes it afterwards. Previous variable bindings referred to by the sequence are automatically included in this serialisation in their current evaluation state. The second function loads an IO action from a file and executes it. To achieve good performance, both functions use the binary file interface functions defined in Figure 3. These functions can now be used directly at the top level, as sketched here:

```
main = do args <- getArgs
          if not (null args) && head args == "-r"
          then recover "checkpt"
          else do x1 <- computation_1 args
                  actions_1 x1
                  checkpoint "checkpt" $ do
                    actions_2 x1
                    x2 <- computation_2 x1
                    checkpoint "checkpt" $ do
                      more_actions x1 x2
                      ...
```

However, the program needs to be structured in a somewhat unelegant "continuation-capturing" style: every `checkpoint` needs to capture the *entire* remainder of the program. The example code uses the IO monad, and checkpoints therefore have to be established at the very top level; the calling context of a subordinate function cannot be accessed from inside that function. A slightly more elegant solution would be to use the continuation monad instead of the IO monad, and a monad transformer to embed IO actions. A `callCC`-like mechanism can then capture and serialise the entire program continuation–but again, the program needs to be rewritten to use monad `ContT () IO ()` instead of `IO` in every function that involves establishing checkpoints.

So, our diagnosis is that equipping a program with failover safety through checkpoints requires considerable restructuring by the programmer. That said, it seems promising to provide "checkpointed" versions of monadic computation combinators like `sequence` and `mapM` to support and facilitate this manual restructuring (the type of the checkpoint functions in Figure 4 is based on `IO a` instead of a unit return `IO ()` precisely to allow this). A checkpoint will typically be established at a particular stage of execution, for instance after each step of an iteration. Figure 5 shows how to realise a combinator `sequenceC` where previous results are accumulated and stored in a checkpoint after each step of a monadic sequence. A monadic `mapM` with checkpoints can be expressed using `sequenceC`, and used as shown in the `example`. Introducing a number of checkpoints to a program remains an explicit restructuring task for the programmer, but such checkpointed IO-monadic combinators greatly facilitate the job.

```
sequenceC :: Typeable a => FilePath -> [IO a] -> IO [a]
sequenceC name ms = seqC_acc [] ms
    where seqC_acc acc   []    = return (reverse acc)
          seqC_acc acc (m:ms) = do x <- m
                                   checkpoint name (seqC_acc (x:acc) ms)
-- build mapM_C with sequenceC:
mapMC :: Typeable b => FilePath -> (a -> IO b) -> [a] -> IO [b]
mapMC name f xs = sequenceC name (map f xs)


-- usage example:
example args = -- either the recover option "-r" has been given...
              let doRecover = not (null args) && head args == "-r"
                  -- or we read an argument n (if any given)
                      n = if null args then 10 else read (head args)::Int
              in do xs <- if doRecover then recover "seqC_test"
                                       else mapMC "seqC_test" doIt [1..n]
                    putStrLn (show xs)
    where doIt :: Int -> IO Int
          doIt x = ... -- an expensive computation
```

Fig. 5. Combinator for checkpointed sequence, with usage example

4.2   Persistent Memoisation for Frequently Used Applications

A second potential application area for the approach (with its present limitations) is to alleviate the computational load of frequently used applications in a production environment by *memoisation.*

Memoisation [20] is a well-known technique to speed up function calls in a computer program by storing results for previously-processed inputs. This technique is particularly well suited for languages that support higher-order functions: automatic memoisation can be readily provided by a library function. For the language Haskell, several such libraries exist [15,8,21,5], with only small differences between them: both Elliot's `MemoTrie` library [8] and Palmer's `Memocombinators` [21] use a Trie-based store [15], another library we have found [5] relies on Haskell Generics [16].

Extending these memoisation techniques to more than one run of the program is possible using our proposed serialisation. *Persistent memo tables* for supportive data structures and repeatedly used functions can be built up, serialised to persistent storage at shutdown, and loaded (deserialised) into memory at startup. In order to realise persistent memoisation, a program using memoised functions has to be extended by suitable init and shutdown mechanisms. The shutdown routine will serialise all memoised functions to a file with the memo tables obtained so far. The init routine of a subsequent run will then load these existing memo table dumps if they exist, or otherwise use the "fresh" definition in the program.

```
f :: Integer -> Integer
f = memo f' -- assuming a suitable memoisation library
  where f' x = ... -- can use f (not f') recursively

main = do haveFile <- doesFileExist "f_memo.cache"
          f_memo <- if haveFile then decodeFromFile "f_memo.cache"
                                else return f
          ...
          -- all code must use (and pass around) f_memo
          ...
          encodeToFile file_f f_memo
```

Fig. 6. Usage example for a memoised function in a program

A simple way to realise this is sketched in Figure 6. Function f_memo is either loaded from a serialised file or used from the original definition in a file, before doing any work. Then, after the main execution, this function is serialised into a file to be loaded in the next program execution.

A drawback of the code shown here is that the memoised function is loaded inside the main function and has to be passed around as an argument to every function which uses f. This can be remedied by loading the file inside f as an "unsafe global" (using `unsafePerformIO`, see [22]), as we show in Figure 7. In this

```
{-# NOINLINE f_memo2 #-}          -- this will be executed once, because
f_memo2 = unsafePerformIO $ do -- of lazy evaluation.
    haveFile <- doesFileExist "f_memo2.cache"
    if haveFile then decodeFile "f_memo2.cache" >>= deserialize
                else let f = memo f'
                         f' x = ... -- can use f recursively
                     in return f
main = do ...                               -- f_memo2 can be used for f
          ...                               -- in the entire program
          encodeFile "f_memo2.cache" f_memo2 -- and is saved at shutdown
```

Fig. 7. Less intrusive, however `unsafe` memoisation variant

way, the function will be loaded from the given file automatically. Saving it at shutdown still needs to be done explicitly, but the program can remain otherwise identical to the non-memoised version. However, the memo effect in this version relies on the compiler pragma not to inline the function–especially not at the place where the file is written at shutdown.

We have experimented with the different memoisation libraries and did proof-of-concept implementations for all of them, and for a naïve list-based memoisation. For the latter, care had to be taken to prevent the compiler from optimising away the memoisation effect by aggressive inlining or let floating, but the memoisation libraries generally provide suitable compiler pragmas. `MemoTrie` [8] appears to be the most widely accepted, but `Memocombinators` [21] produced slightly smaller memoisation data for our test program (fibonacci). In all, the differences between these libraries are very minor and all can be used with our approach to memoise functions persistently across program runs.

5   Conclusions and Future Work

We have presented an approach to serialisation for Haskell data structures which is orthogonal to both evaluation and data types and which can be fitted with dynamic type checks by suitable Haskell wrapper functions. Haskell heap structures representing data can be serialised independently of their evaluation state and restored later by the same program (but potentially in a different run of it). Our approach is, to a large extent, also orthogonal to data types; no special serialisation type class is used. By Haskell wrapper functions using the `Typeable` class, we have re-established type safety at runtime, ensuring that ill-typed usage will be at least dynamically detected and results in meaningful runtime error messages instead of unspecific internal failure.

The base implementation for our approach is directly carried over from previous research in the area of parallel Haskell implementations. As such, our approach has conceptual and technical limits, the most relevant being that data can only be read by the very same version of a program. This limitation notwithstanding, we have pointed out and demonstrated important application areas for the approach in its current form. Easy-to-use checkpointing constructs for iterative computations in the IO monad have been proposed and we have shown how memoisation techniques can be made persistent with only minor effort. Very few related approaches have been been investigated in the past and, to our knowledge, no previous work has investigated the technical details in comparable depth or exemplified the application areas as we have done.

As future work, we plan to investigate how the Haskell code and the RTS routines should be extended to provide better support for serialisation. The version checksums for serialised data which we have briefly outlined appears to be a straightforward extension at the Haskell level. In contrast, considerable modifications to the packing routine need to be made in order to support data exchange between several (versions of) applications. It would require to make the packet format entirely self-contained and to avoid dependence on any static data which is a very long-term goal. A way to achieve this could be to include dynamically linkable code chunks in the packet. Parallel Haskell implementations for distributed memory systems can as well profit from these improvements, in the form of extended platform independence and flexibility.

Availability. The runtime support on which we build our implementation is available as part of the Eden-version of GHC[4], currently at release 6.12.3. Haskell code is available on request from the author.

Acknowledgements. We would like to thank our colleagues from Marburg, Edinburgh, and St.Andrews who were and are supporting the development of parallel Haskell on distributed memory platforms. Special thanks go to Phil Trinder, who brought up the initial idea to work on serialisation as a separable strand, and to an anonymous referee who pointed us to the continuation monad.

References

1. Augustsson, L.: Personal communication, about a possible Haskell serialisation feature, during the Haskell Symposium (September 2009)
2. Berthold, J.: Explicit and implicit parallel functional programming: Concepts and implementation. Ph.D. thesis, Philipps-Universität Marburg, Germany (June 2008), http://archiv.ub.uni-marburg.de/diss/z2008/0547/
3. Berthold, J., Loidl, H.W., Al Zain, A.: Scheduling Light-Weight Parallelism in ARTCoP. In: Hudak, P., Warren, D. (eds.) PADL 2008. LNCS, vol. 4902, pp. 214–229. Springer, Heidelberg (2008)
4. Berthold, J., Loogen, R.: Parallel Coordination Made Explicit in a Functional Setting. In: Horváth, Z., Zsók, V., Butterfield, A. (eds.) IFL 2006. LNCS, vol. 4449, pp. 73–90. Springer, Heidelberg (2007)

---

[4] http://www.mathematik.uni-marburg.de/~eden/

5. Claessen, K.: Memoisation module based on Haskell generics, `http://www.cse.chalmers.se/~ms/TR0912/Memo.hs` (accessed 2010-03-15)
6. Corona, A.: Refserialize-0.2.7: Write to and read from Strings maintaining internal memory references. Haskell Library on Hackage, `http://hackage.haskell.org/package/RefSerialize` (accessed 2010-10-21)
7. Davie, T., Hammond, K., Quintela, J.: Efficient Persistent Haskell. In: Clack, C., Hammond, K., Davie, T. (eds.) IFL 1998 – Draft Proceedings, London, UK (September 1998)
8. Elliott, C.: Memo trie library. Haskell Library on Hackage, `http://hackage.haskell.org/package/MemoTrie` (accessed 2010-10-20)
9. Marlow, S.: Haskell 2010 Language Report (June 2010), `http://www.haskell.org/`
10. Haskell Hierarchical Libraries: Base library, version 4.2.0.2. Haskell Library on Hackage, `http://hackage.haskell.org/package/base` (accessed 2010-10-21)
11. Haskell Wiki. Wiki, `http://www.haskell.org/haskellwiki/` (accessed 2010-10-20)
12. Haskell Café: Discussion on "bulk synchronous parallel", `http://www.haskell.org/pipermail/haskell-cafe/2010-April/076593.html` (accessed 2010-07-20)
13. Haskell Café: Discussion on "how to serialize thunks?", `http://www.haskell.org/pipermail/haskell-cafe/2006-December/020786.html` (accessed 2010-07-23)
14. Haskell Café: Discussion "persist and retrieve of IO type?", `http://www.haskell.org/pipermail/haskell-cafe/2010-April/076121.html` (accessed 2010-07-20)
15. Hinze, R.: Memo functions, polytypically! In: Jeuring, J. (ed.) Proc. of 2nd Workshop on Generic Programming, WGP 2000, Ponte de Lima, Portugal, pp. 17–32 (July 2000); Tech. Report UU-CS-2000-19, Utrecht Universiteit
16. Lämmel, R., Jones, S.P.: Scrap your boilerplate: a practical design pattern for generic programming. ACM SIGPLAN Notices 38(3), 26–37 (2003)
17. Loogen, R., Ortega-Mallén, Y., Peña-Marí, R.: Parallel Functional Programming in Eden. Journal of Functional Programming 15(3), 431–475 (2005)
18. McNally, D.J.: Models for Persistence in Lazy Functional Programming. Ph.D. thesis, University of St.Andrews (1993)
19. McNally, D.J., Davie, A.J.T.: Two models for integrating persistence and lazy functional languages. ACM SIGPLAN Notices 26(5), 43–52 (1991)
20. Michie, D.: 'Memo' functions and machine learning. Nature 218, 19–22 (1968)
21. Palmer, L.: Memo combinator library (data-memocombinators). Haskell Library on Hackage, `http://hackage.haskell.org/package/data-memocombinators` (accessed 2010-10-20)
22. Peyton Jones, S.: Tackling the Awkward Squad: monadic input/output, concurrency, exceptions, and foreign-language calls in Haskell (2002), `http://research.microsoft.com/~simonpj/`
23. Plasmeier, R.J., Koopman, P.: Personal communication (September 2010), about the Clean Dynamics implementation in practical use and its pragmatic limitations, during IFL (2010)
24. Quintela, J.J., Sánchez, J.J.: Persistent Haskell. In: Moreno-Díaz, R., Buchberger, B., Freire, J.L. (eds.) EUROCAST 2001. LNCS, vol. 2178, pp. 657–667. Springer, Heidelberg (2001); presented earlier, at IFL 1998, as [7]

25. Santos, A., Abdon Monteiro, B.: A Persistence Library for Haskell. In: Musicante, M.A., Haeusler, E.H. (eds.) Proceedings of SBLP 2001 - V Simpósio Brasileiro de Linguagens de Programação, Curitiba (May 2001)
26. Trinder, P., Hammond, K., Mattson Jr., J., Partridge, A., Peyton Jones, S.: GUM: a Portable Parallel Implementation of Haskell. In: PLDI 1996, pp. 78–88. ACM Press, Philadephia (1996)
27. Vervoort, M., Plasmeijer, R.J.: Lazy Dynamic Input/Output in the Lazy Functional Language Clean. In: Peña, R., Arts, T. (eds.) IFL 2002. LNCS, vol. 2670, pp. 101–117. Springer, Heidelberg (2003)

Introducing the PilGRIM: A Processor for Executing Lazy Functional Languages

Arjan Boeijink, Philip K.F. Hölzenspies, and Jan Kuper

University of Twente
Enschede, The Netherlands
w.a.boeijink@utwente.nl

Abstract. Processor designs specialized for functional languages received very little attention in the past 20 years. The potential for exploiting more parallelism and the developments in hardware technology, ask for renewed investigation of this topic. In this paper, we use ideas from modern processor architectures and the state of the art in compilation, to guide the design of our processor, the PilGRIM. We define a high-level instruction set for lazy functional languages and show the processor architecture, that can efficiently execute these instructions.

1 Introduction

The big gap between the functional evaluation model, based on graph reduction, and the imperative execution model of most processors, has made (efficient) implementation of functional languages a topic of extensive research. Until about 20 years ago, several projects have been undertaken to solve the implementation problem by designing processors specifically for executing functional languages. However, advances in the compilation strategies for conventional hardware and the rapid developments in clock speed of mainstream processor architectures made it very hard for language specific hardware to show convincing benefits.

In the last 20 years, the processors in PCs have evolved a lot. The number of transistors of a single core has grown from hundreds of thousands to hundreds of millions following Moore's law and the clock speed has risen from a few MHz to a few GHz [5]. Introduction of deep pipelines, superscalar, and out-of-order execution changed the microarchitecture of processors completely. Currently, processor designs are limited by power usage instead of transistor count, which is known as the *power wall*. Two other "walls" limiting the single thread performance of modern processors are the memory wall (memory latency and bandwidth bottleneck) and the Instruction Level Parallelism (ILP) wall (mostly due to the unpredictability of control flow). These three walls have shifted the focus in processor architectures from increasing frequencies to building multicore processors.

Recent work on the Reduceron [9] showed encouraging results demonstrating what can be gained by using low-level parallelism to design a processor specifically for a functional language. The emphasis of this low-level parallelism is on

J. Hage, M.T. Morazán (Eds.): IFL 2010, LNCS 6647, pp. 54–71, 2011.

simultaneous data movements, but also includes instruction level parallelism. Functional languages are well suited for applications that are hard to parallelize, such as complex symbolic manipulations. Single thread performance will be critical when all easy parallelism has been fully exploited. Laziness and first-class functions make Haskell very data and control flow intensive [10]. Unlike research done in previous decades, language specific hardware modifications are now bounded by complexity (of design and verification) and not the number of transistors.

Performance gains for specialized pure functional architectures might influence conventional processor architectures, because the trend in mainstream programming languages is towards more abstraction, first-class functions, and immutable data structures.

The changes in hardware technology, the resulting modern hardware architectures, and the positive results of the Reduceron suggest it is time to evaluate processors for functional languages again.

2   The Pipelined Graph Reduction Instruction Machine

In this paper, we introduce the PilGRIM (the name is an acronym of the section title). The PilGRIM is a processor with a design that is specialized for executing lazy functional languages. The architecture is derived from modern general purpose architectures, with a 64-bit datapath and using a standard memory hierarchy: separate L1 instruction and data caches, an L2 cache, and DDR-memory interface. The design targets silicon and is intended to be a realistic design for current hardware technology. The instruction set is designed to exploit benefits of extensive higher level compiler optimizations (using the output of GHC). This is especially important for performance of primitive (arithmetic) operations. The processor executes a high-level instruction set that is close to a functional core language and that allows code generation to be simple. The PilGRIM reuses some of the basic principles behind the Big Word Machine (BWM) [1] and the Reduceron [8].

We intend to pipeline this processor deep enough to make a clock frequency of 1GHz a feasible target. The details of the pipeline structure are work in progress. For space reasons, we will not discuss pipelining in this paper, but many design choices are made in preparation of a deep pipeline.

The contributions of this paper are:

- A high-level and coarse-grained instruction set for lazy functional languages, with a simple compilation scheme from a functional core language.
- Proposal of a hardware architecture that can efficiently execute this instruction set, where this design is made with a deep pipeline in mind.

3   Instruction Set and Compilation

Before designing the hardware, we first want to find a suitable evaluation model and an instruction set, because designing hardware and an instruction set simultaneously is too complex. We chose to use GHC as the Haskell compiler frontend,

because its External Core [15] feature is a convenient starting point on which to
base a code generator for our new architecture. The extensive set of high-level
optimizations provided by GHC is a big additional benefit.

While External Core is a much smaller language than Haskell, it is still too
complex and too abstract for efficient execution in hardware. Before compiling to
an instruction set, we transform External Core to a simplified and low-level intermediate language, defined in the next section. The instruction set and assembly
language is derived from Graph Reduction Intermediate Notation (GRIN) [4,3]
(an intermediate language, in the form of a first-order monadic functional language). GRIN has been chosen as our basis, because it is a simple sequential
language, that has a small set of instructions and that is close to a functional
language.

---

function definition:

$d ::= \mathfrak{f}\ x^+ = e$

$\quad |\ \mathfrak{g} = e$

toplevel expression:

$e ::= s$ *(simple expr.)*

$\quad |\ \textbf{let}\ b\ \textbf{in}\ e$ *(lazy let expr.)*

$\quad |\ \textbf{letS}\ b\ \textbf{in}\ e$ *(strict let expr.)*

$\quad |\ \textbf{case}\ s\ \textbf{of}\ \{\ a^+\ \}$ *(case expr.)*

$\quad |\ \textbf{if}\ c\ \textbf{then}\ e\ \textbf{else}\ e$ *(if expr.)*

$\quad |\ \textbf{fix}\ (\lambda r.\mathfrak{f}\ r\ x^\star)$ *(fixpoint expr.)[†]*

$\quad |\ \textbf{try}\ \mathfrak{f}\ x^+\ \textbf{catch}\ x$ *(catch expr.)[†]*

$\quad |\ \textbf{throw}\ x$ *(throw expr.)*

$\quad$ [†]*where $\mathfrak{f}$ is saturated*

$a ::= C\ x^\star \to e$ *(constructor alternative)*

$b ::= x = s$ *(binding)*

$c ::= x \bowtie x$ *(primitive comparison)*

simple expression:

$s ::= x$ *(variable)*

$\quad |\ n$ *(integer)*

$\quad |\ C\ x^\star$ *(constructor [application])*

$\quad |\ \mathfrak{f}\ x^\star$ *(function [application])*

$\quad |\ \mathfrak{g}\ x^\star$ *(global const. [application])*

$\quad |\ y\ x^+$ *(variable application)*

$\quad |\ \otimes\ x^+$ *(primitive operation)*

$\quad |\ \pi_n\ x$ *(proj. of a product type)*

Fig. 1. Grammar of the simple core language

3.1 A Simple Functional Core Language

As an intermediate step in the compilation process, we want a language that
is both simpler and more explicit, with special and primitive constructs, than
External Core. The simple core language is (like GRIN) structured using supercombinators, which means that all lambdas need to be transformed to toplevel
functions (lambda lifting). The grammar of the simple core language is given
in Figure 1. Subexpressions and arguments are restricted to plain variables,
achieved by introducing let expressions for complex subexpressions. An explicit
distinction is made between top level functions and global constants (both have
globally unique names, denoted by $\mathfrak{f}$ and $\mathfrak{g}$). All constructors and primitive operations are fully saturated (all arguments applied). From the advanced type
system in External Core, the types are simplified to the point where only the
distinction between reference and primitive types remains. Strictness is explicit
in this core language, using a strict let, a strict case scrutinee, and strict primitive variables. This core language has primitive (arithmetic) operations and an

if-construct for primitive comparison and branching. Exception handling is supported by a try/catch construct and a throw expression. Let expressions are not recursive; for recursive values a fixed point combinator is used instead. Selection from a product type could be done using a case expression, but is specialized with a projection expression.

3.2 Evaluation Model and Memory Layout

Almost all modern implementations of lazy functional languages use a variation of the G-machine, which introduced compiled graph reduction [6]. The evaluation model and memory layout described in this section are derived largely from a mix of the spineless tagless G-machine (STG), as used in GHC [12], and GRIN [3]. The machine model (from GRIN) consists of an environment and a heap. The environment maps variables to values, where values can be either *primitive values* or *heap references*. The environment is implemented as a stack of call frames. The heap maps references to *nodes*, where a node is a data structure consisting of a tag and zero-or-more arguments (values). Node tags specify the node's type and contain additional metadata, in particular a bitmask denoting which of the node's arguments are primitive values and which are references. This simplifies garbage collection. Using metadata in tags—as opposed to using info pointers, as in STG—makes handling tags more involved, but reduces the number of memory accesses.

Table 1. Node types

Node Type	Represents	Contents
C	Constructor	Constructor arguments
P	Partially applied function	Args. and number of missing args.
F	Fully applied function	All arguments for the function

Tags distinguish three basic node types (see Table 1). Both C- and P-nodes are in Weak Head Normal Form (WHNF), while F-nodes are not. Tags for C-nodes contain a unique number for the data type they belong to and the index of the constructor therein. The P- and F-tags contain a pointer to the applied function. The F-nodes are closures, that can be evaluated when required. To implement laziness, F-nodes are overwritten (updated) with the result after evaluation.

A program is a set of functions, each resulting in an evaluated node on the stack (i.e., a C- or P-node). Every function has a fixed list of arguments and consists of a sequence of instructions. Next, we introduce the instruction set, on the level of an assembly language (i.e., with variables as opposed to registers).

3.3 Assembly Language

Similar to GRIN, PilGRIM's assembly language can be seen as a first-order, untyped, strict, and monadic language. The monad, in this case, is abstract and implicit. That is, the programmer can not access its internal state other than through the predefined instructions. This internal state is, in fact, the state of the heap and the stack. Unlike GRIN, the syntax of PilGRIM's assembly language is not based on a "built-in bind structure," [3] but rather on Haskell's do-notation. This, however, imposes considerably more restrictions, viz. in

$$pattern \leftarrow instruction \; ; \; rest$$

the variables in *pattern* are bound in *rest* to the corresponding parts of the result of *instruction*. Which pattern is allowed is determined by the instruction. The grammar of the assembly language (including extensions) is shown in Figure 2.

---

function implementation:
$fun ::= \mathsf{f} \; a^+ = block$
$\quad | \quad \mathsf{g} = block$
basic block:
$block ::= instr;^* \; term$
instruction:
$instr ::= x \leftarrow \mathsf{Store} \; T \; a^*$
$\quad | \quad x \leftarrow \mathsf{Push_{CAF}} \; \mathsf{g}$
$\quad | \quad y \leftarrow \mathsf{PrimOp} \; \otimes \; y \; y$
$\quad | \quad y \leftarrow \mathsf{Constant} \; n$
$\quad | \quad T \; a^* \leftarrow \mathsf{Call} \; call \; cont$
$\quad | \quad x \leftarrow \mathsf{Force} \; call \; cont$
terminator instruction:
$term ::= \mathsf{Return} \; T \; a^*$
$\quad | \quad \mathsf{Jump} \; call \; cont$
$\quad | \quad \mathsf{Case} \; call \; cont \; alt^+$
$\quad | \quad \mathsf{If} \; (y \bowtie y) \; block \; block$
$\quad | \quad \mathsf{Throw} \; x$

case alternative:
$alt ::= T \; a^* \rightarrow block$
callable expression:
$call ::= (\mathsf{Eval} \; x)$
$\quad | \quad (\mathsf{Eval_{CAF}} \; \mathsf{g})$
$\quad | \quad (\mathsf{TLF} \; \mathsf{f} \; a^+)$
$\quad | \quad (\mathsf{Fix} \; \mathsf{f} \; a^*)$
evaluation continuation:
$cont ::= ()$
$\quad | \quad (\mathsf{Apply} \; a^+)$
$\quad | \quad (\mathsf{Select} \; n)$
$\quad | \quad (\mathsf{Catch} \; x)$
node tag:
$T \quad ::= \mathsf{C_{con}}$
$\quad | \quad \mathsf{F_{fun}}$
$\quad | \quad \mathsf{P_{fun}^m}$
argument or parameter:
$a \quad ::= x \qquad \qquad (ref. \; var.)$
$\quad | \quad y \qquad \qquad (prim. \; var.)$

Fig. 2. Grammar of PilGRIM's assembly language

Like the simple core language, PilGRIM programs are structured using supercombinators (i.e., only top-level functions have formal parameters). A program is a set of function definitions, where a function is defined by its name, its formal parameters, and a code block. A block can be thought of as a unit, in that control flow does not enter a block other than at its beginning and once a block is entered, all instructions in that block will be executed. Only the last instruction can redirect control flow to another block. Thus, we distinguish between *instructions* and *terminator instructions*. The former can not be the last of a block, whereas the latter must be. It follows, that a block is a (possibly empty) sequence of instructions, followed by a terminator instruction.

As discussed in Section 3.2, nodes consist of a tag and a list of arguments. When functions return their result, they do this in the form of a node on the top of the stack. This is why the pattern to bind variables to the result of a `Call` must be in the form of a tag with a list of parameters.

Basic instructions. We will continue with an informal description of all instructions that are essential for a lazy functional language. The appendix contains a more formal description of the semantics of the assembly language in an operational style.

First, we only consider top-level functions. A top-level function is called by forming a *callable*, using `TLF` with the name of the function to call and all the arguments to call it with. Given such a callable, `Call` pushes the return address and the arguments onto the stack and jumps to the called function's code block. In all cases, a `Call` has a corresponding `Return`. `Return` clears the stack down to (and including) the return address pushed by `Call`. Next, it pushes its result node (tag and arguments) onto the stack, before returning control flow to the return address.

Next, we consider calls to non-top-level functions. As discussed above, F-nodes contain fully applied functions. Therefore, F-nodes can be considered callable. On the level of PilGRIM's assembly language, however, different types of nodes can not be identified in the program. To this end, `Eval` takes a heap reference to any type of node, loads that node from the heap onto the stack, and turns it into a callable. Calling `Eval` x thus behaves differently for different types of nodes. Since C- and P-nodes are already in WHNF, a `Call` to such a node will implicitly return immediately (i.e., it simply leaves the node on the stack). F-nodes are called using the same mechanism as top-level functions.

In Figure 2, `Call` has another argument, namely a *continuation*. In PilGRIM's assembly language, continuations are transformations of the result of a call, so they can be seen as part of the return. The empty continuation, (), leaves the result unchanged. `Select` n takes the nth argument from the C-node residing at the top of the stack and (if that argument is a reference) loads the corresponding node from the heap onto the stack. Similarly, `Apply` works on the P-node at the top of the stack. Given a list of arguments, `Apply` appends its arguments to those of the P-node. If this saturates the P-node (i.e., if this reduces the number of missing arguments to nil), the resulting F-node is automatically called, as if using `Call` and `Eval`.

Instead of returning, another way to transfer control flow from the end of a block to the beginning of another is by using `Case`. `Case` can be understood as a `Call` combined with a switch statement, or `Call` as a `Case` with only one alternative. After the callable returns a result and the continuation is applied, the C-node at the top of the stack is matched against a number of cases. If a case matches, the arguments of the node are bound to the corresponding parameters of the case and control flow is transferred to the case's block. Note that in this transfer of control flow, the stack is unaltered (i.e., the top-most return address remains the return address for the next `Return`).

Finally, a node can be written to the heap by the `Store` instruction. Since the heap is garbage collected, the address where a node is stored is not in the program's control. `Store` takes its arguments from the stack, allocates a new heap node, and then pushes the reference to the new heap node onto the stack.

Extensions. Because some patterns of instructions are very common and, thus far, the instruction set is very small, a few extra instructions and combined instructions are added as optimizations.

First, support for primitive values and operations is added. As a load immediate instruction, `Constant` produces a primitive constant. Primitive constants can be fed to primitive operations by means of `PrimOp`. Control flow can be determined by comparison operations on primitive values in `If`. The implementation of arithmetic operations in PilGRIM is such, that it can be seen as an independent coprocessor. By letting the operation be a parameter of `PrimOp` and `If`, the instruction set is easily extended with more primitive operations.

Second, we add support for functions in Constant Applicative Form (CAF). These are functions without arguments (i.e., global constants). They are stored in a fixed position on the heap and require special treatment in case of garbage collection [11]. To this end, `Push`$_{\mathrm{CAF}}$ generates a constant reference to a function in CAF. Furthermore, `Eval`$_{\mathrm{CAF}}$ is used to make such a function callable. `Eval`$_{\mathrm{CAF}}$ can be interpreted as a `Push`$_{\mathrm{CAF}}$, followed by an `Eval`.

Third, there are some useful optimizations with regards to control flow instructions. The common occurrence of tail recursion in lazy functional programming languages calls for a cheaper means than having to `Call` every recursion. The `Jump` instruction is a terminator instruction that redirects control to the code block of the recursive call, without instantiating a new call frame on the stack. Another combination with calls is having a `Call` immediately followed by a `Store`. This happens in the case of evaluating references in a strict context. `Force` is a `Call`, followed immediately by a `Store` of the call's result.

Finally, for exception handling, we add a terminator instruction `Throw` and a continuation `Catch`. The latter places a reference to an exception handler on the stack. The former unwinds the stack, down to the first exception handler and calls that handler with the thrown value as argument.

3.4   Translation of the Core Language to the Instruction Set

The translation from the core language (presented in Section 3.1) to PilGRIM's assembly language (Section 3.3) is defined by a four-level scheme. The entry-point of the translation is $\mathcal{T}$ (Figure 3). This scheme translates (strict) top-level expressions of the core language. It is quite straightforward, except maybe for the translation of function applications. At this point, the distinction must be made between saturated an unsaturated function application. The notation $\alpha(\mathfrak{f})$ refers to the arity of function $\mathfrak{f}$, whereas $|\vec{x}|$ denotes the number of arguments in the core language expression.

Subexpressions can be translated for lazy evaluation (by means of scheme $\mathcal{V}$), or strict evaluation (scheme $\mathcal{S}$). Note that some subexpressions are only in scheme $\mathcal{S}$, because they are strict by definition. The lowest level of the translation is scheme $\mathcal{E}$. This scheme determines the calling method for every expression (i.e., both the callable *and* the continuation).

toplevel expression translation:

$\mathcal{T}\llbracket\, C\ \vec{x}\ \rrbracket = \mathtt{Return}\ \mathtt{C}_c\ \vec{x}$

$\mathcal{T}\llbracket\, \mathfrak{f}\ \vec{x}\ \rrbracket = \begin{cases} \mathtt{Jump}\ \mathcal{E}\llbracket \mathfrak{f}\ \vec{x} \rrbracket & \text{if } \alpha(\mathfrak{f}) \le |\vec{x}| \\ \mathtt{Return}\ \mathtt{P}_{\mathfrak{f}}\ \vec{x} & \text{if } \alpha(\mathfrak{f}) > |\vec{x}| \end{cases}$

$\mathcal{T}\llbracket\, s\ \rrbracket = \mathtt{Jump}\ \mathcal{E}\llbracket s \rrbracket \qquad \text{(other simple expressions)}$

$\mathcal{T}\llbracket\, \mathbf{let}\ x = s\ \mathbf{in}\ e\ \rrbracket = x \leftarrow \mathcal{V}\llbracket s \rrbracket\,;\,\mathcal{T}\llbracket e \rrbracket$

$\mathcal{T}\llbracket\, \mathbf{letS}\ x = s\ \mathbf{in}\ e\ \rrbracket = x \leftarrow \mathcal{S}\llbracket s \rrbracket\,;\,\mathcal{T}\llbracket e \rrbracket$

$\mathcal{T}\llbracket\, \mathbf{fix}\ (\lambda r.\mathfrak{f}\ r\ \vec{x})\ \rrbracket = \mathtt{Jump}\ (\mathtt{Fix}\ \mathfrak{f}\ \vec{x})\ ()$

$\mathcal{T}\llbracket\, \mathbf{try}\ \mathfrak{f}\ \vec{x}\ \mathbf{catch}\ h\ \rrbracket = \mathtt{Jump}\ (\mathtt{TLF}\ \mathfrak{f}\ \vec{x})\ (\mathtt{Catch}\ h)$

$\mathcal{T}\llbracket\, \mathbf{throw}\ x\ \rrbracket = \mathtt{Throw}\ x$

$\mathcal{T}\llbracket\, \mathbf{case}\ s\ \mathbf{of}\ \{\ C\ \vec{y} \to e\ \}\ \rrbracket = C\ \vec{y} \leftarrow \mathtt{Call}\ \mathcal{E}\llbracket s \rrbracket\,;\,\mathcal{T}\llbracket e \rrbracket$

$\mathcal{T}\llbracket\, \mathbf{case}\ s\ \mathbf{of}\ \{\ \vec{a}\ \}\ \rrbracket = \mathtt{Case}\ \mathcal{E}\llbracket s \rrbracket\ [C\ \vec{y} \to \mathcal{T}\llbracket e \rrbracket\ |\ (C\ \vec{y} \to e) \leftarrow \vec{a}]$

$\mathcal{T}\llbracket\, \mathbf{if}\ c\ \mathbf{then}\ p\ \mathbf{else}\ q\ \rrbracket = \mathtt{If}\ c\ \mathcal{T}\llbracket p \rrbracket\ \mathcal{T}\llbracket q \rrbracket$

lazy subexpression translation:

$\mathcal{V}\llbracket\, \mathfrak{g}\ \vec{x}\ \rrbracket = \begin{cases} \mathtt{Push}_{\mathtt{CAF}}\ \mathfrak{g} & \text{if } |\vec{x}| = 0 \\ h \leftarrow \mathtt{Push}_{\mathtt{CAF}}\ \mathfrak{g}\,; & \text{if } |\vec{x}| > 0 \\ \quad \mathtt{Store}\ \mathtt{F}_{\mathtt{ap}}\ h\ \vec{x} & \end{cases}$

$\mathcal{V}\llbracket\, \mathfrak{f}\ \vec{x}\ \rrbracket = \begin{cases} \mathtt{Store}\ \mathtt{P}_{\mathfrak{f}}\ \vec{x} & \text{if } \alpha(\mathfrak{f}) > |\vec{x}| \\ \mathtt{Store}\ \mathtt{F}_{\mathfrak{f}}\ \vec{x} & \text{if } \alpha(\mathfrak{f}) = |\vec{x}| \\ h \leftarrow \mathtt{Store}\ \mathtt{F}_{\mathfrak{f}}\ \vec{y}\,; & \text{where } \vec{y} = x_1, \ldots, x_{\alpha(\mathfrak{f})} \quad \text{if } \alpha(\mathfrak{f}) < |\vec{x}| \\ \quad \mathtt{Store}\ \mathtt{F}_{\mathtt{ap}}\ h\ \vec{z} & \text{where } \vec{z} = x_{\alpha(\mathfrak{f})+1}, \ldots, x_{|\vec{x}|} \end{cases}$

$\mathcal{V}\llbracket\, y\ \vec{x}\ \rrbracket = \mathtt{Store}\ \mathtt{F}_{\mathtt{ap}}\ y\ \vec{x}$

$\mathcal{V}\llbracket\, \pi_n\ x\ \rrbracket = \mathtt{Store}\ \mathtt{F}_{\mathtt{Sel\_n}}\ x$

strict subexpression translation:

$\mathcal{S}\llbracket\, n\ \rrbracket = \mathtt{Constant}\ n$

$\mathcal{S}\llbracket\, \otimes\ \vec{x}\ \rrbracket = \mathtt{PrimOp}\ \otimes\ \vec{x}$

$\mathcal{S}\llbracket\, x\ \rrbracket = \mathtt{Force}\ \mathcal{E}\llbracket x \rrbracket$

$\mathcal{S}\llbracket\, C\ \vec{x}\ \rrbracket = \mathtt{Store}\ \mathtt{C}_c\ \vec{x}$

$\mathcal{S}\llbracket\, y\ \vec{x}\ \rrbracket = \mathtt{Force}\ \mathcal{E}\llbracket y\ \vec{x} \rrbracket$

$\mathcal{S}\llbracket\, \pi_n\ x\ \rrbracket = \mathtt{Force}\ \mathcal{E}\llbracket \pi_n\ x \rrbracket$

$\mathcal{S}\llbracket\, \mathfrak{f}\ \vec{x}\ \rrbracket = \begin{cases} \mathtt{Force}\ \mathcal{E}\llbracket \mathfrak{f}\ \vec{x} \rrbracket & \text{if } \alpha(\mathfrak{f}) \le |\vec{x}| \\ \mathtt{Store}\ \mathtt{P}_{\mathfrak{f}}^{m}\ \vec{x} & \text{where } m = \alpha(\mathfrak{f}) - |\vec{x}| \quad \text{if } \alpha(\mathfrak{f}) > |\vec{x}| \end{cases}$

evaluation expression translation:

$\mathcal{E}\llbracket\, x\ \rrbracket = (\mathtt{Eval}\ x)()$

$\mathcal{E}\llbracket\, \pi_n\ x\ \rrbracket = (\mathtt{Eval}\ x)(\mathtt{Select}\ n)$

$\mathcal{E}\llbracket\, \mathfrak{g}\ \vec{x}\ \rrbracket = \begin{cases} (\mathtt{Eval}_{\mathtt{CAF}}\ \mathfrak{g})() & \text{if } |\vec{x}| = 0 \\ (\mathtt{Eval}_{\mathtt{CAF}}\ \mathfrak{g})(\mathtt{Apply}\ \vec{x}) & \text{if } |\vec{x}| > 0 \end{cases}$

$\mathcal{E}\llbracket\, \mathfrak{f}\ \vec{x}\ \rrbracket = \begin{cases} (\mathtt{TLF}\ \mathfrak{f}\ \vec{x})() & \text{if } \alpha(\mathfrak{f}) = |\vec{x}| \\ (\mathtt{TLF}\ \mathfrak{f}\ \vec{y})(\mathtt{Apply}\ \vec{z}) & \text{where } \vec{y}, \vec{z} \text{ as in } \mathcal{V}\llbracket \mathfrak{f}\ \vec{x} \rrbracket \text{ above} \quad \text{if } \alpha(\mathfrak{f}) < |\vec{x}| \end{cases}$

$\mathcal{E}\llbracket\, y\ \vec{x}\ \rrbracket = (\mathtt{Eval}\ y)(\mathtt{Apply}\ \vec{x})$

Fig. 3. Translation from simple core to PilGRIM's assembly language

4   The PilGRIM Architecture

In this section, we describe a simplified variant of the PilGRIM architecture, which is complete with regards to the instruction set defined in the previous section. This variant is not pipelined and does not include many hardware optimizations.

The Structure of the Architecture

Essential to the understanding of the structure of PilGRIM, is the partitioning of the memory components. The main memory element is the *heap*. The heap contains whole nodes (i.e., addressing and alignment are both based on the size and format of nodes which is discussed in more detail in Section 4.3). Loads from and stores to the heap are performed in a single step. That is, memory buses are also node-aligned. For the larger part, the heap consists of external DDR-memory. However, PilGRIM has a small allocation heap (see Section 4.2) to exploit the memory locality present in typical functional programs.

PilGRIM's assembly language (Section 3.3) is based on a stack-model. The *stack* supports (random access) reading and pushing everything that is required for the execution of an instruction in a single cycle. The stack contains nodes, values, and call frames. Call frames always contain a return address and may contain an update continuation and zero or more application continuations. As discussed in Section 4.1, the stack is not implemented as a monolithic component, but split up to make parallel access less costly in hardware.

At the logistic heart of the architecture sits a *crossbar*, which connects the stack, the heap, and an ALU (used for primitive operations). The crossbar can combine parts from different sources in parallel to build a whole node, or anything else that can be stored or pushed on the stack in a single step. PilGRIM's control comes from a *sequencer*, that calculates instruction addresses, decodes instructions, and controls all other components of the architecture. The sequencer reads instructions from a dedicated *code memory*.

4.1   Splitting the Stack

The stack contains many different kinds of values: nodes read from memory, function arguments, return addresses, update pointers, intermediate primitive values, and temporary references to stored nodes. Every instruction reads and/or writes multiple values from/to the stack. All these data movements make the stack and the attached crossbar a critical central point of the core. The mix of multi-word nodes, single-word values, and variable-sized groups of arguments makes it very hard to implement a stack as parallelized as required, without making it big and slow. A solution to this problem is to split the stack into multiple special-purpose stacks. The second reason to split up the stack is to make it possible to execute a complete instruction at once (by having a separate stack for each aspect of an instruction).

The *return/update stack* contains the return addresses, update references, and counters for the number of nodes and continuations that belong to a callframe.

The *continuation stack* contains arguments to be applied or other simple continuations to be executed, between a return instruction and the actual jump to the return address. The *node stack* only contains complete nodes (including their tag). Values in the topmost few entries of the node stack can be read directly. Every instruction can read from and pop off any combination of these top entries. Reading from, popping from and pushing onto the node stack can take place simultaneously. The *reference queue* contains the references to the most recently stored nodes. The *primitive queue* contains the most recently produced primitive values.

The return stack and continuation stack are simple stacks with only push/pop functionality. The queues are register file structures with multiple read ports, that contain the n most recently written values. When writing a new value into a queue, the oldest value in the queue is lost.

A very parallel stack, such as the node stack, requires many read and write ports in its hardware implementation, which make it slow and big. By storing the top of the stack in separate registers, the number of read ports for the rest of the stack can be reduced, because the top element is accessed most often. Pushing can be faster, because the pushed data can only go to a single place and the *top of stack register* can be placed close to the local heap memory. The other stacks also have a top of stack register for fast access (not shown in Figure 4). All stacks are implemented using register files for the top few entries and backed up by a local memory. Transfers between the stack registers and the stack memory are handled automatically in the background by the hardware.

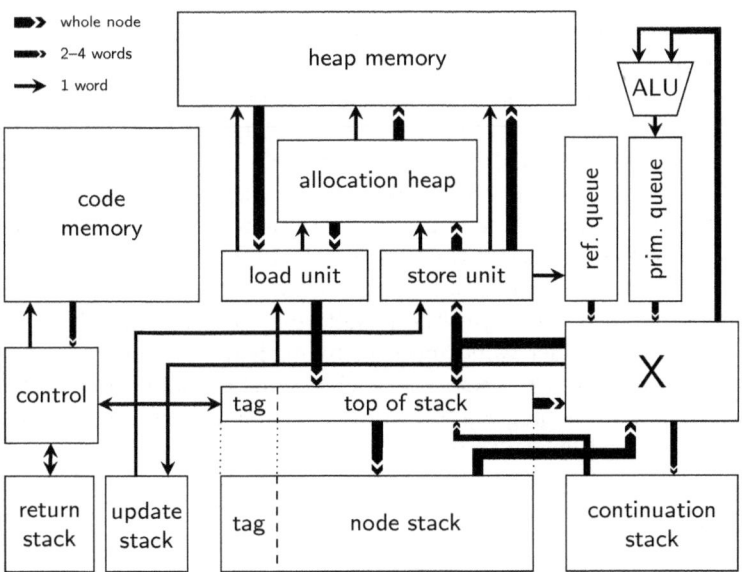

Fig. 4. The basic PilGRIM architecture

4.2   Allocation Heap

Typically as much as 25% of the executed instructions are stores, requiring a lot of allocation bandwidth. The percentage of instructions reading from the heap can be even higher than that. It is crucial that most loads and stores be fast, which can be achieved by using a small local memory.

We can make allocation more efficient, by storing all newly allocated nodes in a sizable buffer (the allocation heap) of several hundreds of nodes first. The allocation heap serves, in effect, as a fast, directly mapped, tagless data cache. We have chosen 512 elements of four words as the size for the allocation heap. This is 16 kilobytes of memory. The allocation heap exploits the temporal locality between the allocation of and reading back of the same data. To save bandwidth to external memory, nodes with a short lifetime are garbage collected while still in the allocation heap. This is implemented in hardware using a reference counting mechanism (extending the one-bit reference counters from SKIM [14]).

4.3   Hardware Component Sizes and Constraints

We have chosen the sizes of hardware components to be small enough to ensure that the cost in area and latency are reasonable, but also big enough to not limit performance too much. Some hardware constraints need transformations in the code generator to work around them.

- The datapath is 64 bits wide and all data in memory and registers is organized and addressed in 64 bit words.
- Nodes are limited to eight words (one tag word and seven values). The compiler has to transform the code to eliminate all constructors and function applications that are too big, as is done in the BWM and the Reduceron.
- The heap is divided in four word elements, because most of the nodes on the heap fit in four words [1,9]. Using wider elements adds a lot to hardware cost and only gives a small performance benefit. If a node is wider than four words, reading or writing nodes takes extra cycles. Updating a small F-node with a big result node is done using indirection nodes, as in the STG [12].
- Only the top four entries of the node stack can be read. The code generator ensures that all required values from the stack are in the top four nodes.
- Both the reference queue and the primitive queue are limited to the last 16 values produced. Older values need to be pushed onto the node stack.
- The continuation stack is two words wide. This is enough for most function applications [7]. For bigger applications, arguments can be pushed onto the continuation stack in multiple steps.

4.4   Instruction Set

The assembly language (defined in Section 3.3) and the instruction set differ only in two important details. First, all variables are replaced by explicit indices to elements on the stacks or queues. For reference values, copying/destructive reads are explicitly encoded, to have accurate live reference information for garbage collection. Second, the structure of programs is transformed to a linear sequence of instructions, by using jump offsets for the else branches and case alternatives.

Instruction Set Encoding. All instructions can be encoded in 128 bits, although the majority of instructions fit within 64 bits. The mix of two instruction lengths is a trade off between fast (fixed length) instruction decoding and small code size (where variable length instructions are better). Small instructions are all arithmetic operations, constant generation, if-with-compare, and many other instructions with only a few operands. Operands are not only stack and queue indices, but can also be small constant values. The distinction between primitive and reference values is explicit in the operands. All instructions have a common header structure, with the opcode and a bitmask to optionally clear the queues or any of the top stack nodes.

Generating Instructions. The process of generating actual instructions from the assembly language is straightforward. Every constructor is assigned a unique number, where the numbers are grouped in such a way, that the lowest bits distinguish between the alternatives within a data type. Values on the node stack are indexed from the top by a number starting with zero, and values in the queues are indexed from the most recently produced entry in the queue. Every instruction that produces a result pushes its result on either the node stack or one of the queues. Thus the *sequence of executed instructions* within a supercombinator determines the translation of variables in the assembly to stack or queue indices (without any 'register' allocation). The last step is linking together all supercombinators, which assigns an instruction address to every use of a function name.

4.5 Hardware Implementation Strategy

The implementation of the PilGRIM is done in a series of Haskell programs, each one more detailed and lower level than the previous one. A high-level evaluator of the instruction set is the first step in this process. Following steps include: choosing sizes for memory structures, adding lower level optimizations, and splitting up functions to follow the structure of the hardware architecture.

We intend to use CλaSH [2] in the final step to produce a synthesizable implementation of the PilGRIM. CλaSH is a subset of Haskell that can be compiled to VHDL (a hardware description language supported by many existing tools).

We have gone through several iterations of the first few steps of this design process, starting from roughly GRIN as the instruction set on a simple single stack architecture, up to the current design. Making the step from a single cycle model to a fully pipelined architecture is ongoing work.

5 Evaluation and Comparison

For measurements in this section, we make use of the benchmark set of the Reduceron [9]. We selected these benchmarks, because they require only minimal

Table 2. Measurements of the performance of the instruction set

program	PilGRIM instrs. [million]	instr. rate to match PC [MHz]	arithmetic instrs. [%]	node store instrs. [%]	Reduceron cycles [million]
PermSort	166	231	4	34	154
Queens	84	645	42	10	96
Braun	83	347	2	35	66
OrdList	98	271	0	32	94
Queens2	111	278	0	32	120
MSS	86	728	24	1	66
Adjoxo	23	378	23	13	37
Taut	39	352	5	18	54
CountDown	16	324	25	17	18
Clausify	46	284	5	17	67
While	46	359	9	24	56
SumPuz	277	338	12	18	362
Cichelli	29	587	19	6	39
Mate	343	528	15	6	628
KnuthBendix	15	302	8	18	16

support of primitive operations and the memory usage and run times are small enough to use them in simulation. The results come from an instruction-level simulator we developed for the PilGRIM. All measurements exclude the garbage collection overhead. GHC 6.10.4 (with the option -O2) was used for running the benchmarks on a PC and to produce to the simple core language for the PilGRIM code generator.

For 11 out of the 15 benchmarks in Table 2, 400 million PilGRIM instructions per second is enough to match the performance of GHC on a 2.66GHz Intel i5 PC. The benchmarks with a high percentage of arithmetic instructions do not perform so well on the PilGRIM, while the best performing ones are store intensive. The arithmetic performance of the PilGRIM could be improved, but the architecture has no inherent advantage on this aspect over other architectures.

For a deeply pipelined processor the performance in instructions says little about the actual performance. Pipeline stalls due to control flow and latency of memory operations are a big factor.

It is too early to compare with the Reduceron directly on performance, but we can compare the instruction set approach of the PilGRIM versus template instantiation in the Reduceron. For most benchmark programs the difference is fairly small (note that one is measured in instructions and the other in cycles). The Reduceron does better on Braun and MSS, due to requiring one step less in a critical small inner 'loop' in both programs. Where the numbers for PilGRIM are significantly lower, such as in Adjoxo and Mate, we believe they can entirely attributed to the optimizations applied by GHC.

5.1   Related Work

Between roughly 1975 and 1990, a lot of work was done on the design of Lisp machines and combinator based processors [14,13]. Big differences in implementation strategy and hardware technology leaves little to directly compare this work to. The only processor designs comparable to our work are Augustsson's Big Word Machine (BWM) [1] from 1991 and the recent work by Naylor and Runciman on the Reduceron [8,9]. Our work was inspired by the Reduceron, because of its promising results. The unusual architecture of the Reduceron leaves room (from a hardware perspective) for improvements and many alternative design choices. The BWM, Reduceron and PilGRIM have in common that they all focus on exploiting the potential parallelism in data movements inherent to functional languages, by reading multiple values in parallel from the stack and rearranging them through a large crossbar in every cycle. Advances in hardware technology allowed the Reduceron and the PilGRIM to go a step further than the BWM, by also using a wide heap memory and adding special-purpose stacks, that can be used in parallel. Both the BWM and the Reduceron choose to encode data constructors and case expression in functions for hardware simplicity. The Reduceron adds special hardware to speed up handling these function-application-encoded case expressions. The Reduceron is based on template instantiation, while the BWM uses a small instruction set, based on the G-machine [6]. Unfortunately, the BWM was only simulated and never built. The Reduceron has been implemented on an FPGA, achieving a clock speed close to 100MHz. The Reduceron executes one complete reduction step per cycle.

While the Reduceron achieves surprisingly high performance given its simplicity, the single cycle nature of its design is the limiting factor in performance. It will have a relatively low clock speed even in a silicon implementation, because the latency of memory reads and writes performed within every cycle. With the extensive use of pipelining the PilGRIM targets a high clock frequency which comes with a strong increase in the complexity of the design.

6   Conclusions

It is feasible to design an efficient processor for lazy functional languages using a high-level instruction set. We designed the instruction set to match closely with the source language, so that code generation is (relatively) simple. Lazy functional languages can expose a lot of low-level parallelism, even in an instruction set based architecture. Most of this parallelism is in data movements, and can be exploited by using wide memories and many parallel stacks. A large part of the abstraction overhead typically incurred by high-level languages can be removed, by adding specialized hardware.

Measurements have shown that the designed instruction set is better suited for the functional language domain than the instruction set of typical general purpose processors. Combined with the results from the Reduceron, we conclude that the potential exploitation of low-level parallelism is inherent to lazy functional languages. This form of parallelism is not restricted to a single implementation strategy, but works both for template instantiation and a GRIN-derived instruction set. The advantage of using an instruction set based and pipelined design is that many existing hardware optimization techniques can be applied to the PilGRIM.

As for absolute performance numbers compared to desktop processors: the big open question is how often the pipeline of this core will stall on cache misses and branches. To become competitive with current general purpose processors, the PilGRIM needs to execute about 500 million instructions per second. We might be able to achieve that with the not unreasonable numbers of a 1 GHz operating frequency and executing an instruction every other cycle on average. The optimal trade off between frequency and pipeline stalls is an open question, and we might need to settle for a lower frequency in a first version, due to the complexity of a deep pipelined design.

Future Work. The next step is finishing a fully pipelined, cycle accurate simulation model with all optimizations applied. Most optimizations under consideration are to avoid pipeline stalls and to reduce the latency and bandwidth of memory accesses. Another area for optimization is the exploitation of potential parallelism in arithmetic operations. Then, we plan to transform the simulation model into a synthesizable hardware description of this architecture, and make it work on an FPGA, so that real programs can be benchmarked with it. Once this processor is complete, a lot of interesting research possibilities open up, like building a multicore system with it and making the core run threads concurrently by fine-grained multithreading.

Acknowledgements. We are grateful to the Reduceron team for making their benchmark set available online and providing raw numbers of the Reduceron. We also thank the anonymous reviewers, Kenneth Rovers, Christiaan Baaij and Raphael Poss for their extensive and helpful comments on earlier versions of this paper.

References

1. Augustsson, L.: BWM: A concrete machine for graph reduction. Functional Programming, 36–50 (1991)
2. Baaij, C.P.R., Kooijman, M., Kuper, J., Boeijink, W.A., Gerards, M.E.T.: CΛash: Structural descriptions of synchronous hardware using haskell. In: Proceedings of the 13th EUROMICRO Conference on Digital System Design: Architectures, Methods and Tools, pp. 714–721 (September 2010)
3. Boquist, U.: Code Optimisation Techniques for Lazy Functional Languages. Ph.D. thesis, Chalmers University of Technology (April 1999),
   http://www.cs.chalmers.se/~boquist/phd/phd.ps.gz
4. Boquist, U., Johnsson, T.: The GRIN project: A highly optimising back end for lazy functional languages. Implementation of Functional Languages, 58–84 (1996)
5. Hennessy, J.L., Patterson, D.A.: Computer Architecture: A Quantitative Approach, 4th edn. Morgan Kaufmann, San Francisco (2006)

6. Johnsson, T.: Efficient compilation of lazy evaluation. In: SIGPLAN Symposium on Compiler Construction, pp. 58–69 (1984)
7. Marlow, S., Peyton Jones, S.L.: Making a fast curry: push/enter vs. eval/apply for higher-order languages. In: ICFP, pp. 4–15 (2004)
8. Naylor, M., Runciman, C.: The reduceron: Widening the von neumann bottleneck for graph reduction using an FPGA. In: Chitil, O., Horváth, Z., Zsók, V. (eds.) IFL 2007. LNCS, vol. 5083, pp. 129–146. Springer, Heidelberg (2008)
9. Naylor, M., Runciman, C.: The reduceron reconfigured. In: ICFP (2010)
10. Nethercote, N., Mycroft, A.: The cache behaviour of large lazy functional programs on stock hardware. In: MSP/ISMM, pp. 44–55 (2002)
11. Peyton Jones, S.L.: The Implementation of Functional Programming Languages. Prentice-Hall, Inc., Englewood Cliffs (1987)
12. Peyton Jones, S.L.: Implementing lazy functional languages on stock hardware: The spineless tagless g-machine. J. Funct. Program. 2(2), 127–202 (1992)
13. Scheevel, M.: Norma: A graph reduction processor. In: LISP and Functional Programming, pp. 212–219 (1986)
14. Stoye, W.R., Clarke, T.J.W., Norman, A.C.: Some practical methods for rapid combinator reduction. In: LISP and Functional Programming, pp. 159–166 (1984)
15. Tolmach, A.: An external representation for the GHC core language (2001)

A   Semantics

We chose to present the semantics on the level of assembly language, instead of the instruction set, in order to describe how the PilGRIM works without getting lost in less important details.

The processor state $\langle H|S|Q \rangle$ is a triple consisting of the *heap* H with bindings from references to nodes, the *stack* S (a sequence of stack frames), and a *queue* Q (a local sequence of temporary values). Each frame $\langle N|C|R \rangle$ on stack S has three parts: the local node stack N (a nonempty sequence of nodes), the optional local update/apply/select continuation stack C, and a return target R. Possible return targets are: returning a node or reference ($R^n$to/$R^r$to) to an instruction sequence, returning into case statement $\mathtt{Rcase}$, continuing with the next stack frame $\mathtt{Rnext}$, or completing the main function $\mathtt{Rmain}$.

The semantics are written in an operational style, structured by the various modes of operation. These modes $\mathcal{I}$, $\mathcal{C}$, $\mathcal{R}$, $\mathcal{E}$, and $\mathcal{W}$, are explained below. Figure 5 contains the semantics for executing instructions indicated by the mode $\mathcal{I}$, with the instruction block as first argument. The callee mode $\mathcal{C}$ is only a notational construct to avoid the combinatorial explosion between what is called and how it is called. Underlining of variables denotes the conversion from stack/queue indices to values (by reading from the stack and/or queue).

A program starts in evaluation $\mathcal{E}$ mode, with the following initial state: $\langle \overrightarrow{g \mapsto \mathbf{F}_g} | \langle \mathbf{F}_{entry}\vec{a} | \epsilon | \mathtt{Rmain} \rangle | \epsilon \rangle$. The heap is initialized with a vector of bindings from constant references to nullary function nodes corresponding to all CAFs in the program. Initially the stack contains a single frame with the entry function with its arguments $\mathbf{F}_{entry}\vec{a}$ on the node stack. The queue and the extra continuation stack start empty, denoted by ϵ.

$\mathcal{I}(\mathtt{Store}\ t\ \vec{x}); \vec{\imath}$	$\langle H|S|Q \rangle \rightsquigarrow \mathcal{I}\ \vec{\imath}$	$\langle H, y \mapsto t\ \underline{\vec{x}}|S|y, Q \rangle$	, $y = newRef(H)$
$\mathcal{I}(\mathtt{Push}_{\mathtt{CAF}}\ g); \vec{\imath}$	$\langle H|S|Q \rangle \rightsquigarrow \mathcal{I}\ \vec{\imath}$	$\langle H|S|g, Q \rangle$	
$\mathcal{I}(\mathtt{PrimOp} \otimes \vec{x}); \vec{\imath}$	$\langle H|S|Q \rangle \rightsquigarrow \mathcal{I}\ \vec{\imath}$	$\langle H|S|y, Q \rangle$	, $y = \otimes\ \underline{\vec{x}}$
$\mathcal{I}(\mathtt{Constant}\ n); \vec{\imath}$	$\langle H|S|Q \rangle \rightsquigarrow \mathcal{I}\ \vec{\imath}$	$\langle H|S|n, Q \rangle$	
$\mathcal{I}(\mathtt{Call}\ c\ e); \vec{\imath}$	$\langle H|S|Q \rangle \rightsquigarrow \mathcal{C}\ c\ e\ (R^n\mathtt{to}\ \vec{\imath})$	$\langle H|S|Q \rangle$	
$\mathcal{I}(\mathtt{Force}\ c\ e); \vec{\imath}$	$\langle H|S|Q \rangle \rightsquigarrow \mathcal{C}\ c\ e\ (R^r\mathtt{to}\ \vec{\imath})$	$\langle H|S|Q \rangle$	
$\mathcal{I}(\mathtt{Jump}\ c\ e)$	$\langle H|S|Q \rangle \rightsquigarrow \mathcal{C}\ c\ e\ \mathtt{Rnext}$	$\langle H|S|Q \rangle$	
$\mathcal{I}(\mathtt{Case}\ c\ e\ \vec{a})$	$\langle H|S|Q \rangle \rightsquigarrow \mathcal{C}\ c\ e\ (\mathtt{Rcase}\ \vec{a})$	$\langle H|S|Q \rangle$	
$\mathcal{I}(\mathtt{Return}\ t\ \vec{x})$	$\langle H|S|Q \rangle \rightsquigarrow \mathcal{R}\ (t\ \underline{\vec{x}})$	$\langle H|S|Q \rangle$	
$\mathcal{I}(\mathtt{If}\ (x \bowtie y)\ t\ e)$	$\langle H|S|Q \rangle \rightsquigarrow \mathcal{I}\ t$	$\langle H|S|Q \rangle$	, *if* $\underline{x} \bowtie \underline{y}$
	$\rightsquigarrow \mathcal{I}\ e$	$\langle H|S|Q \rangle$	, *otherwise*
$\mathcal{I}(\mathtt{Throw}\ x)$	$\langle H|S|Q \rangle \rightsquigarrow \mathcal{W}\ \underline{x}$	$\langle H|S|\epsilon \rangle$	
$\mathcal{C}(\mathtt{Eval}\ x)$	$e\ r\ \langle H|S|Q \rangle \rightsquigarrow \mathcal{E}$	$\langle H|\langle n|\underline{e}|r \rangle, S|\underline{x} \rangle$	, $n = load(H,\underline{x})$
$\mathcal{C}(\mathtt{Eval}_{\mathtt{CAF}}\ g)$	$e\ r\ \langle H|S|Q \rangle \rightsquigarrow \mathcal{E}$	$\langle H|\langle n|\underline{e}|r \rangle, S|g \rangle$	, $n = load(H,g)$
$\mathcal{C}(\mathtt{TLF}\ f\ \vec{x})$	$e\ r\ \langle H|S|Q \rangle \rightsquigarrow \mathcal{I}\ \vec{\imath}\ \langle H|\langle \mathbf{F}_f\underline{\vec{x}}|\underline{e}|r \rangle, S|Q \rangle$		, $\vec{\imath} = code(f)$
$\mathcal{C}(\mathtt{Fix}\ f\ \vec{x})$	$e\ r\ \langle H|S|Q \rangle \rightsquigarrow \mathcal{I}\ \vec{\imath}\ \langle H|\langle \mathbf{F}_f\underline{\vec{x}}|\mathtt{Update}\ y,\underline{e}|r \rangle, S|y, Q \rangle$		, $y = newRef(H)$

Fig. 5. Semantics of the assembly language instructions

$\mathcal{R}\ n\ \langle H|\langle N|C|R\rangle, S|Q\rangle \qquad\qquad \rightsquigarrow \mathcal{E}\ \langle H|\langle n|C|R\rangle, S|\epsilon\rangle$

$\mathcal{E}\ \langle H|\langle \mathbf{F}_f\vec{x}\,|C|R\rangle, S|u\rangle \qquad\qquad \rightsquigarrow \mathcal{I}\ \vec{\imath}\ \langle H|\langle \mathbf{F}_f\vec{x}\,|\mathtt{Update}\ u, C|R\rangle, S|\epsilon\rangle$, $\vec{\imath} = code(f)$

$\mathcal{E}\ \langle H|\langle \mathbf{F}_f\vec{x}\,|C|R\rangle, S|\epsilon\rangle \qquad\qquad \rightsquigarrow \mathcal{I}\ \vec{\imath}\ \langle H|\langle \mathbf{F}_f\vec{x}\,|C|R\rangle, S|\epsilon\rangle$, $\vec{\imath} = code(f)$

$\mathcal{E}\ \langle H|\langle n|\mathtt{Update}\ u, C|R\rangle, S|\epsilon\rangle \quad \rightsquigarrow \mathcal{E}\ \langle H, u\mapsto n|\langle n|C|R\rangle, S|\epsilon\rangle$

$\mathcal{E}\ \langle H|\langle n|\mathtt{Catch}\ h, C|R\rangle, S|\epsilon\rangle \quad \rightsquigarrow \mathcal{E}\ \langle H|\langle n|C|R\rangle, S|\epsilon\rangle$

$\mathcal{E}\ \langle H|\langle \mathbf{C}_c\vec{x}\,|\mathtt{Select}\ i, C|R\rangle, S|\epsilon\rangle \rightsquigarrow \mathcal{E}\ \langle H|\langle n|C|R\rangle, S|x_i\rangle$, $n = load(H, x_i)$

$\mathcal{E}\ \langle H|\langle \mathbf{P}_f^m\vec{x}\,|\mathtt{Apply}\ \vec{a}, C|R\rangle, S|\epsilon\rangle$

$\qquad \rightsquigarrow \mathcal{E}\ \langle H|\langle \mathbf{P}_f^{m-|\vec{a}|}[\vec{x}, \vec{a}]\,|C|R\rangle, S|\epsilon\rangle$, if $m > |\vec{a}|$

$\qquad \rightsquigarrow \mathcal{E}\ \langle H|\langle \mathbf{F}_f[\vec{x}, \vec{a}]\,|C|R\rangle, S|\epsilon\rangle$, if $m = |\vec{a}|$

$\qquad \rightsquigarrow \mathcal{E}\ \langle H|\langle \mathbf{F}_f[\vec{x}, a_0, .., a_{m-1}]\,|\mathtt{Apply}\ [a_m, .., a_{|\vec{a}|-1}], C|R\rangle, S|\epsilon\rangle$, if $m < |\vec{a}|$

$\mathcal{E}\ \langle H|\langle n|\epsilon|\mathtt{Rnext}\rangle, \langle N|C|R\rangle, S|\epsilon\rangle \qquad \rightsquigarrow \mathcal{E}\ \langle H|\langle n|C|R\rangle, S|\epsilon\rangle$

$\mathcal{E}\ \langle H|\langle n|\epsilon|\mathbf{R}^\mathtt{n}\mathtt{to}\ \vec{\imath}\rangle, \langle N|C|R\rangle, S|\epsilon\rangle \qquad \rightsquigarrow \mathcal{I}\ \vec{\imath}\ \langle H|\langle n, N|C|R\rangle, S|\epsilon\rangle$

$\mathcal{E}\ \langle H|\langle n|\epsilon|\mathbf{R}^\mathtt{r}\mathtt{to}\ \vec{\imath}\rangle, S|\epsilon\rangle \qquad\qquad \rightsquigarrow \mathcal{I}\ \vec{\imath}\ \langle H, y\mapsto n|S|y\rangle$, $y = newRef(H)$

$\mathcal{E}\ \langle H|\langle \mathbf{C}_c\vec{x}\,|\epsilon|\mathtt{Rcase}\ \vec{a}\rangle, \langle N|C|R\rangle, S|\epsilon\rangle \rightsquigarrow \mathcal{I}\ \vec{\imath}\ \langle H|\langle \mathbf{C}_c\vec{x}, N|C|R\rangle, S|\epsilon\rangle$, $\vec{\imath} = selectAlt(\vec{a}, c)$

$\mathcal{E}\ \langle H|\langle n|\epsilon|\mathtt{Rmain}\rangle|\epsilon\rangle \qquad\qquad \rightsquigarrow \langle H|\langle n|\epsilon\rangle|\epsilon\rangle$ (end of program)

$\mathcal{W}\ x\ \langle H|\langle N|\mathtt{Catch}\ h, C|R\rangle, S|\epsilon\rangle \rightsquigarrow \mathcal{E}\ \langle H|\langle n|\mathtt{Apply}\ x, C|R\rangle, S|h\rangle$, $n = load(H, h)$

$\mathcal{W}\ x\ \langle H|\langle N|c, C|R\rangle, S|\epsilon\rangle \qquad \rightsquigarrow \mathcal{W}\ x\ \langle H|\langle N|C|R\rangle, S|\epsilon\rangle$

$\mathcal{W}\ x\ \langle H|\langle N|\epsilon|\mathtt{Rmain}\rangle|\epsilon\rangle \qquad \rightsquigarrow \langle H|\epsilon|\epsilon\rangle$ (exit with exception)

$\mathcal{W}\ x\ \langle H|\langle N|\epsilon|R\rangle, S|\epsilon\rangle \qquad\quad \rightsquigarrow \mathcal{W}\ x\ \langle H|S|\epsilon\rangle$

Fig. 6. Semantics of the stack evaluation/unwinding

Figure 6 contains the stack evaluation mode $\mathcal{E}$, and exception unwinding mode $\mathcal{W}$. Here, the order of the rules does matter: if multiple rules could match, the topmost one is taken. To avoid too many combinations, the rules for the evaluation mode are split up in multiple small steps. Returning a node in mode $\mathcal{R}$ is (after pushing the node onto the stack) identical to evaluation (of a node loaded from the heap). Thus it can share the following steps.

Automating Derivations of Abstract Machines from Reduction Semantics:
A Generic Formalization of Refocusing in Coq

Filip Sieczkowski*, Małgorzata Biernacka, and Dariusz Biernacki

Institute of Computer Science, University of Wrocław
`fisi@itu.dk`

Abstract. We present a generic formalization of the refocusing transformation for functional languages in the Coq proof assistant. The refocusing technique, due to Danvy and Nielsen, allows for mechanical transformation of an evaluator implementing a reduction semantics into an equivalent abstract machine via a succession of simple program transformations. So far, refocusing has been used only as an informal procedure: the conditions required of a reduction semantics have not been formally captured, and the transformation has not been formally proved correct.

The aim of this work is to formalize and prove correct the refocusing technique. To this end, we first propose an axiomatization of reduction semantics that is sufficient to automatically apply the refocusing method. Next, we prove that any reduction semantics conforming to this axiomatization can be automatically transformed into an abstract machine equivalent to it. The article is accompanied by a Coq development that contains the formalization of the refocusing method and a number of case studies that serve both as an illustration of the method and as a sanity check on the axiomatization.

1 Introduction

Refocusing has been introduced by Danvy and Nielsen [12] as a method for optimizing functions that directly implement the transitive closure of the following three steps: (1) decomposition of a term in order to locate a reduction site, (2) contraction of a redex, (3) recomposition of the entire term. Such an implementation induces an overhead due to the recomposition of a term that will immediately be decomposed in the next iteration; in such cases, refocusing can be applied to eliminate the overhead and produce more efficient functions.

In particular, Danvy and Nielsen showed how to mechanically derive an abstract machine from an evaluator implementing a reduction semantics (i.e., a small-step operational semantics with explicit representation of reduction contexts).

The original derivation method was applied to substitution-based reduction semantics and accounted for local contractions. It has later been used by Biernacka and Danvy to derive abstract machines for context-sensitive reduction

---

* Author's current affiliation: IT University of Copenhagen.

J. Hage, M.T. Morazán (Eds.): IFL 2010, LNCS 6647, pp. 72–88, 2011.

semantics [3], and it has been extended to a syntactic correspondence in order to facilitate derivations of environment-based machines from reduction semantics using explicit substitutions [2]. The refocusing method has been applied to a variety of languages [4,7,8,9,11,13,14,16]. This transformation can serve not only to derive new abstract machines, but also as a tool for interderiving different semantic specifications of the same language that are often designed independently from each other. For example, Danvy and Biernacka have shown the underlying reduction semantics of several well-known abstract machines and confirmed their correctness by applying refocusing [2].

The goal of this work is to formalize the refocusing transformation and prove it correct in the Coq proof assistant. In the article introducing the vanilla version of refocusing, Danvy and Nielsen define a set of conditions on a reduction semantics sufficient for constructing a refocused evaluation function, and they sketch a correctness proof of this function. However, they focus on the final efficient definition of an evaluation function and their representation of reduction semantics is not adequate for a formalization on a computer. In contrast, we formalize refocusing as a succession of simple intensional transformations of the evaluation relation induced by reduction semantics and we formally prove the correctness of all steps of the transformation.

To this end, we first give an axiomatization of reduction semantics that is sufficient to automatically apply the refocusing method. Next, we prove that any reduction semantics conforming to this axiomatization can be automatically transformed into an abstract machine equivalent to it. We formalize each intermediate step of the derivation and we state and prove its correctness. Our work is based on preliminary results by Biernacka and Biernacki [1] which we extend to a general framework.

Apart from the formalization of the basic refocusing transformation of Danvy and Nielsen, we also consider its variant used by Biernacka and Danvy for context-sensitive reduction semantics (useful, e.g., for expressing languages with control operators such as `call/cc`), and also a syntactic correspondence that for variants of calculi of closures leads to abstract machines with environments (rather than with meta-level substitutions) [2,3].

The formalization is carried out in the Coq proof assistant.[1] It includes a number of case studies: the language of arithmetic expressions, the lambda calculi (both pure and with `call/cc`) under call-by-value (accounting for Felleisen's CEK machine [15]) and call-by-name (accounting for Krivine's abstract machine [17]), as well as Mini-ML. These case studies serve both as an illustration of how to use the formalization in practice and as a sanity check on the axiomatization. However, due to space constraints, these examples are left out of this article—the reader is welcome to consult the Coq development.

---

[1] The Coq development accompanying this article can be found at `<http://fsieczkowski.com>`. Sections 2 and 3 refer to the subdirectory `substitutions`, Section 4 to the subdirectory `environments`, and Section 5 to the subdirectory `substitutions_cs` of the Coq development.

The implementation makes essential use of the Coq module system [5] that is based on the module system known from the ML family of languages. In Coq, however, a module type (i.e., a signature in SML parlance) may contain not only data declarations, but also logical axioms that capture extra properties of the data. In consequence, in an implementation of any module of such a signature one must provide proofs of the required properties. In our formalization, we first gather all the properties characterizing a reduction semantics into a module type, and similarly we define further signatures describing each of the intermediate semantic artefacts of the refocusing transformation. Then we define a series of functors each implementing one step of the derivation (i.e., the transformation from one module to the next). The formalization is engineered as a generic framework, so one can use it to transform one's own reduction semantics into an abstract machine. To this end, one has to specify the reduction semantics in the format prescribed by the signature, and then to apply the sequence of functors in order to obtain the abstract machine that is extensionally equivalent to the initial semantics.

The rest of this article is structured as follows. In Section 2 we define an axiomatization for the substitution-based reduction semantics amenable to refocusing. In Section 3 we give a brief summary of the refocusing method starting with the semantics given in Section 2 and we show the resulting abstract machine semantics in two versions: an *eval/continue* abstract machine and an *eval* abstract machine.[2] In Section 4 we formalize the extension of refocusing for a language with closures. In Section 5 we turn to context-sensitive reduction semantics and sketch the formalization for this extension. We conclude in Section 6.

2   An Axiomatization of a Substitution-Based Reduction Semantics

In this section we describe an axiomatization of a generic reduction semantics that defines sufficient conditions for the semantics to be automatically refocused. The description is similar to the one given by Danvy and Nielsen in [12], though it differs in several points, e.g., we require potential redexes to be explicitly provided, whereas Danvy and Nielsen specify them by their properties. The differences we introduce arise from the need to completely formalize the language and its reduction semantics in a proof assistant. We use the call-by-value lambda calculus (λ_v) as a running example in this section and in the next.

2.1   Syntactic Categories

We begin by specifying the syntactic categories used throughout the formalization: terms, values, potential redexes, and context frames, which we denote with

---

[2] We distinguish between eval/continue abstract machines, e.g., the CK abstract machine [15], that make transitions between two kinds of configurations: one focused on the term under evaluation and one focused on the context of the evaluation, and eval abstract machines, e.g., the Krivine Abstract Machine [17], that operate on configurations of one kind.

t, v, r and f, respectively. All these sets are declared as parameters of the language signature and have to be provided by the user in the implementation of that signature. The set of values and the set of potential redexes should be disjoint subsets of the set of terms. As traditional, values are terms irreducible in a given strategy (i.e., results of evaluation), and potential redexes can be thought of as minimal non-value terms.

Further, we introduce the syntactic category of reduction contexts (denoted as E). A reduction context is defined as a list of context frames and is interpreted similarly to the standard inside-out reduction context (i.e., as a stack). The composition of two reduction contexts is denoted as $E_1 \circ E_2$, while a context extended with a single frame is denoted as $f :: E$. The meaning of reduction contexts is usually specified by a *plug* function[3], which describes the effect of plugging a term into the context. Since reduction contexts are defined constructs in our approach, we can specify *plug* as a (left) folding of an *atomic plug* function over a reduction context, where *atomic plug* describes the effect of plugging a term into a context frame and has to be provided by the user. We denote with $E[t]$ the term obtained by plugging a term t into a context E. Our approach enforces that the composition of contexts and *plug* satisfy the property

$$(\text{plug-compose}) \quad (E_1 \circ E_2)[t] = E_2[E_1[t]],$$

which otherwise would have to be proved. In the example language λ_v, the syntactic categories can be defined with the following grammars, where x ranges over the (unspecified) set of variables:

$$t ::= x \mid \lambda x.t \mid t\,t \qquad \text{(terms)}$$
$$v ::= x \mid \lambda x.t \qquad \text{(values)}$$
$$r ::= v\,v \qquad \text{(potential redexes)}$$
$$f ::= [\,]\,t \mid v\,[\,] \qquad \text{(context frames)}$$

The grammar of potential redexes includes both standard beta redexes ("actual redexes") and stuck terms, e.g., $x\,v$.

2.2   Decompositions and Contraction

The notion of decomposition is defined as in Danvy and Nielsen [12]: any pair (E, t) is a decomposition of the term $E[t]$. A decomposition of the form (E, v) is said to be *trivial*, while the decomposition $([\,], t)$ is called *empty*. Our axiomatization requires that for both values and potential redexes every nonempty decomposition is trivial and that every term that has only trivial or empty decompositions is either a value or a potential redex.[4] We also define a partial

---

[3] In some recent articles [11,13,14] this function is called *recompose*.

[4] It is tempting to use a stronger requirement for values: a value can only have the empty decomposition. However, such a condition would preclude, i.e., values of the form $\mathsf{S}\,v$ (representing natural numbers), where v is a value.

function *contract* that takes a potential redex as argument and returns the term resulting from reducing it. For stuck terms, the function *contract* is undefined. All the definitions and properties introduced so far are specified in the module type RED_LANG.

Let us now look at the λ_v-calculus. It is easy to see that a value can never be decomposed into a term and a nonempty context. It follows that potential redexes can only be decomposed trivially or into the empty context and the redex itself: any redex $r = v\,v'$ can be decomposed either as $([\,],r)$, $([\,]\,v',v)$, or as $(v\,[\,],v')$, so the obligations on decompositions of values and redexes are fulfilled. The requirement that a term with only trivial or empty decompositions is either a value or a redex is also easy to prove by case analysis on the term.

Contraction in our example is defined using the standard capture-avoiding substitution: $(\lambda x.t)\,v$ reduces to $t[x/v]$. Both the semantics before and after the refocusing transformation are defined using contraction as a black box, and for the basic transformation we do not require any specific properties of this function.

2.3   Reduction Semantics

For a language satisfying the conditions stated above we can now specify a reduction semantics. First, we notice that a decomposition of any term t can lead to one of three possibilities:

1. t is a redex r that cannot be further decomposed
2. t is a value v that cannot be decomposed (e.g., a lambda form or a lazy constructor)
3. t can be decomposed into a term t' and a context frame f

The first and the third case are straightforward—either we have found a decomposition by locating the next potential redex, or we need to further decompose t' in the context extended with f. In the second case, we have to look at the current context: if it is empty, we have finished decomposing and reached a value. Otherwise, we have to examine the innermost context frame f in the surrounding context, and the value v. Together they can either form a potential redex or a value (in the case when all the decompositions of $f[v]$ are trivial, e.g., when $f[v]$ is a pair constructed of two values), or they can be decomposed into a new term t' and a new context frame f'. We require the user to provide two functions that capture this insight: $\mathbf{dec_t}$, that for a given term describes how it can be decomposed in one step, and an analogous function $\mathbf{dec_f}$, that does the same but for a pair of a context frame and a value. These "atomic" decomposition functions let us build a generic decomposition predicate. We require the user to provide not only the definitions of these two functions $\mathbf{dec_t}$ and $\mathbf{dec_f}$, but also a proof of their correctness with respect to the (atomic) plug function, i.e., that these functions are inverses of the atomic plug function. The decomposition relation can now be defined by iterating these user-defined functions until a decomposition is found. Formally, it is defined as an indexed family of inductive predicates in Coq, and its transcribed definition is presented in the top part of Figure 1.

In the case of the λ_v-calculus, we can define the atomic decomposition functions as follows:

$$\mathsf{dec}_t \, v = v \qquad\qquad \mathsf{dec}_f \, ([\,]\,t)\,v = (t, v\,[\,])$$
$$\mathsf{dec}_t \, (t_1\,t_2) = (t_1, [\,]\,t_2) \qquad\qquad \mathsf{dec}_f \, (v\,[\,])\,v' = v\,v'$$

Next, we introduce two strict, well-founded orderings: a subterm order $\prec_t$ that characterizes the relation of being a subterm of another term (and is defined using the atomic plug function), and an order on context frames $\prec_f$ that describes the order of evaluation of subterms (intuitively, $f \prec_f f'$ means that f' has more subterms left to be visited than f). The latter order is left to be provided by the user, together with a proof that this order is compatible with what the atomic decomposition functions describe. The relation might be definable in a similar manner to $\prec_t$, however, it seems that the required proofs are easier when the relation is defined by the user. Specifically, we require the following properties to hold:

- if $\mathsf{dec}_t \, t = (t', f)$, then f is maximal with respect to $\prec_f$
- if $\mathsf{dec}_f \, f \, v = (t, f')$, then $f' \prec_f f$ and $\forall f''.f'' \prec_f f \implies f'' \preceq_f f'$
- if $\mathsf{dec}_f \, f \, v$ returns a redex or a value, then f is minimal with respect to $\prec_f$
- if $\mathsf{dec}_t \, t \neq (t', f)$ for all t', f, then t has only the empty decomposition

Additionally, we require that all the elementary decompositions of a given term are comparable, i.e., if $f[t] = f'[t']$, then $f \prec_f f' \vee f' \prec_f f \vee (f = f' \wedge t = t')$, and that if $f[t] = f'[t'] \wedge f \prec_f f'$, then t' is a value, which effectively fixes the order of evaluation. Of course, both the structure of terms and the order of evaluation exist without specifying these orders: their explicit definition, however, allows us to conduct inductive reasoning without knowing the precise structure of terms. We need this kind of reasoning to prove the necessary properties of the semantics, such as the unique-decomposition lemma.

In our example of the λ_v-calculus, the order on context frames can be defined as the smallest strict order with the property $v\,[\,] \prec_f [\,]\,t$ for any term t and value v. This relation should hold for any t and v, because the term $(v\,t)$ can be decomposed into both contexts. It is also easy to see that the orders satisfy all the required conditions.

The properties of orders stated above are similar to those specified in Danvy and Nielsen [12], but they are in general more lax for the purpose of a formalization in a proof assistant. For example, unlike Danvy and Nielsen, we do not impose a fixed evaluation order but we leave it to the user to specify it.

The module type `RED_REF_LANG` contains all the requirements on the language stated above in the form of parameter declarations to be provided by the implementation, definitions (including inductive definitions), and axioms expressing required properties to be proved in the implementation. The definition of the reduction semantics is then given by the module types `RED_SEM` and `RED_REF_SEM` parameterized by `RED_LANG`.

$$\text{dec}\,t\,E\,d \iff \begin{cases} d = (r, E) & \text{if } \text{dec}_t\,t = r \\ \text{dec}_{\text{ctx}}\,E\,v\,d & \text{if } \text{dec}_t\,t = v \\ \text{dec}\,t'\,(f :: E)\,d & \text{if } \text{dec}_t\,t = (t', f) \end{cases}$$

$$\text{dec}_{\text{ctx}}\,[\,]\,v\,d \iff d = v$$

$$\text{dec}_{\text{ctx}}\,(f :: E)\,v\,d \iff \begin{cases} d = (r, E) & \text{if } \text{dec}_f\,f\,v = r \\ \text{dec}_{\text{ctx}}\,E\,v'\,d & \text{if } \text{dec}_f\,f\,v = v' \\ \text{dec}\,t\,(f' :: E)\,d & \text{if } \text{dec}_f\,f\,v = (t, f') \end{cases}$$

$$\text{iter}\,v\,v' \iff v = v'$$

$$\text{iter}\,(r, E)\,v \iff r \mapsto t \wedge \boxed{\text{dec}\,(E[t])\,[\,]\,d} \wedge \text{iter}\,d\,v \quad \text{for some } d$$

$$\text{eval}\,t\,v \iff \text{dec}\,t\,[\,]\,d \wedge \text{iter}\,d\,v \quad \text{for some } d$$

Fig. 1. A generic evaluator for reduction semantics

3   From Reduction Semantics to Abstract Machine by Refocusing

In this section, we present the formalization of the refocusing transformation for a language conforming to the axiomatization of reduction semantics specified in Section 2.3. The transformation follows the steps of the original refocusing method as presented by Danvy and Nielsen [12] and it consists of a series of semantics, each obtained in a systematic way from the preceding one and provably equivalent to it. Each of the semantics is given by an inductively defined relation that in the Coq formalization can be obtained by instantiating a functor with the module implementing the language under consideration.

3.1   An Evaluator

The starting point of the refocusing transformation is the evaluation function obtained by naively iterating the reduce-plug-decompose procedure that uses the components introduced in the previous section. This semantics is shown in Figure 1, where successful contraction of a potential redex is denoted with $\mapsto$, and the dec_t and dec_f functions are the elementary decomposition functions from Section 2.3. Both the iterating function iter and the evaluation function eval are represented as inductively defined relations (see module type RED_SEM).

3.2   A Small-Step Abstract Machine

The first step of the transformation, where the actual *refocusing* happens, builds on the observation that in a deterministic reduction semantics the following property should hold

$$\text{dec}\,(E[t])\,[\,]\,d \iff \text{dec}\,t\,E\,d.$$

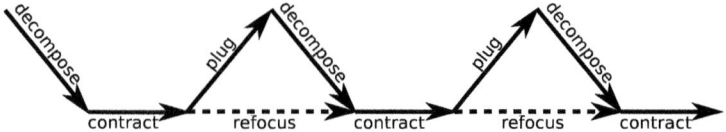

Fig. 2. A schematic view of the refocusing transformation

$$\texttt{iter}_{\texttt{ssam}}\, v\, v' \iff v = v'$$

$$\texttt{iter}_{\texttt{ssam}}\, (r, E)\, v \iff r \mapsto t \wedge \boxed{\texttt{dec}\, t\, E\, d} \wedge \texttt{iter}_{\texttt{ssam}}\, d\, v \quad \text{for some } d$$

$$\texttt{eval}_{\texttt{ssam}}\, t\, v \iff \texttt{dec}\, t\, [\,]\, d \wedge \texttt{iter}_{\texttt{ssam}}\, d\, v \quad \text{for some } d$$

Fig. 3. A generic small-step abstract machine for reduction semantics

Indeed, this property is a special case of (plug-compose), which we have asserted in Section 2. Thus, we can substitute the right-hand side of this equivalence for the left-hand side in the definition of the $\texttt{iter}$ function in the naive evaluator (the place where this change takes place is indicated with a gray box in Figure 1). The resulting definition is more efficient in that it avoids reconstructing the entire term after a contraction and then decomposing it again. The situation is shown in Figure 2, where "refocus" denotes the more efficient procedure that bypasses the successive *plug* and *decompose* steps, and instead it continues to decompose with the term obtained after contraction in the current context. Hence we arrive at a more efficient evaluator, a small-step abstract machine (a.k.a. a pre-abstract machine) [3,12]. The definition of this machine is presented in Figure 3, where the only change compared to Figure 1 is in the contents of the gray box (the $\texttt{dec}$ relation is defined as before and omitted).

The correctness of this step of transformation is captured by the following proposition.

Proposition 1. *For any term t and any value v of a language satisfying the axioms of Section 2, the equivalence $\texttt{eval}\, t\, v \iff \texttt{eval}_{\texttt{ssam}}\, t\, v$ holds.*

The proof follows immediately from a similar equivalence defined for $\texttt{iter}$ and $\texttt{iter}_{\texttt{ssam}}$, which in turn is done by induction on the derivation and uses the (plug-compose) property.

The specification of a small-step abstract machine is captured in the module type `SS_ABSTRACT_MACHINE` in the Coq development, and it is constructed by the functor `SSAbstractMachine` given a module implementing the reduction semantics.

3.3   A Staged Abstract Machine

The next step of the transformation consists in fusing computations, using lightweight fusion [10], so that the definitions of the relations $\texttt{dec}$ and $\texttt{dec}_{\texttt{ctx}}$

$$\mathbf{dec_{sam}}\, t\, E\, v \iff \begin{cases} \mathtt{iter_{sam}}\,(r, E)\, v & \text{if } \mathbf{dec_t}\, t = r \\ \mathbf{dec_{ctx\text{-}sam}}\, E\, v'\, v & \text{if } \mathbf{dec_t}\, t = v' \\ \mathbf{dec_{sam}}\, t'\, (f :: E)\, v & \text{if } \mathbf{dec_t}\, t = (t', f) \end{cases}$$

$$\mathbf{dec_{ctx\text{-}sam}}\, [\,]\, v\, v' \iff \mathtt{iter_{sam}}\, v\, v'$$

$$\mathbf{dec_{ctx\text{-}sam}}\, (f :: E)\, v\, v' \iff \begin{cases} \mathtt{iter_{sam}}\,(r, E)\, v' & \text{if } \mathbf{dec_f}\, f\, v = r \\ \mathbf{dec_{ctx\text{-}sam}}\, E\, v''\, v' & \text{if } \mathbf{dec_f}\, f\, v = v'' \\ \mathbf{dec_{sam}}\, t\, (f' :: E)\, v' & \text{if } \mathbf{dec_f}\, f\, v = (t, f') \end{cases}$$

$$\mathtt{iter_{sam}}\, v\, v' \iff v = v'$$

$$\mathtt{iter_{sam}}\,(r, E)\, v \iff r \mapsto t \wedge \mathbf{dec_{sam}}\, t\, E\, v$$

$$\mathbf{eval_{sam}}\, t\, v \iff \mathbf{dec_{sam}}\, t\, [\,]\, v$$

Fig. 4. A generic staged abstract machine for reduction semantics

are now made recursively dependent on the iter relation. The definition of the generic staged abstract machine is shown in Figure 4.

The correctness of this step of derivation is captured by the following proposition:

Proposition 2. *For any term t and any value v of a language satisfying the axioms of Section 3, the equivalence* $\mathbf{eval_{ssam}}\, t\, v \iff \mathbf{eval_{sam}}\, t\, v$ *holds.*

The proof is a little more complicated than in the case of the small-step abstract machine. To prove the "only if" case we need the following lemma:

Lemma 1. *For any term t, context E, decomposition d, and value v of a language satisfying the axioms of Section 2, the following implications hold:*

$$\mathbf{dec}\, t\, E\, d \wedge \mathtt{iter_{sam}}\, d\, v \implies \mathbf{dec_{sam}}\, t\, E\, v,$$

$$\mathtt{iter_{ssam}}\, d\, v \implies \mathtt{iter_{sam}}\, d\, v.$$

The lemma is proved by induction on the derivations of $\mathbf{dec}\, t\, E\, d$ and $\mathtt{iter_{ssam}}\, d\, v$, respectively. For the "if" case, we need the property stating that dec is a total function, which follows from the axiomatization, and a similar lemma:

Lemma 2. *For any term t, context E, decomposition d and value v of a language satisfying the axioms of Section 2, the following implication holds:*

$$\mathbf{dec_{sam}}\, t\, E\, v \wedge \mathbf{dec}\, t\, E\, d \implies \mathtt{iter_{ssam}}\, d\, v.$$

The lemma is proved by induction on the derivation of $\mathbf{dec_{sam}}$.

The specification of a staged abstract machine is captured in the module type STAGED_ABSTRACT_MACHINE in the Coq development, and it is constructed by the functor StagedAbstractMachine given a module implementing the reduction semantics.

$$\langle t \rangle_{\texttt{init}} \quad \triangleright \quad \langle t, [\,] \rangle_{\texttt{e}}$$

$$\langle t, E \rangle_{\texttt{e}} \quad \triangleright \quad \begin{cases} \langle t', E \rangle_{\texttt{e}} & \text{if } \textbf{dec}_{\texttt{t}}\, t = r \text{ and } r \mapsto t' \\ \langle E, v \rangle_{\texttt{c}} & \text{if } \textbf{dec}_{\texttt{t}}\, t = v \\ \langle t', f :: E \rangle_{\texttt{e}} & \text{if } \textbf{dec}_{\texttt{t}}\, t = (t', f) \end{cases}$$

$$\langle [\,], v \rangle_{\texttt{c}} \quad \triangleright \quad \langle v \rangle_{\texttt{fin}}$$

$$\langle f :: E, v \rangle_{\texttt{c}} \quad \triangleright \quad \begin{cases} \langle t, E \rangle_{\texttt{e}} & \text{if } \textbf{dec}_{\texttt{f}}\, f\, v = r \text{ and } r \mapsto t' \\ \langle E, v' \rangle_{\texttt{c}} & \text{if } \textbf{dec}_{\texttt{f}}\, f\, v = v' \\ \langle t, f' :: E \rangle_{\texttt{e}} & \text{if } \textbf{dec}_{\texttt{f}}\, f\, v = (t, f') \end{cases}$$

$$\textbf{eval}_{\texttt{ecam}}\, t\, v \iff \langle t \rangle_{\texttt{init}} \triangleright^{+} \langle v \rangle_{\texttt{fin}}$$

Fig. 5. A generic eval/continue abstract machine semantics derived from reduction semantics

3.4   The Result: An Eval/Continue Abstract Machine

The final step of the transformation yields an eval/continue abstract machine by inlining the definition of $\texttt{iter}_{\texttt{sam}}$ in $\textbf{dec}_{\texttt{sam}}$ and $\textbf{dec}_{\texttt{ctx-sam}}$ and by introducing the relation $\triangleright$ (and its transitive closure) between configurations defined by the latter two. The grammar of configurations of the machine reads as follows:

$$c ::= \langle t \rangle_{\texttt{init}} \mid \langle t, E \rangle_{\texttt{e}} \mid \langle E, v \rangle_{\texttt{c}} \mid \langle v \rangle_{\texttt{fin}}$$

Apart from the initial $\langle t \rangle_{\texttt{init}}$ and the final $\langle v \rangle_{\texttt{fin}}$ configurations corresponding to the "loading" and the "unloading" of the machine, there are two other kinds of configurations: an *eval*-configuration of the form $\langle t, E \rangle_{\texttt{e}}$ and a *continue*-configuration of the form $\langle E, v \rangle_{\texttt{c}}$. The *eval*-configurations arise from decompositions of terms in the reduction semantics, and the *continue*-configurations arise from analyzing values in context. The transitions of the machine and the induced evaluation function are presented in Figure 5.

The correctness of the overall transformation can then be stated with the following theorem, which follows from the correctness of individual transformation steps.

Theorem 1. *For any term t and any value v of a language satisfying the axioms of Section 2, the equivalence $\textbf{eval}\, t\, v \iff \textbf{eval}_{\texttt{ecam}}\, t\, v$ holds.*

The specification of an eval/continue machine is captured in the module type EVAL_CONTINUE_MACHINE in the Coq development, and it is constructed by the functor EvalContinueMachine given a module implementing the reduction semantics.

Redundancies in the generic abstract machine. Due to the transformation working in a very general setting, the resulting abstract machine may contain transitions that are not actually possible, e.g., in the case of the λ_v-calculus, the transition from $\langle f :: E, v \rangle_{\texttt{c}}$ to $\langle E, v' \rangle_{\texttt{c}}$ is present in the derived machine,

$$\langle t \rangle_{\texttt{init}} \quad \triangleright \quad \langle t, [\,] \rangle_{\texttt{e}}$$

$$\langle t, E \rangle_{\texttt{e}} \quad \triangleright \quad \begin{cases} \langle v \rangle_{\texttt{fin}} & \text{if } \textbf{dec}_{\texttt{t}}\, t = v \text{ and } E = [\,] \\ \langle t', E \rangle_{\texttt{e}} & \text{if } \textbf{dec}_{\texttt{t}}\, t = r \text{ and } r \mapsto t' \\ \langle t', E' \rangle_{\texttt{e}} & \text{if } \textbf{dec}_{\texttt{t}}\, t = v, E = f :: E', \textbf{dec}_{\texttt{f}}\, f\, v = r, \text{ and } r \mapsto t \\ \langle t', f' :: E' \rangle_{\texttt{e}} & \text{if } \textbf{dec}_{\texttt{t}}\, t = v, E = f :: E', \text{ and } \textbf{dec}_{\texttt{f}}\, f\, v = (t', f') \\ \langle t', f :: E \rangle_{\texttt{e}} & \text{if } \textbf{dec}_{\texttt{t}}\, t = (t', f) \end{cases}$$

$$\texttt{eval}_{\texttt{eam}}\, t\, v \iff \langle t \rangle_{\texttt{init}} \triangleright^{+} \langle v \rangle_{\texttt{fin}}$$

Fig. 6. A generic eval abstract machine semantics derived from reduction semantics

but it is never made because the side condition can never arise. It is however possible to simplify the machine by replacing the $\textbf{dec}_{\texttt{t}}$ and $\textbf{dec}_{\texttt{f}}$ functions with their definitions, compressing corridor transitions, and then removing unreachable transitions. In the case of the λ_v-calculus the obtained abstract machine coincides with Felleisen's CK machine [15].

3.5   An Eval Abstract Machine

In some cases we can obtain an eval abstract machine from an eval/continue abstract machine. It is possible when the reduction semantics satisfies an extra property that amounts to the condition that values have only empty decompositions. When this condition is fulfilled, it is possible to eliminate the *continue*-configurations since then the machine never makes a single transition from one *continue*-configuration to another *continue*-configuration. This step of the transformation has also been shown in Danvy and Nielsen [12], but the authors do not specify conditions on the reduction semantics under which it can be performed.

In the case of an eval abstract machine there are no *continue*-configurations in the machine:

$$c ::= \langle t \rangle_{\texttt{init}} \mid \langle t, E \rangle_{\texttt{e}} \mid \langle v \rangle_{\texttt{fin}}$$

The transitions of the machine and the induced evaluation function are presented in Figure 6.

The correctness of the overall transformation to an eval machine follows from the correctness of each of its steps, and is summarized by the following theorem:

Theorem 2. *Let L be a language satisfying the axioms of Section 2 and such that for any frame f and any value v, $\textbf{dec}_{\texttt{f}}\, f\, v$ is not a value. Then for any term t and any value v of L, the equivalence $\texttt{eval}\, t\, v \iff \texttt{eval}_{\texttt{eam}}\, t\, v$ holds.*

The specification of an eval abstract machine is captured in the module type `EVAL_MACHINE` in the Coq development, and it is constructed by the functor `EvalMachine` given a module implementing the reduction semantics.

4 Refocusing in Reduction Semantics with Explicit Substitutions

In this section we sketch the formalization of a derivation method that produces environment-based abstract machines for languages with closures. A closure is a purely syntactic entity that consists of a term together with an explicit substitution. The idea that a language with closures corresponds more faithfully to abstract machines using environments than a language with substitution as a meta-level operation originates in Curien's work: he introduced the calculus of closures $\lambda\rho$ as the simplest calculus of closures accounting for environment machines for the λ-calculus [6].

The extension of refocusing that operates on languages with closures is due to Biernacka and Danvy [2]. The method uses an intermediate calculus (the $\lambda\widehat{\rho}$-calculus) that minimally extends Curien's $\lambda\rho$-calculus in order to accommodate all the necessary refocusing steps, but the final result it produces, i.e., an environment-based abstract machine, operates on terms of the smaller $\lambda\rho$-calculus. In the formalization we also use two calculi: one denoted by C (the calculus corresponding to Curien's $\lambda\rho$-calculus) and the other denoted by $\widehat{C}$, which is an extended version of C amenable to refocusing (the calculus corresponding to Biernacka and Danvy's $\lambda\widehat{\rho}$-calculus). It might seem that given C one should be able to compute $\widehat{C}$, however, this is a task that requires some insight, and so we formalize both connected calculi.

4.1 Axiomatization of Closure Calculi

For both the calculi C and $\widehat{C}$ we need to specify the syntactic categories of closures, values and context frames, denoted c, v, and f in the C-calculus, and $\hat{c}$, $\hat{v}$, and $\hat{f}$ in the $\widehat{C}$-calculus, respectively. Since $\widehat{C}$ is an extension of C, we require that $c \subseteq \hat{c}$, $v \subseteq \hat{v}$, and $f \subseteq \hat{f}$ hold. We will apply the refocusing transformation to the $\widehat{C}$-calculus, hence we require that it fulfills all the obligations of Section 2.3 with closures taking on the role of terms.

Furthermore, we require that in the C-calculus each closure is either a term with an explicit substitution (i.e., with a list of closures) or a value, and that a closure has only the empty decomposition.

Finally, we also need the following compatibility properties expressing the fact that the syntactic extension in the $\widehat{C}$-calculus is inessential with respect to the C-calculus:

$$\mathsf{dec_t}\, c = \hat{r} \wedge \hat{r} \mapsto \hat{c}' \implies \hat{c}' \text{ is a } C\text{-closure} \vee \exists c', f.f[c'] = \hat{c}'$$
$$\mathsf{dec_t}\, c = \hat{v} \implies \hat{v} \text{ is a } C\text{-value}$$
$$\mathsf{dec_f}\, f\, v = \hat{r} \wedge \hat{r} \mapsto \hat{c} \implies \hat{c} \text{ is a } C\text{-closure} \vee \exists c, f'.f'[c] = \hat{c}$$
$$\mathsf{dec_f}\, f\, v = \hat{v}' \implies \hat{v}' \text{ is a } C\text{-value}$$
$$\mathsf{dec_f}\, f\, v = (\hat{c}, \hat{f}) \implies \exists c', f'.f' = \hat{f} \wedge c' = \hat{c}$$

$$\mathbf{dec}_{\text{ecamc}}\, c\, E\, v \iff \begin{cases} \mathbf{dec}_{\text{ecamc}}\, c'\, (E' \cdot E)\, v & \text{if } \mathbf{dec}_t\, c = \hat{r}, \hat{r} \mapsto \hat{c}' \\ & \text{and } E'[c'] = \hat{c}' \\ \mathbf{dec}_{\text{ctx-ecamc}}\, E\, v'\, v & \text{if } \mathbf{dec}_t\, c = \hat{v}' \text{ and } v' = \hat{v}' \end{cases}$$

$$\mathbf{dec}_{\text{ctx-ecamc}}\, [\,]\, v\, v' \iff v = v'$$

$$\mathbf{dec}_{\text{ctx-ecamc}}\, (f :: E)\, v\, v' \iff \begin{cases} \mathbf{dec}_{\text{ecamc}}\, c'\, (E' \cdot E)\, v' & \text{if } \mathbf{dec}_f\, f\, v = \hat{r}, \hat{r} \mapsto \hat{c}' \\ & \text{and } E'[c'] = \hat{c}' \\ \mathbf{dec}_{\text{ctx-ecamc}}\, E\, v''\, v' & \text{if } \mathbf{dec}_f\, f\, v = v'' \\ \mathbf{dec}_{\text{ecamc}}\, c\, (f' :: E)\, v' & \text{if } \mathbf{dec}_f\, f\, v = (\hat{c}, \hat{f}'), \\ & \quad c = \hat{c} \text{ and } f' = \hat{f}' \end{cases}$$

$$\mathbf{eval}_{\text{ecamc}}\, t\, v \iff \mathbf{dec}_{\text{ecamc}}\, (t[\bullet])\, [\,]\, v$$

Fig. 7. A generic eval/continue like semantics utilizing the C calculus

4.2   Towards an Efficient Eval/Continue Machine

Most of the derivation is adapted directly from Section 3 with the transformation working over the closures of the $\widehat{C}$-calculus. However, the properties stated in Section 4.1 allow us to make two additional steps in the derivation just before changing the format of the semantics to the abstract machine. The purpose of these two steps is to expose the environment in the resulting abstract machine.

Transition compression—back to the C-calculus. After performing the refocusing steps as in the standard version, we obtain a semantics in the form of an eval/continue machine for the $\widehat{C}$-calculus. We can now exploit the connection between the two calculi C and $\widehat{C}$ to arrive at a semantics defined only on C-closures. We do this by compressing transitions that first introduce, and then immediately consume the extra syntactic constructs of the $\widehat{C}$-calculus that are not present in the C-calculus. This step results in the semantics presented in Figure 7 and it relies on the compatibility properties stated in the previous subsection. For example, we observe that the existence of the context E' and the closure c' that appear in the first clause of the definition is ensured by the first of the compatibility properties.

The correctness of this step of the derivation is summarized by the following proposition:

Proposition 3. *For any term t and any value v of a language satisfying the axioms of Section 4.2, the equivalence* $\mathbf{eval}_{\text{ecam}}\, t\, v \iff \mathbf{eval}_{\text{ecamc}}\, t\, v$ *holds.*

Unfolding the closures. The final step of the extended transformation consists in "unfolding" the closures into their components (i.e., terms and substitutions) and it yields an eval/continue environment-based machine. As before, we introduce the transition relation $\triangleright$ together with its transitive closure. The grammar of configurations of the machine reads as follows:

$$c ::= \langle t \rangle_{\text{init}} \mid \langle t, s, E \rangle_{\text{e}} \mid \langle E, v \rangle_{\text{c}} \mid \langle v \rangle_{\text{fin}}$$

$$\langle t \rangle_{\texttt{init}} \quad \triangleright \quad \langle t, \bullet, [\,] \rangle_{\texttt{e}}$$

$$\langle t, s, E \rangle_{\texttt{e}} \quad \triangleright \quad \begin{cases} \langle t', s', E' \cdot E \rangle_{\texttt{e}} & \text{if } \texttt{dec}_\texttt{t}\, t[s] = \hat{r}, \hat{r} \mapsto \hat{c} \text{ and } E'[t'[s']] = \hat{c} \\ \langle E' \cdot E, v \rangle_{\texttt{c}} & \text{if } \texttt{dec}_\texttt{t}\, t[s] = \hat{r}, \hat{r} \mapsto \hat{c} \text{ and } E'[v] = \hat{c} \\ \langle E, v \rangle_{\texttt{c}} & \text{if } \texttt{dec}_\texttt{t}\, t[s] = v \end{cases}$$

$$\langle [\,], v \rangle_{\texttt{c}} \quad \triangleright \quad \langle v \rangle_{\texttt{fin}}$$

$$\langle f :: E, v \rangle_{\texttt{c}} \quad \triangleright \quad \begin{cases} \langle t, s, E' \cdot E \rangle_{\texttt{e}} & \text{if } \texttt{dec}_\texttt{f}\, f\, v = \hat{r}, \hat{r} \mapsto \hat{c} \text{ and } E'[t[s]] = \hat{c} \\ \langle E' \cdot E, v' \rangle_{\texttt{c}} & \text{if } \texttt{dec}_\texttt{f}\, f\, v = \hat{r}, \hat{r} \mapsto \hat{c} \text{ and } E'[v'] = \hat{c} \\ \langle E, v' \rangle_{\texttt{c}} & \text{if } \texttt{dec}_\texttt{f}\, f\, v = v' \\ \langle t, s, f' :: E \rangle_{\texttt{e}} & \text{if } \texttt{dec}_\texttt{f}\, f\, v = (t[s], f') \\ \langle f' :: E, v' \rangle_{\texttt{c}} & \text{if } \texttt{dec}_\texttt{f}\, f\, v = (v', f') \end{cases}$$

$$\texttt{eval}_{\texttt{ecam-env}}\, t\, v \iff \langle t \rangle_{\texttt{init}} \triangleright^+ \langle v \rangle_{\texttt{fin}}$$

Fig. 8. A generic eval/continue environment-based abstract machine semantics derived from reduction semantics

Note the change in the *eval* configuration, which now operates separately on terms and on substitutions that have become environments. The transitions of the machine and the induced evaluation function are presented in Figure 8.

The correctness of the transformation can then be stated with the following theorem, which follows from the correctness of individual transformation steps.

Theorem 3. *For any term t and any value v of a language satisfying the axioms of Section 4.2, the equivalence $\texttt{eval}\, t\, v \iff \texttt{eval}_{\texttt{ecam-env}}\, t\, v$ holds.*

Under conditions similar to those for the substitution-based eval/continue abstract machine of Section 3.5, one can transform the environment-based eval/continue abstract machine into an environment-based eval abstract machine.

5   Refocusing in Context-Sensitive Reduction Semantics

In this section we sketch the (minor) changes needed to adapt the formalization from Sections 2, 3 and 4 to languages with context-sensitive reduction. The refocusing method has been formalized for both substitution-based and closure-based source languages.

The notion of *context-sensitive reduction semantics* was first introduced by Biernacka and Danvy in order to deal with languages with multiple binders in the refocusing framework [2]. They also used it to account for languages with control effects such as the control operators call/cc or shift and reset [3].

In a standard reduction semantics the contracting function has type redex → term. This, however, can be insufficient for languages that contain more sophisticated constructs, where contraction depends not only on the redex, but also on the shape of the entire context surrounding that redex. For example, the control operator call/cc can be seen as a binding construct that captures the context which can then be applied to a value inside its body. Now, when we plug a term built with `call/cc` in a context, we trigger a contraction, where the structure of the contracted term depends on the structure of the context.

This more general notion of reduction requires only a small adaptation in the reduction semantics: we need to change the type of the contracting function into `redex × context → term × context`. Such a formulation of reduction semantics admits refocusing, as no part of the transformation depends on any specific properties of contraction.

The changes in the formalization needed to account for context-sensitive reduction are minor. In the axiomatization, they consist only in changing the type of contraction and propagating this change in the `dec`, `iter`, and `eval` relations. This change is then propagated through definitions of the refocusing steps and proofs without any impact on the structure or difficulty of proofs. As mentioned above, besides introducing context-sensitive reductions in the standard transformation, a combination with the environment-based extension is provided, as this is the setting in which context-sensitive reduction semantics have appeared and is a source of many interesting case studies.

6   Conclusion

We have formalized and proved correct the refocusing derivation method in the Coq proof assistant. The formalization is done as a generic framework and can be used to derive abstract machines for any language satisfying the requirements described in Section 2 (and in Section 4 for closure calculi). These (standard) requirements have to be packaged in a Coq module as specified in the signature. The output is an abstract machine extensionally equivalent to the initial semantics and is obtained by applying a sequence of functors to the module implementing the reduction semantics. The correctness of the final machine is a consequence of the correctness of each step of the transformation which in turn is ensured by each functor. The framework is quite general: it allows one to express languages with meta-level substitutions or with explicit substitutions, as well as languages with context-sensitive reduction. It is also possible to express the transition function of the final abstract machine as a Coq function and to employ the code extraction mechanism of Coq to generate a certified executable implementation of the machine.

The axiomatization of reduction semantics that we present in this article seems usable in practice, but it would be interesting to see if there are other, simpler axiomatizations, especially for languages with closures. Also, further automatization of some of the tasks that are now delegated to the user—including providing atomic decomposition functions—should be investigated.

Whereas the current article shows the subsequent semantics in the derivation chain are extensionally equivalent, there is ongoing work on characterizing such equivalence in terms of execution traces keeping track of the reduction sequence. This approach can further lead, with the help of coinductive reasoning of Coq, to refocusing and its correctness proof for potentially infinite computations.

Acknowledgements. We would like to thank Olivier Danvy and the anonymous reviewers of IFL'10 for numerous useful comments on the presentation of this work.

References

1. Biernacka, M., Biernacki, D.: Formalizing constructions of abstract machines for functional languages in Coq. In: Giesl, J. (ed.) Preliminary proceedings of the Seventh International Workshop on Reduction Strategies in Rewriting and Programming (WRS 2007), Paris, France (June 2007)
2. Biernacka, M., Danvy, O.: A concrete framework for environment machines. ACM Transactions on Computational Logic 9(1), 1–30 (2007)
3. Biernacka, M., Danvy, O.: A syntactic correspondence between context-sensitive calculi and abstract machines. Theoretical Computer Science 375(1-3), 76–108 (2007)
4. Biernacka, M., Danvy, O.: Towards compatible and interderivable semantic specifications for the Scheme programming language, Part II: Reduction semantics and abstract machines. In: Palsberg, J. (ed.) Semantics and Algebraic Specification. LNCS, vol. 5700, pp. 186–206. Springer, Heidelberg (2009)
5. Chrząszcz, J.: Implementing modules in the Coq system. In: Basin, D.A., Wolff, B. (eds.) TPHOLs 2003. LNCS, vol. 2758, pp. 270–286. Springer, Heidelberg (2003)
6. Curien, P.-L.: An abstract framework for environment machines. Theoretical Computer Science 82, 389–402 (1991)
7. Danvy, O.: Defunctionalized interpreters for programming languages. In: Thiemann, P. (ed.) Proceedings of the 2008 ACM SIGPLAN International Conference on Functional Programming (ICFP 2008), Victoria, British Columbia. SIGPLAN Notices, vol. 43(9), ACM Press, New York (September 2008)
8. Danvy, O.: From reduction-based to reduction-free normalization. In: Koopman, P., Plasmeijer, R., Swierstra, D. (eds.) AFP 2008. LNCS, vol. 5832, pp. 66–164. Springer, Heidelberg (2009)
9. Danvy, O., Johannsen, J.: Inter-deriving semantic artifacts for object-oriented programming. Journal of Computer and System Sciences 76, 302–323 (2010)
10. Danvy, O., Millikin, K.: On the equivalence between small-step and big-step abstract machines: a simple application of lightweight fusion. Information Processing Letters 106(3), 100–109 (2008)
11. Danvy, O., Millikin, K., Munk, J., Zerny, I.: Defunctionalized interpreters for call-by-need evaluation. In: Blume, M., Kobayashi, N., Vidal, G. (eds.) FLOPS 2010. LNCS, vol. 6009, pp. 240–256. Springer, Heidelberg (2010)
12. Danvy, O., Nielsen, L.R.: Refocusing in reduction semantics. Research Report BRICS RS-04-26, DAIMI, Department of Computer Science, Aarhus University, Aarhus, Denmark, A preliminary version appeared in the informal proceedings of the Second International Workshop on Rule-Based Programming (RULE 2001). Electronic Notes in Theoretical Computer Science, Vol. 59(4) (November 2004)
13. Danvy, O., Zerny, I.: Three syntactic theories for combinatory graph reduction. In: Alpuente, M. (ed.) LOPSTR 2010. LNCS, vol. 6564, pp. 1–20. Springer, Heidelberg (2011)
14. Danvy, O., Zerny, I., Johannsen, J.: A walk in the semantic park. In: Proceedings of the 2011 ACM SIGPLAN Symposium on Partial Evaluation and Semantics-Based Program Manipulation (PEPM 2011), Austin, USA. ACM Press, New York (January 2011) Invited talk

15. Felleisen, M., Friedman, D.P.: Control operators, the SECD machine, and the λ-calculus. In: Wirsing, M. (ed.) Formal Description of Programming Concepts III, pp. 193–217. Elsevier Science Publishers B.V., North-Holland (1986)
16. Garcia, R., Lumsdaine, A., Sabry, A.: Lazy evaluation and delimited control. Logical Methods in Computer Science 6(3:1), 1–39 (2010)
17. Krivine, J.-L.: A call-by-name lambda-calculus machine. Higher-Order and Symbolic Computation 20(3), 199–207 (2007)

From Bayesian Notation to Pure Racket via Discrete Measure-Theoretic Probability in λ_{ZFC}

Neil Toronto and Jay McCarthy

PLT @ Brigham Young University, Provo, Utah, USA
neil.toronto@gmail.com, jay@cs.byu.edu

Abstract. Bayesian practitioners build models of the world without re-garding how difficult it will be to answer questions about them. When answering questions, they put off approximating as long as possible, and usually must write programs to compute converging approximations. Writing the programs is distracting, tedious and error-prone, and we wish to relieve them of it by providing languages and compilers.

Their style constrains our work: the tools we provide cannot approximate early. Our approach to meeting this constraint is to 1) determine their notation's meaning in a suitable theoretical framework; 2) general-ize our interpretation in an uncomputable, *exact* semantics; 3) *approximate* the exact semantics and prove convergence; and 4) implement the approximating semantics in Racket (formerly PLT Scheme). In this way, we define languages with at least as much exactness as Bayesian practi-tioners have in mind, and also put off approximating as long as possible.

In this paper, we demonstrate the approach using our preliminary work on discrete (countably infinite) Bayesian models.

Keywords: Semantics, Domain-specific languages, Probability theory.

1 Introduction

Bayesian practitioners define *models*, or probabilistic relationships among ob-jects of study, without regard to whether future calculations are closed-form or tractable. They are loath to make simplifying assumptions. (If some probabilis-tic phenomenon is best described by an unsolvable integral or infinitely many distributions, so be it.) When they must approximate, they often create two models: an "ideal" model first, and a second model that approximates it.

Because they create models without regard to future calculations, they usually must accept approximate answers to queries about them. Typically, they adapt algorithms that compute converging approximations in programming languages they are familiar with. The process is tedious and error-prone, and involves much performance tuning and manual optimization. It is by far the most time-consuming part of their work—and also the most automatable part.

They follow this process to adhere to an overriding philosophy: an approxi-mate answer to the right question is worth more than an exact answer to an approximate question. Thus, they put off approximating as long as possible.

J. Hage, M.T. Morazán (Eds.): IFL 2010, LNCS 6647, pp. 89–104, 2011.

We must also adhere to this philosophy, because Bayesian practitioners are unlikely to use a language that requires them to approximate early, or that approximates earlier than they would. We have found that a good way to put the philosophy into practice in language design is to create two semantics: an "ideal," or *exact* semantics first, and a converging, *approximating* semantics.

1.1 Theory of Probability

Measure-theoretic probability is the most successful theory of probability in precision, maturity, and explanatory power. In particular, it explains every Bayesian model. We therefore define the exact semantics as a transformation from Bayesian notation to measure-theoretic calculations.

Measure theory treats finite, countably infinite, and uncountably infinite probabilistic outcomes uniformly, but with significant complexity. Though there are relatively few important Bayesian models that require countably many outcomes but not uncountably many, in our preliminary work, we deal with only countable sets. This choice avoids most of measure theory's complexity while retaining its functional structure, and still requires approximation.

1.2 Approach and Target Language

For three categories of Bayesian notation, we

1. manually interpret an unambiguous subclass of typical notation,
2. mechanize the interpretation with a semantic function,
3. if necessary, create an approximation and prove convergence, and
4. implement the approximation in Racket [3] (formerly PLT Scheme).

This approach is most effective if the target language can express measure-theoretic calculations and is similar to Racket in structure and semantics.

To this end, we are concurrently developing λ_{ZFC}: an untyped, call-by-value lambda calculus extended with sets as values, and primitive set operators that correspond with the Zermelo-Fraenkel axioms and Choice. Mixing lambdas and sets has been done in automated theorem proving [17,18,5]; it is possible to define exact real arithmetic, and easy to express infinite set operations and infinite sums. For this paper, we assume those operations are already defined. We freely use syntactic sugar like infix, summation, set comprehensions, and pattern-matching definitions. In short, we intend λ_{ZFC} to be contemporary mathematics with well-defined lambdas, or a practical lambda calculus with infinite sets.

For example, ***image*** is a `map`-like primitive set operator corresponding to the replacement axiom schema. If f is a lambda and A is a set, ***image*** f A = $\{f\ x \mid x \in A\}$ applies f to every element of A and returns the set of results.

Besides lambdas, λ_{ZFC} has an another class of applicable values: set-theoretic functions, or **mappings**. A mapping is just a set of pairs (x, y) where each x is unique. If g is a mapping and x is in its domain, $g\ x$ returns the y for which $(x, y) \in g$. Restricting a lambda f to a domain A returns a mapping:

$$f\big|_A \;=\; \{(x, f\ x) \mid x \in A\} \;=\; \textbf{\textit{image}}\ (\lambda x.\,(x, f\ x))\ A \tag{1}$$

Mappings can also be restricted using (1). We often write mappings as $\lambda(x \in A).e$ instead of $(\lambda x.e)\big|_A$. We think of (A, f) as a *lazy* mapping.

Though λ_{ZFC} has no formal type system, we find it helpful to reason about types informally. When we do, $A \Rightarrow B$ is a lambda or mapping type, $A \rightarrow B$ is the set of total mappings from A to B, and a set is a membership proposition.

1.3   Bayesian Languages

The Bayesian notation we interpret falls into three categories:

1. **Expressions**, which have no side effects, with $\mathcal{R}[\![\cdot]\!] : \lambda_{\mathrm{ZFC}} \Rightarrow \lambda_{\mathrm{ZFC}}$.
2. **Queries**, which observe side effects, with $\mathbf{P}[\![\cdot]\!], \mathbf{D}[\![\cdot]\!] : propositions \Rightarrow \lambda_{\mathrm{ZFC}}$.
3. **Statements**, which create side effects, with $\mathcal{M}[\![\cdot]\!] : statements \Rightarrow \lambda_{\mathrm{ZFC}}$.

We use λ_{ZFC} as a term language for all of our mathematics. We write Bayesian notation in sans serif, Racket in `fixed width`, common keywords in **bold** and invented keywords in ***bold italics***. We omit proofs for space.

2   The Expression Language

2.1   Background Theory: Random Variables

Most practitioners of probability understand random variables as free variables whose values have ambient probabilities. But measure-theoretic probability defines a **random variable** X as a total mapping

$$X : \Omega \rightarrow S_X \tag{2}$$

where Ω and S_X are sets called **sample spaces**, with elements called **outcomes**. Random variables define and limit what is observable about any outcome $\omega \in \Omega$, so we call outcomes in S_X ***observable outcomes***.

Example 1. Suppose we want to encode, as a random variable E, the act of observing whether the outcome of a die roll is even or odd.

A complicated way is to define Ω as the possible states of the universe. $E : \Omega \rightarrow \{even, odd\}$ must simulate the universe until the die is still, and then recognize the outcome. Hopefully, the probability that $E\ \omega = even$ is $\frac{1}{2}$.

A tractable way defines $\Omega = \{1, 2, 3, 4, 5, 6\}$ and $E\ \omega = even$ if $\omega \in \{2, 4, 6\}$, otherwise *odd*. The probability that $E\ \omega = even$ is the sum of probabilities of every even $\omega \in \Omega$, or $\frac{1}{6} + \frac{1}{6} + \frac{1}{6} = \frac{1}{2}$.

If we are interested in observing only evenness, we can define $\Omega = \{even, odd\}$, each with probability $\frac{1}{2}$, and $E\ \omega = \omega$. □

Random variables enable a kind of probabilistic abstraction. The example does it twice. The first makes calculating the probability that $E\ \omega = even$ tractable. The second is an optimization. In fact, redefining Ω, the random variables, and the probabilities of outcomes—without changing the probabilities of *observable* outcomes—is the essence of measure-theoretic optimization.

Defining random variables as functions is also a good factorization: it separates nondeterminism from assigning probabilities. It allows us to interpret expressions involving random variables without considering probabilities at all.

$$\mathcal{R}[\![X]\!] = X \quad \mathcal{R}[\![x]\!] = \textbf{\textit{pure}}\ x \quad \mathcal{R}[\![v]\!] = \textbf{\textit{pure}}\ v$$

$$\mathcal{R}[\![(e_f\ e_1\ \ldots\ e_n)]\!] = \textbf{\textit{ap}}^*\ \mathcal{R}[\![e_f]\!]\ \mathcal{R}[\![e_1]\!]\ \ldots\ \mathcal{R}[\![e_n]\!]$$

$$\mathcal{R}[\![\lambda x_1 \ldots x_n.e]\!] = \lambda\omega.\lambda x_1 \ldots x_n.\,(\mathcal{R}[\![e]\!]\ \omega)$$

$$\textbf{\textit{pure}}\ c = \lambda\omega.c, \quad \textbf{\textit{ap}}^*\ F\ X_1\ \ldots\ X_n = \lambda\omega.\,((F\ \omega)\ (X_1\ \omega)\ \ldots\ (X_n\ \omega))$$

Fig. 1. Random variable expression semantics. The source and target language are both λ_{ZFC}. Conditionals and primitive operators are trivial special cases of application.

2.2 Interpreting Random Variable Expressions as Computations

When random variables are regarded as free variables, arithmetic with random variables is no different from deterministic arithmetic. Measure-theoretic probability uses the same notation, but regards it as implicit pointwise lifting (as in vector arithmetic). For example, if A, B and C are random variables, $\mathsf{C} = \mathsf{A} + \mathsf{B}$ means $C\ \omega = (A\ \omega) + (B\ \omega)$, and $\mathsf{B} = 4 + \mathsf{A}$ means $B\ \omega = 4 + (A\ \omega)$.

Because we write all of our math in λ_{ZFC}, we can extend the class of random variables from $\Omega \to S_X$ to $\Omega \Rightarrow S_X$. Including lambdas as well as mappings makes it easy to interpret unnamed random variables: $4 + \mathsf{A}$, or $(+\ 4\ \mathsf{A})$, means $\lambda\omega.\,(+\ 4\ (A\ \omega))$. Lifting constants allows us to interpret expressions uniformly: if we interpret $+$ as $Plus = \lambda\omega.+$ and 4 as $Four = \lambda\omega.4$, then $(+\ 4\ \mathsf{A})$ means

$$\lambda\omega.\,((Plus\ \omega)\ (Four\ \omega)\ (A\ \omega)) \tag{3}$$

We abstract lifting and application with the combinators

$$\begin{aligned}\textbf{\textit{pure}}\ c &= \lambda\omega.c \\ \textbf{\textit{ap}}^*\ F\ X_1\ \ldots\ X_n &= \lambda\omega.\,((F\ \omega)\ (X_1\ \omega)\ \ldots\ (X_n\ \omega))\end{aligned} \tag{4}$$

so that $(+\ 4\ \mathsf{A})$ means $\textbf{\textit{ap}}^*\ (\textbf{\textit{pure}}\ +)\ (\textbf{\textit{pure}}\ 4)\ A = \cdots = \lambda\omega.\,(+\ 4\ (A\ \omega))$. These combinators define an **idiom** [13], which is like a monad but can impose a partial order on computations. Our *random variable idiom* instantiates the environment idiom with the type constructor $(I\ a) = (\Omega \Rightarrow a)$ for some Ω.

$\mathcal{R}[\![\cdot]\!]$ (Figure 1), the semantic function that interprets random variable expressions, targets this idiom. It does mechanically what we have done manually, and additionally interprets lambdas. For simplicity, it follows probability convention by assuming single uppercase letters are random variables. Figure 1 assumes syntactic sugar has been replaced; e.g. that application is in prefix form.

$\mathcal{R}[\![\cdot]\!]$ may return lambdas that do not converge when applied. These lambdas do not represent random variables, which are total. We will be able to recover mappings by restricting them, as in $\mathcal{R}[\![(+\ 4\ \mathsf{A})]\!]\big|_{\Omega}$.

2.3 Implementation in Racket

Figure 2 shows RV and a snippet of RV/kernel, the macros that implement $\mathcal{R}[\![\cdot]\!]$. RV fully expands expressions into Racket's kernel language, allowing RV/kernel to

```
(define-syntax (RV/kernel stx)
  (syntax-parse stx
    [(_ Xs:ids e:expr)
     (syntax-parse #'e #:literal-sets (kernel-literals)
       [X:id  #:when (free-id-in? #'Xs #'X)  #'X]
       [x:id          #'(pure x)]
       [(quote c)    #'(pure (quote c))]
       [(%#plain-app e ...)  #'(ap* (RV/kernel Xs e) ...)]
       ....)])]))
(define-syntax (RV stx)
  (syntax-parse stx
    [(_ Xs:ids e:expr)
     #'(RV/kernel Xs #,(local-expand #'e 'expression empty))]))
```

Fig. 2. A fragment of our implementation of $\mathcal{R}[\![\cdot]\!]$ in Racket

transform any pure Racket expression into a random variable. Both use Racket's new `syntax-parse` library [2]. `RV/kernel` raises a syntax error on `set!`, but there is no way to disallow applying functions that have effects.

Rather than differentiate between kinds of identifiers, `RV` takes a list of known random variable identifiers as an additional argument. It wraps other identifiers with `pure`, allowing arbitrary Racket values to be random variables.

3   The Query Language

It is best to regard statements in Bayesian notation as specifications for the results of later observations. We therefore interpret queries before interpreting statements. First, however, we must define the state objects that queries observe.

3.1   Background Theory: Probability Spaces

In practice, functions called **distributions** assign probabilities or probability densities to observable outcomes. Practitioners state distributions for certain random variables, and then calculate the distributions of others.

Measure-theoretic probability generalizes assigning probabilities and densities using **probability measures**, which assign probabilities to *sets* of outcomes. There are typically no special random variables: all random variable distributions are calculated from one global probability measure.

It is generally not possible to assign meaningful probabilities to all subsets of a sample space Ω—except when Ω is countable. We thus deal here with **discrete probability measures** $\mathbb{P} : \mathcal{P}(\Omega) \to [0,1]$. Any discrete probability measure is uniquely determined by its value on singleton sets, or by a **probability mass function** $P : \Omega \to [0,1]$. It is easy to convert P to a probability measure:

$$\mathit{sum}\ P\ A = \sum_{\omega \in A} P\ \omega \tag{5}$$

Then $\mathbb{P} = \boldsymbol{sum}\ P$. Converting the other direction is also easy: $P\ e = \mathbb{P}\ \{e\}$.

A **discrete probability space** (Ω, P) embodies all probabilistic nondeterminism introduced by statements. It is fine to think of Ω as the set of all possible states of a write-once memory, with P assigning a probability to each state.

3.2   Background Theory: Queries

Any probability can be calculated from (Ω, P). For example, suppose we want to calculate, as in Example 1, the probability of an even die outcome. We must apply $\mathbb{P}$ to the correct subset of Ω. Suppose that $\Omega = \{1, 2, 3, 4, 5, 6\}$ and that $P = [1, 2, 3, 4, 5, 6 \rightarrow \frac{1}{6}]$ determines $\mathbb{P}$. The probability that E outputs *even* is

$$\mathbb{P}\ \{\omega \in \Omega \mid E\ \omega = even\}\ =\ \mathbb{P}\ \{2, 4, 6\}\ =\ \boldsymbol{sum}\ P\ \{2, 4, 6\}\ =\ \tfrac{1}{2} \qquad (6)$$

This is a **probability query**.

Alternatively, we could use a **distribution query** to calculate E's distribution $\mathbb{P}_E$, and then apply it to $\{even\}$. Measure-theoretic probability elegantly defines $\mathbb{P}_E$ as $\mathbb{P} \circ E^{-1}$, but for now we do not need a measure. We only need the probability mass function $P_E\ e = \boldsymbol{sum}\ P\ (E^{-1}\ \{e\})$. Applying it yields

$$P_E\ even\ =\ \boldsymbol{sum}\ P\ (E^{-1}\ \{even\})\ =\ \boldsymbol{sum}\ P\ \{2, 4, 6\}\ =\ \tfrac{1}{2} \qquad (7)$$

More abstractly, we can calculate discrete distribution queries using

$$\boldsymbol{dist}\ X\ (\Omega, P)\ =\ \lambda(x \in S_X).\boldsymbol{sum}\ P\ \left(X\big|_\Omega^{-1}\ \{x\} \right) \qquad (8)$$

where $S_X = \boldsymbol{image}\ X\ \Omega$. Recall that $X\big|_\Omega$ converts X, which may be a lambda, to a mapping with domain Ω, on which preimages are well-defined.

3.3   Interpreting Query Notation

When random variables are regarded as free variables, special notation $\mathsf{P}[\cdot]$ replaces applying $\mathbb{P}$ and sets become propositions. For example, a common way to write "the probability of an even die outcome" in practice is $\mathsf{P}[E = \mathsf{even}]$.

The semantic function $\mathcal{R}[\![\cdot]\!]$ turns propositions about random variables into predicates on Ω. The set corresponding to the proposition is the preimage of $\{true\}$. For $E = \mathsf{even}$, for example, it is $\mathcal{R}[\![E = \mathsf{even}]\!]\big|_\Omega^{-1}\ \{true\}$. In general,

$$\boldsymbol{sum}\ P\ \left(\mathcal{R}[\![e]\!]\big|_\Omega^{-1}\ \{true\} \right)\ =\ \boldsymbol{dist}\ \mathcal{R}[\![e]\!]\ (\Omega, P)\ true \qquad (9)$$

calculates $\mathsf{P}[e]$ when e is a proposition; i.e. when $\mathcal{R}[\![e]\!] : \Omega \Rightarrow \{true, false\}$.

Although probability queries have common notation, there seems to be no common notation that denotes distributions *per se*. The typical workarounds are to write implicit formulas like $\mathsf{P}[E = e]$ and to give distributions suggestive names like P_E. Some theorists use $\mathcal{L}[\cdot]$, with $\mathcal{L}$ for *law*, an obscure synonym of *distribution*. We define $\mathbf{D}[\![\cdot]\!]$ in place of $\mathcal{L}[\cdot]$. Then $\mathbf{D}[\![E]\!]$ denotes E's distribution.

Though we could define semantic functions $\mathbf{P}[\![\cdot]\!]$ and $\mathbf{D}[\![\cdot]\!]$ right now, we are putting them off until after interpreting statements.

```
(struct mapping (domain proc)
  #:property prop:procedure (λ (f x) ((mapping-proc f) x)))
(struct fmapping (default hash)
  #:property prop:procedure
  (λ (f x) (hash-ref (fmapping-hash f) x (fmapping-default f))))

(define appx-z (make-parameter +inf.0))
(define (finitize ps)
  (match-let* ([(mapping Ω P)  ps]
               [Ωn  (cotake Ω (appx-z))]
               [qn  (apply + (map P Ωn))])
    (mapping Ωn (λ (ω) (/ (P ω) qn)))))

(define ((dist X) ps)
  (match-define (mapping Ω P) ps)
  (fmapping 0 (for/fold ([h (hash)]) ([ω (in-list Ω)])
                (hash-set h (X ω) (+ (P ω) (hash-ref h (X ω) 0))))))
```

Fig. 3. Implementation of finite approximation and distribution queries in Racket

3.4 Approximating Queries

Probabilities are real numbers. They remain real in the approximating semantics; we use floating-point approximation and exact rationals in the implementation.

Arbitrary countable sets are not finitely representable. In the approximating semantics, we restrict Ω to recursively enumerable sets. The implementation encodes them as lazy lists. We trust users to not create "sets" with duplicates.

When A is infinite, *sum P A* is an infinite series. With A as a lazy list, it is easy to compute a converging approximation—but then approximate answers to distribution queries sum to values less than 1. Instead, we approximate Ω and normalize P, which makes the sum finite and the distributions proper.

Suppose $(\omega_1, \omega_2, \ldots)$ is an enumeration of Ω. Let $z \in \mathbb{N}$ be the length of the prefix $\Omega_z = \{\omega_1, \ldots, \omega_z\}$ and let $P_z\, \omega = (P\, \omega)/(sum\, P\, \Omega_z)$. Then P_z converges to P. We define *finitize* $(\Omega, P) = (\Omega_z, P_z)$ with $z \in \mathbb{N}$ as a free variable.

3.5 Implementation in Racket

Figure 3 shows the implementations of *finitize* and *dist* in Racket. The free variable z appears as a *parameter* `appx-z`: a variable with static scope but dynamic extent. The `cotake` procedure returns the prefix of a lazy list as a finite list.

To implement *dist*, we need to represent mappings in Racket. The applicable struct type `mapping` represents lazy mappings with possibly infinite domains. A `mapping` named f can be applied with (f x). We do not ensure x is in the domain because checking is semidecidable and nontermination is a terrible error message. For distributions, checking is not important; the observable domain is.

However, we do not want `dist` to return lazy mappings. Doing so is inefficient: every application of the mapping would filter Ω. Further, `dist` always receives a `finitized` probability space. We therefore define `fmapping` for mappings that are constant on all but a finite set. For these values, `dist` builds a hash table by computing the probabilities of all preimages in one pass through Ω.

We do use `mapping`, but only for probability spaces and stated distributions.

4 Conditional Queries

For Bayesian practitioners, the most meaningful queries are **conditional** queries: those *conditioned on*, or *given*, some random variable's value. (For example, the probability an email is spam given it contains words like "madam," or the distribution over suspects given security footage.) A language without conditional queries is of little more use to them than a general-purpose language.

Measure-theoretic conditional probability is too involved to accurately summarize here. When $\mathbb{P}$ is discrete, however, the conditional probability of set A given set B (i.e. asserting that $\omega \in B$), simplifies to

$$P[A \mid B] = (\mathbb{P}\ A \cap B)/(\mathbb{P}\ B) \tag{10}$$

In theory and practice, $P[\cdot \mid \cdot]$ is special notation. As with $P[\cdot]$, practitioners apply it to propositions. They define it with $P[e_A \mid e_B] = P[e_A \wedge e_B]/P[e_B]$.

Example 2. Extend Example 1 with random variable $L\ \omega = low$ if $\omega \leq 3$, else *high*. The probability that $E = even$ given $L = low$ is

$$P[E = even \mid L = low] = \frac{P[E = even \wedge L = low]}{P[L = low]} = \frac{\sum\limits_{\omega \in \{2\}} P\ \omega}{\sum\limits_{\omega \in \{1,2,3\}} P\ \omega} = \frac{\frac{1}{6}}{\frac{1}{2}} = \frac{1}{3} \tag{11}$$

Less precisely, there are proportionally fewer even outcomes when $L = low$. □

Conditional *distribution* queries ask how one random variable's output influences the distribution of another. As with unconditional distribution queries, practitioners work around a lack of common notation. For example, they might write the distribution of E given L as $P[E = e \mid L = l]$ or $P_{E|L}$.

It is tempting to define $\mathbf{P}[\![\cdot \mid \cdot]\!]$ in terms of $\mathbf{P}[\![\cdot]\!]$ (and $\mathbf{D}[\![\cdot \mid \cdot]\!]$ in terms of $\mathbf{D}[\![\cdot]\!]$). However, defining conditioning as an operation on probability spaces instead of on queries is more flexible, and it better matches the unsimplified measure theory. The following abstraction returns a discrete probability space in which Ω is restricted to the subset where random variable Y returns y:

$$\boldsymbol{cond}\ Y\ y\ (\Omega, P) = (\Omega', P') \text{ where } \Omega' = Y|_{\Omega}^{-1}\ \{y\}$$
$$P' = \lambda(\omega \in \Omega').(P\ \omega)/(\boldsymbol{sum}\ P\ \Omega') \tag{12}$$

Then $P[E = even \mid L = low]$ means $\boldsymbol{dist}\ E\ (\boldsymbol{cond}\ L\ low\ (\Omega, P))\ even$.

We approximate $\boldsymbol{cond}$ by applying $\boldsymbol{finitize}$ to the probability space. Its implementation uses finite list procedures instead of set operators.

5   The Statement Language

Random variables influence each other through global probability spaces. However, because practitioners regard random variables as free variables instead of as functions of a probability space, they state facts about random variable distributions instead of facts about probability spaces. Though they call such collections of statements *models*,[1] to us they are **probabilistic theories**. A **model** is a probability space and random variables that imply the stated facts.

Discrete **conditional theories** can always be written to conform to

$$t_i \ ::= \ X_i \sim e_i; \ t_{i+1} \ | \ X_i := e_i; \ t_{i+1} \ | \ e_a = e_b; \ t_{i+1} \ | \ \epsilon \tag{13}$$

Further, they can always be made **well-formed**: an e_j may refer to some X_i only when $j > i$ (i.e. no circular bindings). We start by interpreting the most common kind of Bayesian theories, which contain only distribution statements.

5.1   Interpreting Common Conditional Theories

Example 3. Suppose we want to know only whether a die outcome is even or odd, high or low. If L's distribution is $P_L = [low, high \mapsto \frac{1}{2}]$, then E's distribution depends on L's output.

Define $P_{E|L} : S_L \to S_E \to [0,1]$ by $P_{E|L} \ low = [even \mapsto \frac{1}{3}, odd \mapsto \frac{2}{3}]$ and $P_{E|L} \ high = [even \mapsto \frac{2}{3}, odd \mapsto \frac{1}{3}]$.[2] The conditional theory could be written

$$\mathsf{L} \sim \mathsf{P_L}; \ \mathsf{E} \sim (\mathsf{P_{E|L}} \ \mathsf{L}) \tag{14}$$

If L is a measure-theoretic random variable, $(\mathsf{P_{E|L}} \ \mathsf{L})$ does not type-check: $L : \Omega \to S_L$ is clearly not in S_L. The *intent* is that E's distribution depends on L, and that $P_{E|L}$ specifies how.   □

We can regard $\mathsf{L} \sim \mathsf{P_L}$ as a constraint: for every model (Ω, P, L), **dist** $L \ (\Omega, P)$ must be P_L. Similarly, $\mathsf{E} \sim (\mathsf{P_{E|L}} \ \mathsf{L})$ means E's conditional distribution is $P_{E|L}$. We have been using the model $\Omega = \{1, 2, 3, 4, 5, 6\}$, $P = [1, 2, 3, 4, 5, 6 \mapsto \frac{1}{6}]$, and the obvious E and L. It is not hard to verify that this is also a model:

$$\Omega = \{low, high\} \times \{even, odd\} \qquad L \ \omega = \omega_1 \qquad E \ \omega = \omega_2$$
$$P = [(low, even), (high, odd) \mapsto \tfrac{1}{6}, (low, odd), (high, even) \mapsto \tfrac{2}{6}] \tag{15}$$

The construction of Ω, L and E in (15) clearly generalizes, but P is trickier. Fully justifying the generalization (including that it meets implicit independence assumptions that we have not mentioned) is rather tedious, so we do not do it here. But, for the present example, it is not hard to check these facts:

$$P \ \omega = (P_L \ (L \ \omega)) \times (P_{E|L} \ (L \ \omega) \ (E \ \omega))$$
$$\text{or} \quad P = \mathcal{R}[\![(P_L \ L) \times ((P_{E|L} \ L) \ E)]\!] \tag{16}$$

---

[1] In the colloquial sense, probably to emphasize their essential incompleteness.
[2] Usually, $P_{E|L} : S_E \times S_L \to [0, 1]$. We reorder and curry to simplify interpretation.

$$dist_{ps} \ X \ (\Omega, P) = (\Omega, P, P_X) \quad \text{where} \ \ S_X = \textbf{\textit{image}} \ X \ \Omega$$

$$P_X = \lambda(x \in S_X).\textbf{\textit{sum}} \ P \left(X|_{\Omega}^{-1} \{x\} \right)$$

$$cond_{ps} \ Y \ y \ (\Omega, P) = \left(\Omega', P', \_ \right) \quad \text{where} \ \ \Omega' = Y|_{\Omega}^{-1} \{y\}$$

$$P' = \lambda(\omega \in \Omega').(P \ \omega)/(\textbf{\textit{sum}} \ P \ \Omega')$$

$$extend_{ps} \ K_i \ (\Omega_{i-1}, P_{i-1}) = (\Omega_i, P_i, X_i)$$

$$\text{where} \ \ S_i' \ \omega = \textbf{\textit{domain}} \ (K_i \ \omega), \quad \Omega_i = (\omega \in \Omega_{i-1}) \times (S_i' \ \omega)$$

$$X_i \ \omega = \omega_j \ \ (\text{where} \ j = \text{length of any} \ \omega \in \Omega_{i-1}), \quad P_i = \mathcal{R}[\![P_{i-1} \times (K_i \ X_i)]\!]$$

$$run_{ps} \ m = x \quad \text{where} \ \ (\Omega, P, x) = m \ (\{()\}, \lambda\omega.1)$$

Fig. 4. State monad functions that represent queries and statements. The state is probability-space-valued.

If $K_L = \mathcal{R}[\![\mathsf{P_L}]\!]$ and $K_E = \mathcal{R}[\![(\mathsf{P_{E|L}} \ \mathsf{L})]\!]$—which interpret (14)'s statements' right-hand sides—then $P = \mathcal{R}[\![(K_L \ \mathsf{L}) \times (K_E \ \mathsf{E})]\!]$. This can be generalized.

Definition 1 (discrete product model). *Given a well-formed, discrete conditional theory* $X_1 \sim e_1; \ldots; X_n \sim e_n$, *let* $K_i : \Omega \Rightarrow S_i \to [0, 1]$, $K_i = \mathcal{R}[\![e_i]\!]$ *for each* $1 \leq i \leq n$. *The* **discrete product model** *of the theory is*

$$\Omega = \bigtimes_{i=1}^{n} S_i \quad X_i \ \omega = \omega_i \ (1 \leq i \leq n) \quad P = \mathcal{R} \left[\!\!\left[\prod_{i=1}^{n} (K_i \ X_i) \right]\!\!\right] \quad (17)$$

Theorem 1 (semantic intent). *The discrete product model induces the stated conditional distributions and meets implicit independence assumptions.*

When writing distribution statements, practitioners tend to apply first-order distributions to simple random variables. But the discrete product model allows any λ_{ZFC} term e_i whose interpretation is a discrete **transition kernel** $\mathcal{R}[\![e_i]\!]$: $\Omega \Rightarrow S_i \to [0, 1]$. In measure theory, transition kernels are used to build **product spaces** such as (Ω, P). Thus, $\mathcal{R}[\![\cdot]\!]$ links Bayesian practice to measure theory and represents an increase in expressive power in specifying distributions, by turning properly typed λ_{ZFC} terms into precisely what measure theory requires.

5.2 Interpreting Statements as Monadic Computations

Some conditional theories state more than just distributions [12,21]. Interpreting theories with different kinds of statements requires recursive, rather than whole-theory, interpretation. Fortunately, well-formedness amounts to lexical scope, making it straightforward to interpret statements as monadic computations. We use the state monad with probability-space-valued state.

We assume the state monad's $\textbf{\textit{return}}_s$ and $\textbf{\textit{bind}}_s$. Figure 4 shows the additional $\textbf{\textit{dist}}_{ps}$, $\textbf{\textit{cond}}_{ps}$ and $\textbf{\textit{extend}}_{ps}$. The first two simply reimplement $\textbf{\textit{dist}}$ and $\textbf{\textit{cond}}$. But $\textbf{\textit{extend}}_{ps}$, which interprets statements, needs more explanation.

$$\mathcal{M}[\![X_i := e_i;\ t_{i+1}]\!] = \boldsymbol{bind}_s\ (\boldsymbol{return}_s\ \mathcal{R}[\![e_i]\!])\ \lambda X_i.\mathcal{M}[\![t_{i+1}]\!]$$

$$\mathcal{M}[\![X_i \sim e_i;\ t_{i+1}]\!] = \boldsymbol{bind}_s\ (\boldsymbol{extend}_{ps}\ \mathcal{R}[\![e_i]\!])\ \lambda X_i.\mathcal{M}[\![t_{i+1}]\!]$$

$$\mathcal{M}[\![e_a = e_b;\ t_{i+1}]\!] = \boldsymbol{bind}_s\ (\boldsymbol{cond}_{ps}\ \mathcal{R}[\![e_a]\!]\ \mathcal{R}[\![e_b]\!])\ \lambda\_.\mathcal{M}[\![t_{i+1}]\!]$$

$$\mathcal{M}[\![\epsilon]\!] = \boldsymbol{return}_s\ (X_1,\ldots,X_n)$$

$$\mathbf{D}[\![e]\!]\ m = \boldsymbol{run}_{ps}\ (\boldsymbol{bind}_s\ m\ \lambda(X_1,\ldots,X_n).\boldsymbol{dist}_{ps}\ \mathcal{R}[\![e]\!])$$

$$\mathbf{D}[\![e_X\,|\,e_Y]\!]\ m = \lambda y.\mathbf{D}[\![e_X]\!]\ (\boldsymbol{bind}_s\ m\ \lambda(X_1,\ldots,X_n).\mathcal{M}[\![e_Y = y]\!])$$

$$\mathbf{P}[\![e]\!]\ m = \mathbf{D}[\![e]\!]\ m\ true, \quad \mathbf{P}[\![e_A\,|\,e_B]\!]\ m = \mathbf{D}[\![e_A\,|\,e_B]\!]\ m\ true\ true$$

Fig. 5. The conditional theory and query semantic functions

According to (17), interpreting $X_i \sim e_i$ results in $\Omega_i = \Omega_{i-1} \times S_i$, with S_i extracted from $K_i : \Omega_{i-1} \Rightarrow S_i \to [0,1]$. A more precise type for K_i is the dependent type $(\omega : \Omega_{i-1}) \Rightarrow (S_i'\ \omega) \to [0,1]$, which reveals a complication. To extract S_i, we first must extract the random variable $S_i' : \Omega_{i-1} \to \mathcal{P}(S_i)$. So let $S_i'\ \omega = \boldsymbol{domain}\ (K_i\ \omega)$; then $S_i = \bigcup (\boldsymbol{image}\ S_i'\ \Omega_{i-1})$.

But this makes query implementation inefficient: if the union has little overlap or is disjoint, P will assign 0 to most ω. In more general terms, we actually have a *dependent* cartesian product $(\omega \in \Omega_{i-1}) \times (S_i'\ \omega)$, a generalization of the cartesian product.[3] To extend Ω, $\boldsymbol{extend}_{ps}$ calculates this product instead.

Dependent cartesian products are elegantly expressed using the set monad:

$$\boldsymbol{return}_v\ x = \{x\} \qquad \boldsymbol{bind}_v\ m\ f = \bigcup (\boldsymbol{image}\ f\ m) \tag{18}$$

Then $(a \in A) \times (B\ a) = \boldsymbol{bind}_v\ A\ \lambda a.\boldsymbol{bind}_v\ (B\ a)\ \lambda b.\boldsymbol{return}_v\ (a,b)$.

Figure 5 defines $\mathcal{M}[\![\cdot]\!]$, which interprets conditional theories containing definition, distribution, and conditioning statements as probability space monad computations. After it exhausts the statements, it returns the random variables. Returning their names as well would be an obfuscating complication, which we avoid by implicitly extracting them from the theory before interpretation. (However, the implementation explicitly extracts and returns names.)

$\mathbf{D}[\![e]\!]$ expands to a distribution-valued computation and runs it with the **empty probability space** $(\Omega_0, P_0) = (\{()\}, \lambda\omega.1)$. $\mathbf{D}[\![e_X\,|\,e_Y]\!]$ conditions the probability space and hands off to $\mathbf{D}[\![e_X]\!]$. $\mathbf{P}[\![\cdot]\!]$ is defined in terms of $\mathbf{D}[\![\cdot]\!]$.

5.3 Approximating Models and Queries

We compute dependent cartesian products of sets represented by lazy lists in a way similar to enumerating $\mathbb{N} \times \mathbb{N}$. (It cannot be done with a monad as in the exact semantics, but we do not need it to.) The approximating versions of $\boldsymbol{dist}_{ps}$ and $\boldsymbol{cond}_{ps}$ apply **finitize** to the probability space.

---

[3] The dependent cartesian product also generalizes disjoint union to arbitrary index sets. It is often called a *dependent sum* and denoted $\Sigma a : A.(B\ a)$.

5.4 Implementation in Racket

$\mathcal{M}[\![\cdot]\!]$'s implementation is MDL. Like RV, it passes random variable identifiers; unlike RV, MDL also returns them. For example, (MDL [] ([X ~ Px])) expands to

```
([X] (bind/s (extend/ps (RV [] Px)) (λ (X) (ret/s (list X)))))
```

where [X] is the updated list of identifiers and the rest is a model computation.

We store theories in transformer bindings so queries can expand them later. For example, (define-model die-roll [L ~ Pl] [E ~ (Pe/l L)]) expands to

```
(define-syntax die-roll #'(MDL [] ([L ~ Pl] [E ~ (Pe/l L)])))
```

The macro with-model introduces a scope in which a theory's variables are visible. For example, (with-model die-roll (Dist L E)) looks up die-roll and expands it into its identifiers and computation. Using the identifiers as lambda arguments, Dist (the implementation of $\mathbf{D}[\![\cdot]\!]$) builds a query computation as in Figure 5, and runs it with (mapping (list empty) (λ (ω) 1)), the empty probability space.

Using these identifiers would break hygiene, except that Dist replaces the lambda arguments' lexical context. This puts the theory's exported identifiers in scope, even when the theory and query are defined in separate modules. Because queries can access only the exported identifiers, it is safe.

Aside from passing identifiers and monkeying with hygiene, the macros are almost transcribed from the semantic functions.

Examples. Consider a conditional distribution with the first-order definition

```
(define (Geometric p)
   (mapping N1 (λ (n) (* p (expt (- 1 p) (- n 1))))))
```

where N1 is a lazy list of natural numbers starting at 1. Nahin gives a delightfully morbid use for Geometric in his book of probability puzzlers [15].

Two idiots duel with one gun. They put only one bullet in it, and take turns spinning the chamber and firing at each other. They know that if they each take one shot at a time, player one usually wins. Therefore, player one takes one shot, and after that, the next player takes one more shot than the previous player, spinning the chamber before each shot. How probable is player two's demise?

The distribution over the number of shots when the gun fires is (Geometric 1/6). Using this procedure to determine whether player one fires shot n:

```
(define (p1-fires? n [shots 1])
   (cond [(n . <= . 0)  #f]
         [else  (not (p1-fires? (- n shots) (add1 shots)))]))
```

we compute the probability that player one wins with

```
(with-model (model [winning-shot ~ (Geometric 1/6)])
   (Pr (p1-fires? winning-shot)))
```

Nahin computes 0.5239191275550995247919843—25 decimal digits—with custom MATLAB code. At appx-z ≥ 321, our solution computes the same digits. (Though it appends the digits 9..., so Nahin should have rounded up!) Implementing it took about five minutes. But the problem is not Bayesian.

This is: suppose player one slyly suggests a single coin flip to determine whether they spin the chamber before each shot. You do not see the duel, but learn that player two won. What is the probability they spun the chamber?

Suppose that the well-known `Bernoulli` and discrete `Uniform` conditional distributions are defined. Using these first-order conditional distributions and Racket's `cond`, we can state a fairly direct theory of the duel:

```
(define-model half-idiot-duel
  [spin? ~ (Bernoulli 1/2)]
  [winning-shot ~ (cond [spin?  (Geometric 1/6)]
                        [else   (Uniform 1 6)])])
```

Then `(Pr spin? (not (p1-fires? winning-shot)))` converges to about 0.588.

Bayesian practitioners would normally create a new first-order conditional distribution `WinningShot`, and then state [`winning-shot` ~ (`WinningShot spin?`)]. Most would *like* to state something more direct—such as the above theory, which plainly shows how `spin?`'s value affects `winning-shot`'s distribution. However, without a semantics, they cannot be sure that using the value of a `cond` (or of any "if"-like expression) as a distribution is well-defined. That `winning-shot` has a *different range* for each value of `spin?` makes things more uncertain.

As specified by $\mathcal{R}[\![\cdot]\!]$, our implementation interprets (`cond` ...) above as a stochastic transition kernel. As specified by $\mathcal{M}[\![\cdot]\!]$, it builds the probability space using dependent cartesian products. Thus, the direct theory really is well-defined.

The most direct theory has infinitely many statements, one for each possible shot. Supporting such theories is future work.

6   Why Separate Statements and Queries?

Whether queries should be allowed inside theories is a decision with subtle effects.

Theories are sets of facts. Well-formedness imposes a partial order, but every linearization should be interpreted equivalently. Thus, we can determine whether two kinds of statements can coexist in theories by determining whether they can be exchanged without changing the interpretation. This is equivalent to determining whether the corresponding monad functions commute.

The following definitions suppose a conditional theory $t_1; \ldots; t_n$ in which exchanging some t_i and t_{i+1} (where $i < n$) is well-formed. Applying semantic functions in the definitions yields definitions that are independent of syntax but difficult to read, so we give the syntactic versions.

Definition 2 (commutativity). *We say that t_i and t_{i+1}* **commute** *when*
$$\mathcal{M}[\![t_1; \ldots; t_i; t_{i+1}; \ldots; t_n]\!] \ (\Omega_0, P_0) = \mathcal{M}[\![t_1; \ldots; t_{i+1}; t_i; \ldots; t_n]\!] \ (\Omega_0, P_0).$$

This notion of commutativity is too strong: distribution statements would never commute with each other. We need a weaker test than equality.

Definition 3 (equivalence in distribution). *Suppose $X_1, \ldots, X_k$ are defined in $t_1, \ldots, t_n$. Let $m = \mathcal{M}[\![t_1, \ldots, t_n]\!]$, and m' be a (usually different) probability space monad computation. We write $m \equiv_{\mathbf{D}} m'$ and call m and m'* **equivalent in distribution** *when $\mathbf{D}[\![X_1, \ldots, X_k]\!] \ m = \mathbf{D}[\![X_1, \ldots, X_k]\!] \ m'$.*

The following says $\equiv_D$ is like observational equivalence with query contexts:

Theorem 2 (context). $D[\![e_X \mid e_Y]\!] \; m = D[\![e_X \mid e_Y]\!] \; m'$ *for all random variables* $\mathcal{R}[\![e_X]\!]$ *and* $\mathcal{R}[\![e_Y]\!]$ *if and only if* $m \equiv_D m'$.

Definition 4 (commutativity in distribution). *We say* t_i *and* t_{i+1} *commute in distribution when* $\mathcal{M}[\![t_1; \ldots; t_i; t_{i+1}; \ldots; t_n]\!] \equiv_D \mathcal{M}[\![t_1; \ldots; t_{i+1}; t_i; \ldots; t_n]\!]$.

Theorem 3. *The following table summarizes commutativity of* $cond_{ps}$, $dist_{ps}$ *and* $extend_{ps}$ *in the probability space monad:*

$cond_{ps}$	$=$		
$extend_{ps}$	$=$	$\equiv_D$	
$dist_{ps}$	$\not\equiv_D$	$=$	$=$
	$cond_{ps}$	$extend_{ps}$	$dist_{ps}$

By Theorem 3, if we are to maintain the idea that theories are sets of facts, we cannot allow both conditioning and query statements.

7   Related Work

Our approach to semantics is similar to abstract interpretation: we have a concrete (exact) semantics and a family of abstractions parameterized by z (approximating semantics). We have not framed our approach this way because our approximations are not conservative, and would be difficult to formulate as abstractions when parameterized on a random source (which we intend to do).

Bayesian practitioners occasionally create languages for modeling and queries. Analyzing their properties is usually difficult, as they tend to be defined by implementations. Almost all of them compute converging approximations and support conditional queries. When they work as expected, they are useful.

Koller and Pfeffer [9] efficiently compute exact distributions for the outputs of programs in a Scheme-like language. BUGS [11] focuses on efficient approximate computation for probabilistic theories with a finitely many statements, with distributions that practitioners typically use. BLOG [14] exists specifically to allow stating distributions over countably infinite vectors. BLAISE [1] allows stating both distribution and approximation method for each random variable. Church [4] is a Scheme-like probabilistic language with approximate inference, and focuses on expressiveness.

Kiselyov [8] embeds a probabilistic language in OCaml for efficient computation. It uses continuations to enumerate or sample random variable values, and has a `fail` construct for the *complement* of conditioning. The sampler looks ahead for `fail` and can handle it efficiently. This may be justified by commutativity (Theorem 3), depending on interaction with other language features.

There is a fair amount of semantics work in probabilistic languages. Most of it is not motivated by Bayesian concerns, and thus does not define conditioning. Kozen [10] defines the meaning of bounded-space, imperative "while" programs as functions from probability measures to probability measures. Hurd [6] proves properties about programs with binary random choice by encoding programs and portions of measure theory in HOL.

Jones [7] develops a domain-theoretic variation of probability theory, and with it defines the probability monad, whose discrete version is a distribution-valued variation of the set or list monad. Ramsey and Pfeffer [20] define the probability monad measure-theoretically and implement a language for finite probability. We do not build on this work because the probability monad does not build a probability space, making it difficult to reason about conditioning.

Pfeffer also develops IBAL [19], apparently the only lambda calculus with finite probabilistic choice that also defines conditional queries. Park [16] extends a lambda calculus with probabilistic choice, defining it for a very general class of probability measures using inverse transform sampling.

8   Conclusions and Future Work

For discrete Bayesian theories, we explained a large subclass of notation as measure-theoretic calculations by transformation into λ_{ZFC}. There is now at least one precisely defined set of expressions that denote discrete conditional distributions in conditional theories, and it is very large and expressive. We gave a converging approximating semantics and implemented it in Racket.

Now that we are satisfied that our approach works, we turn our attention to uncountable sample spaces and theories with infinitely many statements.

Following measure-theoretic structure in our preliminary work should make the transition to uncountable spaces fairly smooth. The functional structure of the exact semantics will not change, but some details will. The random variable idiom will be identical, but will require measurability proofs. We will still interpret statements as state monad computations, but with general probability spaces as state instead of discrete probability spaces. We will use regular conditional probability in $cond_{ps}$, $extend_{ps}$ will calculate product σ-algebras and transition kernel products, and $dist_{ps}$ will return probability measures. We will not need to change $\mathcal{R}[\![\cdot]\!]$, $\mathbf{D}[\![\cdot]\!]$ or $\mathbf{P}[\![\cdot]\!]$. Many approximations are available; the most efficient and general are sampling methods. We will likely choose sampling methods that parallelize easily.

The most general constructive way to specify theories with infinitely many primitive random variables is with recursive abstractions, but it is not clear what kind of abstraction we need. Lambdas are suitable for most functional programming, in which it is usually good that intermediate values are unobservable. However, they do not meet Bayesian needs: practitioners define theories to study them, not to obtain single answers. If lambdas were the only abstraction, returning every intermediate value from every lambda would become *good practice*. Because we do not know what form abstraction will take, we will likely develop it independently by allowing theories with infinitely many statements.

Model equivalence in distribution extends readily to uncountable spaces. It defines a standard for measure-theoretic optimizations, which can only be done in the exact semantics. Examples are variable collapse, a probabilistic analogue of constant folding that can increase efficiency by an order of magnitude, and a probabilistic analogue of constraint propagation to speed up conditional queries.

References

1. Bonawitz, K.A.: Composable Probabilistic Inference with Blaise. Ph.D. thesis, Massachusetts Institute of Technology (2008)
2. Culpepper, R.: Refining Syntactic Sugar: Tools for Supporting Macro Development. Ph.D. thesis, Northeastern University(2010) (to appear)
3. Flatt, M.: PLT: Reference: Racket. Tech. Rep. PLT-TR-2010-1, PLT Inc., (2010), http://racket-lang.org/tr1/
4. Goodman, N., Mansinghka, V., Roy, D., Bonawitz, K., Tenenbaum, J.: Church: a language for generative models. Uncertainty in Artificial Intelligence (2008)
5. Gordon, M.: Higher order logic, set theory or both? In: TPHOLs, Turku, Finland (1996) invited talk
6. Hurd, J.: Formal Verification of Probabilistic Algorithms. Ph.D. thesis, University of Cambridge (2002)
7. Jones, C.: Probabilistic Non-Determinism. Ph.D. thesis, University of Edinburgh (1990)
8. Kiselyov, O., Shan, C.: Monolingual probabilistic programming using generalized coroutines. Uncertainty in Artificial Intelligence (2008)
9. Koller, D., McAllester, D., Pfeffer, A.: Effective Bayesian inference for stochastic programs. In: 14th National Conference on Artificial Intelligence (August 1997)
10. Kozen, D.: Semantics of probabilistic programs. Foundations of Computer Science (1979)
11. Lunn, D.J., Thomas, A., Best, N., Spiegelhalter, D.: WinBUGS – a Bayesian modelling framework. Statistics and Computing 10(4) (2000)
12. Mateescu, R., Dechter, R.: Mixed deterministic and probabilistic networks. Annals of Mathematics and Artificial Intelligence (2008)
13. McBride, C., Paterson, R.: Applicative programming with effects. Journal of Functional Programming 18(1) (2008)
14. Milch, B., Marthi, B., Russell, S., Sontag, D., Ong, D., Kolobov, A.: BLOG: Probabilistic models with unknown objects. In: International Joint Conference on Artificial Intelligence (2005)
15. Nahin, P.J.: Duelling Idiots and Other Probability Puzzlers. Princeton University Press, Princeton (2000)
16. Park, S., Pfenning, F., Thrun, S.: A probabilistic language based upon sampling functions. Transactions on Programming Languages and Systems 31(1) (2008)
17. Paulson, L.C.: Set theory for verification: I. From foundations to functions. Journal of Automated Reasoning 11, 353–389 (1993)
18. Paulson, L.C.: Set theory for verification: II. Induction and recursion. Journal of Automated Reasoning 15, 167–215 (1995)
19. Pfeffer, A.: The design and implementation of IBAL: A general-purpose probabilistic language. Statistical Relational Learning (2007)
20. Ramsey, N., Pfeffer, A.: Stochastic lambda calculus and monads of probability distributions. Principles of Programming Languages (2002)
21. Toronto, N., Morse, B.S., Seppi, K., Ventura, D.: Super-resolution via recapture and Bayesian effect modeling. Computer Vision and Pattern Recognition (2009)

Dependently Typed Attribute Grammars

Arie Middelkoop, Atze Dijkstra, and S. Doaitse Swierstra

Universiteit Utrecht,
The Netherlands
{ariem,atze,doaitse}@cs.uu.nl

Abstract. Attribute Grammars (AGs) are a domain-specific language for functional and composable descriptions of tree traversals. Given such a description, it is not immediately clear how to state and prove properties of AGs formally. To meet this challenge, we apply dependent types to AGs. In a dependently typed AG, the type of an attribute may refer to values of attributes. The type of an attribute is an invariant, the value of an attribute a proof for that invariant. Additionally, when an AG is cycle-free, the composition of the attributes is logically consistent. We present a lightweight approach using a preprocessor in combination with the dependently typed language Agda.

1 Introduction

Functional programming languages are known to be convenient languages for implementing a compiler. As part of the compilation process, a compiler computes properties of Abstract Syntax Trees (ASTs), such as environments, types, error messages, and code. In functional programming, these syntax-directed computations are typically written as *catamorphisms*[1]. An *algebra* defines an inductive property in terms of each constructor of the AST, and a catamorphism applies the algebra to the AST. Catamorphisms thus play an important role in a functional implementation of a compiler.

Attribute Grammars (AGs) [3] are a domain-specific language for *composable* descriptions of catamorphisms. AGs facilitate the description of complex catamorphisms that typically occur in complex compiler implementations.

An AG extends a context-free grammar by associating *attributes* with nonterminals. Functional *rules* are associated with productions, and define values for the attributes that occur in the nonterminals of associated productions. As AGs are typically embedded in a host language, the rules are terms in the host language, which may additionally refer to attributes. Attributes can easily be composed to form more complex properties. An AG can be compiled to an efficient functional algorithm that computes the synthesized attributes of the root of the AST, given the root's inherited attributes.

It is not immediately clear how to formally specify and write proofs about programs implemented with AGs. *Dependent types* [1] provide a means to use *types* to encode

---

[1] Catamorphisms are a generalization of folds to tree-like data structures. We consider catamorphisms from the perspective of algebraic data types in functional programming instead of the equivalent notion in terms of functors in category theory. A catamorphism $cata_\tau \ (f_1, ..., f_n)$ replaces each occurrence of a constructor c_i of τ in a data structure with f_i. The product $(f_1, ..., f_n)$ is called an *algebra*. An element f_i of the algebra is called a *semantic function*.

J. Hage, M.T. Morazán (Eds.): IFL 2010, LNCS 6647, pp. 105–120, 2011.
© Springer-Verlag Berlin Heidelberg 2011

properties with the expressiveness of (higher-order) intuitionistic propositional logic, and *terms* to encode proofs. Such programs are called correct by construction, because the program itself is a proof of its invariants. The goal of this paper is therefore to apply dependent types to AGs, in order to formally reason with AGs.

Vice versa, AGs also offer benefits to dependently typed programming. Because of the Curry-Howard correspondence, dependently typed AGs are a domain-specific language to write structurally inductive proofs in a *composable, aspect-oriented* fashion; each attribute represents a separate aspect of the proof. Additionally, AGs alleviate the programmer from the tedious orchestration of multi-pass traversals over data structures, and ensure that the traversals are *total*: totality is required for dependently typed programs for reasons of logical consistency and termination of type checking. Hence, the combination of dependent types and AGs is mutually beneficial.

We make the following contributions in this paper:

- We present the language AG_{DA} (Section 3), a light-weight approach to facilitate dependent types in AGs, and vice versa, AGs in the dependently typed language Agda. AG_{DA} is an embedding in Agda via a preprocessor.
  In contrast to conventional AGs, we can encode invariants in terms of dependently typed attributes, and proofs as values for attributes. This expressiveness comes at a price: to be able to compile to a total Agda program, we restrict ourselves to the class of ordered AGs, and demand the definitions of attributes to be total.
- We define a desugared version of AG_{DA} programs (Section 4) and show how to translate them to plain Agda programs (Section 5).
- Our approach supports a conditional attribution of nonterminals, so that we can give total definitions of what would otherwise be partially defined attributes (Section 6).

In Section 2, we introduce the notation used in this paper. However, we assume that the reader is both familiar with AGs (see [10]) and dependently typed programming in Agda (see [7]).

2 Preliminaries

In this warm-up section, we briefly touch upon the Agda and AG notation used throughout this paper. As an example, we implement the sum of a list of numbers with a catamorphism. We give two implementations: first one that uses plain Agda, then another using AG_{DA}. This example does not yet use dependently typed attributes. These are introduced in the next section.

In the following code snippet, the data type *List* represents a cons-list of natural numbers. The type $T'List$ is the type of the value we compute (a number), and $A'List$ is the type of an algebra for *List*. Such an algebra contains a *semantic function* for each constructor of *List*, which transforms a value of that constructor into the desired value (of type $T'List$), assuming that the transformation has been recursively applied to the fields of the constructor. The catamorphism $cata_{List}$ performs the recursive application.

```
data List : Set where        -- represents a cons-list of natural numbers
  nil  : List                -- constructor has no fields
```

$cons : \mathbb{N} \to List \to List$ -- constructor has a number and tail list as fields

$T'List = \mathbb{N}$	-- defines a type alias $T'List : Set$,
$A'List = (T'List, \mathbb{N} \to T'List \to T'List)$	-- and $A'List : Set$
$cata_{List} : A'List \to List \to T'List$	-- applies algebra to list
$cata_{List}\ (n, \_)\ nil\ = n$	-- in case of nil, replaces nil with n
$cata_{List}\ alg\ l$ **with** $alg\ \|\ l$	-- otherwise, matches on alg and l
$cata_{List}\ alg\ l\ \ \|\ (\_, c)\ \|\ cons\ x\ xs$ **with** $cata_{List}\ alg\ xs$	-- recurses on xs
$cata_{List}\ alg\ l\ \ \|\ (\_, c)\ \|\ cons\ x\ xs\ \ \|\ r\ = c\ x\ r$	-- replaces $cons$ with c

In Agda, a function is defined by one or more equations. A with-construct facilitates pattern matching against intermediate values. An equation that ends with **with** $e_1\ \|$ ... $\|\ e_n$ parameterizes the equations that follow with the values of $e_1, ..., e_n$ as additional arguments. Vertical bars separate the patterns intended for the additional parameters.

The actual algebra itself simply takes 0 for the nil constructor, and $\_ + \_$ for the $cons$ constructor. The function sum_{List} shows how the algebra and catamorphism can be used.

$sem_{nil}\ : T'List$	-- semantic function for nil constructor
$sem_{nil}\ = 0$	-- $T'List = \mathbb{N}$ (defined above)
$sem_{cons} : \mathbb{N} \to T'List \to T'List$	-- semantic function for $cons$ constructor
$sem_{cons} = \_ + \_$	-- $\_ + \_ : \mathbb{N} \to \mathbb{N} \to \mathbb{N}$ (defined in library)
$sum_{List} : List \to T'List$	-- transforms the $List$ into the desired sum
$sum_{List} = cata_{List}\ (sem_{nil}, sem_{cons})$	-- algebra is semantic functions in a tuple

In the example, the sum is defined in a bottom-up fashion. By taking a function type for $T'List$, values can also be passed top-down. Multiple types can be combined by using products. Such algebras quickly become tedious to write. Fortunately, we can use AGs as a domain-specific language for algebras. In the code below, we give an AG implementation: we specify a grammar that describes the structure of the AST, declare attributes on productions, and give rules that define attributes.

We now give an implementation of the same example using AG_{DA}. The code consists of blocks of plain Agda code, and blocks of AG code. To ease the distinction, Agda's keywords are underlined, and keywords of AG_{DA} are typeset in bold.

A grammar specification is a restricted form of a data declaration (for an AST): data constructors are called *productions* and their fields are explicitly marked as *terminal* or *nonterminal*. A nonterminal field represents a *child* in the AST and has attributes, whereas a terminal field only has a value. A plain Agda data-type declaration can be derived from a grammar specification. In such a specification, nonterminal types must have a fully saturated, outermost type constructor that is explicitly introduced by a grammar declaration. Terminal types may be arbitrary Agda types[2].

grammar $List : Set$	-- declares nonterminal $List$ of type Set
prod $nil\ : List$	-- production nil of type $List$ (no fields)
prod $cons : List$	-- production $cons$ of type $List$ (two fields)

---

[2] In general, although not needed in this example, nonterminal types may be parametrized, production types may refer to its field names, and field types may refer to preceding field names.

term $hd : \mathbb{N}$ -- terminal field hd of type $\mathbb{N}$
nonterm tl : *List*   -- nonterminal field tl of type *List*

With an interface specification, we declare attributes for nonterminals. Attributes come in two fashions: *inherited* attributes (used in a later example) must be defined by rules of the parent, and *synthesized* attributes may be used by the parent. Names of inherited attributes are distinct from names of synthesized attributes; an attribute of the same name and fashion may only be declared once per nonterminal. We also partition the attributes in one or more *visits*. These visits impose a partial order on attributes. Inherited attributes may not be defined in terms of a synthesized attributes of the same visit or later. We use this order in Section 4 to derive semantic functions that are total.

itf *List*   -- interface for nonterminal *List*,
    visit *compute*   -- with a single visit that is named *compute*,
        syn *sum* : $\mathbb{N}$ -- and a synthesized attribute named *sum* of type $\mathbb{N}$

Finally, we define each of the production's attributes. We may refer to an attribute using *child.attr* notation. For each production, we give rules that define the inherited attributes of the children and synthesized attributes of the production itself (with *lhs* as special name), using inherited attributes of the production and synthesized attributes of the children. The special name *loc* refers to the terminals, and to local attributes that we may associate with a production.

datasem *List*   -- defines attributes of *List* for constructors of *List*
    prod *nil* $lhs.sum = 0$ -- rule for *sum* of production *nil*
    prod *cons* $lhs.sum = loc.hd + tl.sum$ -- refers to terminal hd and attr $tl.sum$

The left-hand side of a rule is a plain Agda pattern, and the right-hand side is either a plain Agda expression or with-construct (not shown in this example). Additionally, both the left and right-hand sides may contain attribute references.

During attribute evaluation, visits are performed on children to obtain their associated synthesized attributes. We do not have to explicitly specify when to visit these children, neither is the order of appearance of rules relevant. However, an inherited attribute $c.x$ may not depend on a synthesized attribute $c.y$ of the same visit or later (in the interface). This guarantees that the attribute dependencies are acyclic, so that we can derive when children need to be visited and in what order.

AGs are a domain-specific language to write algebras in terms of attributes. From the grammar, we generate the data type and catamorphism. From the interface, we generate the $T'List$ type. From the rules, we generate the semantic functions sem_{nil} and sem_{cons}. AGs pay off when an algebra has many inherited and synthesized attributes. Also, there are many AG extensions that offer abstractions over common usage patterns (not covered in this paper). In the next section we present AGs with dependent types, so that we can formulate properties of attributes (and their proofs).

3   Dependently Typed Example

In this section, we use AG_{DA} to implement a mini-compiler that performs name checking of a simple language *Source*, and translates it to target language *Target* if all used identifiers are declared, or produces errors otherwise. A term in *Source* is a sequence of identifier definitions and identifier uses, for example: *def a ◇ use b ◇ use a*. In this case, *b* is not defined, thus the mini-compiler reports an error. Otherwise, it generates a *Target* term, which is a clone of the *Source* term that additionally carries evidence that the term is free of naming errors. Section 3.2 shows the definition of both *Source* and *Target*.

We show how to prove that the mini-compiler produces only correctly named *Target* terms and errors messages that only mention undeclared identifiers. The proofs are part of the implementation's code. Name checking is only a minor task in a compiler. However, the example shows many aspects of a more realistic compiler.

3.1 Support Code Dealing with Environments

We need some Agda support code to deal with environments. We show the relevant data structures and type signatures for operations on them, but omit the actual implementation. We represent the environment as a cons-list of identifiers.

```
Ident = String      -- Ident : Set
Env   = List Ident  -- Env : Set
```

In intuitionistic type theory, a data type represents a relation, its data constructors deduction rules for such a relation, and values built using these constructors are proofs for instances of the relation. We use some data types to reason with environments.

A value of type $\iota \in \Gamma$ is a proof that an identifier ι is member of an environment Γ. A value *here* indicates that identifier is at the front of the environment. A value *next* means that the identifier can be found in the tail of the environment, as described by the remainder of the proof.

```
data _∈_ : Ident → Env → Set where
    here : {ι : Ident} {Γ : Env} → ι ∈ (ι :: Γ)
    next : {ι₁ : Ident} {ι₂ : Ident} {Γ : Env} → ι₁ ∈ Γ → ι₁ ∈ (ι₂ :: Γ)
```

The type $\Gamma_1 \sqsubseteq \Gamma_2$ represents a proof that an environment Γ_1 is contained as a subsequence of an environment Γ_2. A value *subLeft* means that the environment Γ_1 is a prefix of Γ_2, and *subRight* means that Γ_1 is a suffix. With *trans*, we transitively compose two proofs.

```
data _⊑_ : Env → Env → Set where
    subLeft  : {Γ₁ : Env} {Γ₂ : Env} → Γ₁ ⊑ (Γ₁ ⧺ Γ₂)
    subRight : {Γ₁ : Env} {Γ₂ : Env} → Γ₂ ⊑ (Γ₁ ⧺ Γ₂)
    trans    : {Γ₁ : Env} {Γ₂ : Env} {Γ₃ : Env} → Γ₁ ⊑ Γ₂ → Γ₂ ⊑ Γ₃ → Γ₁ ⊑ Γ₃
```

The following functions operate on proofs. When an identifier occurs in an environment, function *inSubset* produces a proof that the identifier is also in the superset of the environment. Given an identifier and an environment, $\iota \in_? \Gamma$ returns either a proof $\iota \in \Gamma$ that the element is in the environment, or a proof that it is not.

$$inSubset : \{\iota : Ident\} \{\Gamma_1 : Env\} \{\Gamma_2 : Env\} \rightarrow \Gamma_1 \sqsubseteq \Gamma_2 \rightarrow \iota \in \Gamma_1 \rightarrow \iota \in \Gamma_2$$
$$\_ \in_? \_ \quad : (\iota : Ident) \rightarrow (\Gamma : Env) \rightarrow \neg(\iota \in \Gamma) \uplus (\iota \in \Gamma)$$

A value of the sum-type $\alpha \uplus \beta$ either consists of an α wrapped in a constructor inj_1 or of a β wrapped in inj_2.

3.2 Grammar of the Source and Target Language

Below, we give a grammar for both the *Source* and *Target* language, such that we can analyze their ASTs with AGs[3]. The *Target* language is a clone of the *Source* language, except that terms that have identifiers carry a field *proof* that is evidence that the identifiers are properly introduced.

grammar *Root*	: *Set*		-- start symbol of grammar and root of AST
prod *root* : *Root*	**nonterm** *top* : *Source*		-- top of the *Source* tree
grammar *Source*	: *Set*		-- grammar for nonterminal *Source*
prod *use*	: *Source*		-- 'result type' of production
term	ι	: *Ident*	-- terminals may have arbitrary Agda types
prod *def*	: *Source*		-- 'result type' may be parametrized
term	ι	: *Ident*	
prod $\_ \diamond \_$	: *Source*		-- represents sequencing of two *Source* terms
nonterm *left*	: *Source*		-- nonterminal fields must have a nonterm as
nonterm *right*	: *Source*		-- outermost type constructor.
grammar *Target*	: *Env* $\rightarrow$ *Set*		-- grammar for nonterminal *Target*
prod *def*	: *Target* Γ		-- production type may refer to any field,
term$^?$	Γ	: *Env*	-- e.g. Γ. Agda feature: implicit terminal
term	ι	: *Ident*	-- (inferred when building a *def*)
term	ϕ	: $\iota \in \Gamma$	-- field type may refer to preceding fields
prod *use*	: *Target* Γ		
term$^?$	Γ	: *Env*	-- a *Target* term carries evidence: a
term	ι	: *Ident*	-- proof that the identifier is in the
term	ϕ	: $\iota \in \Gamma$	-- environment
$\_ \diamond \_$	: *Target* Γ		
term$^?$	Γ	: *Env*	
nonterm *left*	: *Target* Γ		-- nonterm fields introduce children that
nonterm *right*	: *Target* Γ		-- have attributes
<u>data</u> *Err* : *Env* $\rightarrow$ *Set* **where**			-- data type for errors in Agda notation
scope : $\{\Gamma : Env\}$ $(\iota : Ident) \rightarrow \neg(\iota \in \Gamma) \rightarrow Err\ \Gamma$			
Errs Γ = *List* (*Err* Γ)		-- *Errs* : *Env* $\rightarrow$ *Set*	

As shown in Section 2, we generate Agda data-type definitions and catamorphisms from this specification.

The concrete syntax of the source language *Source* and target language *Target* of the mini-compiler is out of scope for this paper; the grammar defines only the abstract

---

[3] In our example, we could have defined the type *Target* using conventional Agda notation instead. However, the grammar for *Target* serves as an example of a parameterized nonterminal.

syntax. Similarly, we omit a formal operational semantics for *Source* and *Target*: it evaluates to unit if there is an equally named *def* for every *use*, otherwise evaluation diverges.

3.3 Dependent Attributes

In this section, we define *dependently typed* attributes for *Source*. Such a type may contain references to preceding[4] attributes using *inh.attrNm* or *syn.attrNm* notation, which explicitly distinguishes between inherited and synthesized attributes. The type specifies a property of the attributes it references; an attribute with such a type represents a proof of this property.

In our mini-compiler, we compute bottom-up a synthesized attribute *gathEnv* that contains identifiers defined by the *Source* term. At the root, the *gathEnv* attribute contains all the defined identifiers. We output its value as the synthesized attribute *finEnv* (final environment) at the root. Also, we pass its value top-down as the inherited attribute *finEnv*, such that we can refer to this environment deeper down the AST. We also pass down an attribute *gathInFin* that represents a proof that the final environment is a superset of the gathered environment. When we know that an identifier is in the gathered environment, we can thus also find it in the final environment. We pass up the attribute *outcome*, which consists either of errors, or of a correct *Target* term.

itf *Root*   -- attributes for the root of the AST
    visit *compile*   **syn** *finEnv*   : *Env*
                    syn *outcome*   : (*Errs syn.finEnv*) ⊎ (*Target syn.finEnv*)

itf *Source*   -- attributes for *Source*
    visit *analyze*   **syn** *gathEnv*   : *Env*   -- attribute of first visit
    visit *translate*   **inh** *finEnv*   : *Env*   -- attributes of second visit
                    inh *gathInFin* : *syn.gathEnv* ⊑ *inh.finEnv*
                    syn *outcome*   : (*Errs inh.finEnv*) ⊎ (*Target inh.finEnv*)

itf *Target Γ*   -- interface for *Target* (parameterized) is not used in the example.

As we show later, at the root, we need the value of *gathEnv* to define *finEnv*. This requires *gathEnv* to be placed in a strict earlier visit. Hence we define two visits, ordered by appearance.

Attribute *gathInFin* has a dependent type: it specifies that *gathEnv* is a subsequence of *finEnv*. A value of this attribute is a proof that essentially states that we did not forget any identifiers. Similarly, in order to construct *Target* terms, we need to prove that *finEnv* defines the identifiers that occur in the term. In the next section, we construct such proofs by applying data constructors. We may use inherited attributes as *assumptions* and pattern matches against values of attributes as *case distinctions*. Thus, with a

---

[4] We may refer to an attribute that is declared earlier (in order of appearance) in the same interface. There is one exception due to the translation to Agda (Section 5): in the type of an inherited attribute, we may not refer to synthesized attributes of the same visit.

dependently typed AG we can formalize and prove correctness properties of our implementation. Agda's type checker validates such proofs using symbolic evaluation driven by unification.

3.4 Semantics of Attributes

For each production, we give definitions for the declared attributes via rules. At the root, we pass the gathered environment back down as final environment. Thus, these two attributes are equal, and we can trivially prove that the final environment is a subsequence using either *subRight* or *subLeft*.

> **datasem** *Root* **prod** *root*   -- rules for production *root* of nonterm *Root*
> *top.finEnv*   = *top.gathEnv*   -- pass gathered environment down
> *top.gathInFin* = *subRight* {[ ]}   -- subsequence proof, using: [ ] ++ $\Gamma_4 \equiv \Gamma_4$
> *lhs.finEnv*   = *top.gathEnv*   -- pass *gathEnv* up
> *lhs.outcome*   = *top.outcome*   -- pass *outcome* up

For the *use*-production of *Source*, we check if the identifier (terminal *loc.ι*) is in the environment. If it is, we produce a *Target* term as value for the outcome attribute, otherwise we produce a *scope* error. For *def*, we introduce an identifier in the gathered environment. No errors can arise, hence we always produce a *Target* term. We prove ($loc.\phi_1$) that the identifier *loc.ι* is actually in the gathered environment, and prove ($loc.\phi_2$) using *inSubset* and attribute *lhs.gathInFin* that it must also be in the final environment. For _ ⋄ _, we pass *finEnv* down to both children, concatenate their *gathEnv*s, and combine their *outcome*s.

> **datasem** *Source*   -- rules for productions of *Source*
> **prod** *use*
>   *lhs.gathEnv*   = [ ]   -- no names introduced
>   *lhs.outcome*   <u>with</u> $loc.\iota \in_?$ *lhs.finEnv*   -- tests presence of *ι*
> | inj_1 *notIn* = inj_1 [*scope loc.ι notIn*]   -- when not in env
> | inj_2 *isIn*   = inj_2 (*use loc.ι isIn*)   -- when in env
> **prod** *def*
>   *lhs.gathEnv*   = [*loc.ι*]   -- one name introduced
> $loc.\phi_1$ = *here* {*loc.ι*} {*syn.lhs.gathEnv*} -- proof of *ι* in *gathEnv*
> $loc.\phi_2$ = *inSubset lhs.gathInFin* $loc.\phi_1$ -- proof of *ι* in *finEnv*
>   *lhs.outcome*   = inj_2 (*def loc.ι* $loc.\phi_2$)   -- never any errors
> **prod** _ ⋄ _
>   *lhs.gathEnv*   = *left.gathEnv* ++ *right.gathEnv*   -- pass names up
>   *left.finEnv*   = *lhs.finEnv*   -- pass *finEnv* down
>   *right.finEnv*   = *lhs.finEnv*   -- pass *finEnv* down
>   *left.gathInFin* = *trans subLeft lhs.gathInFin*   -- proof for *left*
>   *right.gathInFin* = *trans* (*subRight* {*syn.lhs.gathEnv*} {*lhs.finEnv*})
>   *lhs.gathInFin*   -- proof for *right*
>   *lhs.outcome*   <u>with</u> *left.outcome*   -- four alts.
> | inj_1 *es* <u>with</u> *right.outcome*

$$| \ inj_1 \ es_1 \ | \ inj_1 \ es_2 = inj_1 \ (es_1 + \!\!\!+ \ es_2) \qquad \text{-- 1: both in error}$$
$$| \ inj_1 \ es_1 \ | \ inj_2 \ \_ \quad = inj_1 \ es_1 \qquad\qquad \text{-- 2: only } left$$
$$| \ inj_2 \ t_1 \ \underline{\text{with}} \ left.outcome$$
$$| \ inj_2 \ t_1 \quad | \ inj_1 \ es_2 = inj_1 \ es_2 \qquad\qquad \text{-- 3: only } right$$
$$| \ inj_2 \ t_1 \quad | \ inj_2 \ t_2 \ = inj_2 \ (t_1 \diamond t_2) \qquad \text{-- 4: none in error}$$

Out of the above code, we generate each production's semantic function (and some wrapper code), such that these together with a catamorphism form a function that translates *Source* terms. The advantage of using AGs here is that we can easily add more attributes (and thus more properties and proofs) and refer to them.

4   AG Descriptions and Their Core Representation

In the previous sections, we presented AG_{DA} (by example). To describe the dependently-typed extension to AGs, we do so in terms of the core language AG_{DA}^X (a subset of AG_{DA}). Implicit information in AG descriptions (notational conveniences, the order of rules, visits to children) is made explicit in AG_{DA}^X. We sketch the translation from AG_{DA} to AG_{DA}^X. In previous work [4,5], we described the process in more detail (albeit in a non-dependently typed setting).

AG_{DA}^X contains interface declarations, but grammar declarations are absent and semantic blocks encoded differently. Each production in AG_{DA} is mapped to a *semantic function* in AG_{DA}^X: it is a domain-specific language for the contents of semantic functions. A terminal $x : \tau$ of the production is mapped to a parameter $loc_l x : \tau$. Implicit terminals are mapped to implicit parameters. A nonterminal $x : N \ \overline{\tau}$ is mapped to a parameter $loc_c x : T'N \ \overline{\tau}$. The body of the production consists of the rules for the production given in the original AG_{DA}^X description, plus a number of additional rules that declare children and their visits explicitly.

$$sem\diamond \ : T' Source \rightarrow T' Source \rightarrow T' Source \quad \text{-- derived from (non)terminal types}$$
$$sem\diamond \ loc_c left \ loc_c right = \qquad\qquad \text{-- semantic function for } \diamond$$
  sem : *Source*   -- AG_{DA}^X semantics block
    child *left* : *Source*   = $loc_c left$ -- defines a child *left*
    child *right* : *Source* = $loc_c right$ -- defines a child *right*
    invoke *analyze* **of** *left*   -- rule requires visiting *analyze* on *left*
    invoke *analyze* **of** *right*   -- rule requires visiting *analyze* on *right*
    invoke *translate* **of** *left*
    invoke *translate* **of** *right*
    $lhs.gathEnv = left.gathEnv + \!\!\!+ right.gathEnv$ -- the AG_{DA} rules
    ...   -- etc.

A child rule introduces a child with explicit semantics (a value of the type *T'Source*). Other rules may declare visits and refer to the attributes of the child. An invoke rule declares a visit to a child, and brings the attributes of that visit in scope. Conventional rules define attributes, and may refer to attributes. The dependencies between attributes induces a def-use (partial) order.

Actually, there is one more step to go to end up with a AG_{DA}^X description. A semantics block consists of one of more visit-blocks (in the order specified by the interface), and the rules are partitioned over the blocks. In a block, the *lhs* attributes of that and earlier visits are in scope, as well as those brought in scope by preceding rules. Also, the synthesized attributes of the visit must be defined in the block or in an earlier block. We assign rules to the earliest block that satisfies the def-use order. We convert this partial order into a total order by giving conventional rules precedence over child/invoke rules, and using the order of appearance otherwise:

```
sem◇ : T' Source → T' Source → T' Source     -- signature derived from itf
sem◇  locₑleft locₑright =                    -- semantic function for ◇
  sem : Source                                 -- AGᴅᴀˣ block
    visit analyze                              -- first visit
      child left : Source   = locₑleft         -- defines a child left
      invoke analyze of left                   -- requires child to be defined
      child right : Source = locₑright         -- defines a child right
      invoke analyze of right                  -- requires child to be defined
      syn.lhs.gathEnv = syn.left.gathEnv + syn.right.gathEnv

    visit translate                            -- second visit
      inh.left.finEnv      = inh.lhs.finEnv    -- needs lhs.finEnv
      inh.right.finEnv     = inh.lhs.finEnv    -- needs lhs.finEnv
      inh.left.gathInFin   = trans ...         -- also needs lhs.gathEnv
      inh.right.gathInFin = trans ...          -- also needslhs.gathEnv
      invoke translate of left                 -- needs def of inh attrs of left
      invoke translate of right                -- needs def of inh attrs of right
      syn.lhs.outcome   with ...               -- needs translate attrs of children
```

It is a static error when such an order cannot be satisfied. Another interesting example is the semantic function for the root: it has a child with an interface different from its own, and has two invoke rules in the same visit.

```
sem_root : T' Source → T' Root                 -- semantic function for the root
sem_root locStop =                             -- Source's semantics as parameter
  sem : Root visit compile                      -- only one visit
    child top : Source = locₑtop               -- defines a child top
    invoke analyze of top                       -- invokes first visit of top
    inh.top.finEnv      = syn.top.gathEnv       -- passes gathered environment back
    invoke translate of top                     -- invokes second visit of top
    syn.lhs.output      = syn.top.gathEnv       -- passes up the gathered env
    syn.lhs.output      = syn.top.outcome       -- passes up the result
```

Figure 1 shows the syntax of AG_{DA}^X. In general, interfaces may be parametrized. The interface has a function type τ (equal to the type of the nonterminal declaration in AG_{DA}) that specifies the type of each parameter, and the kind of the interface (an upper bound of the kinds of the parameters). For an evaluation rule, we either use a with-expression when the value of the attribute is conditionally defined, or use a simple

$$
\begin{array}{lll}
e & ::= \text{AGDA}\,[\,\overline{b}\,] & \text{-- embedded blocks } b \text{ in AGDA} \\
b & ::= i \mid s \mid o & \text{-- } \text{AG}^{\text{X}}_{\text{DA}} \text{ blocks} \\
o & ::= inh.c.x \mid syn.c.x \mid loc.x & \text{-- embedded attribute reference} \\
i & ::= \textbf{itf}\ I\ \overline{x} : \tau\ v & \text{-- with first visit } v, \text{ params } x, \text{ and signature } \tau \\
v & ::= \textbf{visit}\ x\ \textbf{inh}\ \overline{a}\ \textbf{syn}\ \overline{a}\ v & \text{-- visit declaration} \\
& \mid \ \square & \text{-- terminator of visit decl. chain} \\
a & ::= x : e & \text{-- attribute decl, with Agda type } e \\
s & ::= \textbf{sem} : I\ \overline{e}\ t & \text{-- semantics expr, uses interface } I\ \overline{e} \\
t & ::= \textbf{visit}\ x\ \overline{r}\ t & \text{-- visit definition, with next visit } t \\
& \mid \ \square & \text{-- terminator of visit def. chain} \\
r & ::= p\ e' & \text{-- evaluation rule} \\
& \mid \ \textbf{invoke}\ x\ \textbf{of}\ c & \text{-- invoke-rule, invokes } x \text{ on child } c \\
& \mid \ \textbf{child}\ c : I = e & \text{-- child-rule, defines a child } c, \text{ with interface } I\ \overline{e} \\
p & ::= o & \text{-- attribute def} \\
& \mid \ .\{e\} & \text{-- Agda dot pattern} \\
& \mid \ x\ \overline{p} & \text{-- constructor match} \\
e' & ::= \underline{\text{with}}\ e\ \overline{p'\ e'^{?}} & \text{-- Agda } \underline{\text{with}} \text{ expression } (e' \text{ absent when } p' \text{ absurd}) \\
& \mid \ = e & \text{-- Agda} = \text{expression} \\
p' & & \text{-- Agda LHS} \\
x, I, c & \text{-- identifiers, interface names, children respectively} \\
\tau & \text{-- plain Agda type}
\end{array}
$$

Fig. 1. Syntax of RULER-CORE

equation as RHS. In the next section, we plug such an expression in a function defined via with-expressions; hence we need knowledge about the with-structure of the RHS.

5 Translation to Agda

To explain the preprocessing of $\text{AG}^{\text{X}}_{\text{DA}}$ to Agda, we give a translation scheme in Figure 2 (explained via examples below). This translation scheme is a denotational semantics for $\text{AG}^{\text{X}}_{\text{DA}}$. Also, if the translation is correct Agda, then the original is correct $\text{AG}^{\text{X}}_{\text{DA}}$.

A semantics block in an $\text{AG}^{\text{X}}_{\text{DA}}$ program is actually an algorithm that makes precise how to compute the attributes as specified by the interface: for each visit, the rules prescribe when to compute an attribute and when to visit a child. The idea is that we map such a block to an Agda function that takes values for its inherited attributes and delivers a dependent product[5] of synthesized attributes. However, such a function would be cyclic: in the presented example, the result *gathEnv* would be needed for as input for *finEnv*. Fortunately, we can bypass this problem: we map to a *k*-visit *coroutine* instead.

---

[5] A dependent product $\Sigma\ \tau\ f = (\tau, f\ \tau)$ parameterizes the RHS f with the LHS τ.

A coroutine is a function that can be invoked k times. We associate each invocation with a visit of the interface. Values for the inherited attributes are inputs to the invocation. Values for the synthesized attributes are the result of the invocation. In a pure functional language (like Agda), we can encode coroutines as one-shot continuations (or *visit functions* [8]).

$$
\begin{aligned}
&[\![\textbf{itf}\ I\ \bar{x}:\overline{\tau_x}\to\tau]\!]\ v && \rightsquigarrow [\![_{\text{iv}}\ v]\!]_{I,\tau}^{\overline{x:\tau_x}}\ ;\quad [\![sig\ I]\!]:[\![\tau]\!]\ ;\quad [\![sig\ I]\!]=[\![sig\ I\ (name\ v)]\!]\\
&[\![_{\text{iv}}\ \textbf{visit}\ x\ \textbf{inh}\ \bar{a}\ \textbf{syn}\ \bar{b}\ v]\!]_{I,\tau}^{\bar{g}} && \rightsquigarrow [\![_{\text{iv}}\ v]\!]_{I,\tau}^{\bar{g}+\bar{a}+\bar{b}}\qquad\text{-- interface type for later visits}\\
& && [\![sig\ I\ x]\!]:[\![_{\text{at}}\ g_1]\!]\to\dots\to[\![_{\text{at}}\ g_n]\!]\to[\![resultty\ \tau]\!]\\
& && [\![sig\ I\ x]\!]\ \overline{[\![_{\text{an}}\ g]\!]}=[\![_{\text{a}}\ inh.a_1]\!]\to\dots\to[\![_{\text{a}}\ inh.a_n]\!]\to\\
& && \qquad[\![typrod\ (\overline{syn}.b)\ (sig\ I\ (name\ v))]\!]\\
&[\![_{\text{iv}}\ \Box]\!]_{I,\tau}^{\bar{g}} && \rightsquigarrow [\![sig\ I\ \Box]\!]=\Box\qquad\text{-- terminator (some unit-value)}\\
&[\![_{\text{a}}\ x:e]\!] && \rightsquigarrow [\![atname\ x]\!]:[\![e]\!]\qquad\text{-- extract attribute name and type}\\
&[\![_{\text{at}}\ x:e]\!] && \rightsquigarrow [\![e]\!]\qquad\text{-- extract attribute type}\\
&[\![_{\text{an}}\ x:e]\!] && \rightsquigarrow [\![atname\ x]\!]\qquad\text{-- extract attribute name}\\
&[\![\textbf{sem}\ x:I\ \bar{e}\ t]\!] && \rightsquigarrow [\![vis\ lhs\ (name\ t)]\!]\ \underline{\text{where}}\ [\![_{\text{ev}}t]\!]_I^{\bar{e},\emptyset}\qquad\text{-- top of semfun}\\
&[\![_{\text{ev}}\textbf{visit}\ x\ \bar{r}\ t]\!]_I^{\bar{e},\bar{g}} && \rightsquigarrow [\![vis\ lhs\ x]\!]:[\![sig\ I\ x]\!]\ [\![\bar{e}]\!]\ \overline{[\![_{\text{an}}\ g]\!]}\qquad\text{-- type of visit fun}\\
& && [\![vis\ lhs\ x]\!]\ [\![inhs\ I\ x]\!]=[\![_{\text{r}}\ \bar{r}]\!]_{[\![\varsigma]\!]}\qquad\text{-- chain of rules}\\
& && [\![\varsigma]\!]\rightsquigarrow\ =[\![valprod\ (syns\ I\ x)\ (vis\ lhs\ (name\ t))]\!]\\
& && \underline{\text{where}}\ [\![_{\text{ev}}t]\!]_I^{\bar{g}+\bar{a}+\bar{b}}\qquad\text{-- next visit}\\
&[\![_{\text{ev}}\Box]\!]_I^{\bar{e},\bar{g}} && \rightsquigarrow [\![vis\ lhs\ \Box]\!]:[\![sig\ I\ \Box]\!]\ [\![\bar{e}]\!]\ \overline{[\![_{\text{an}}\ g]\!]}\ ;\quad[\![vis\ lhs\ \Box]\!]=\Box\\
&[\![_{\text{r}}\ \textbf{child}\ c:I=e]\!]_k && \rightsquigarrow \underline{\text{with}}\ [\![e]\!]\ \dots\ |\ [\![vis\ I\ (firstvisit\ I)]\!]\ [\![k]\!]\qquad\text{-- k: remaining rules}\\
&[\![_{\text{r}}\ \textbf{invoke}\ x\ \textbf{of}\ c]\!]_k && \rightsquigarrow \underline{\text{with}}\ [\![vis\ (itf\ c)\ x]\!]\ [\![inhs\ (itf\ c)\ x]\!]\qquad\text{-- pass inh values}\\
& && \dots\ |\ (valprod\ (syns\ (itf\ c)\ x))\ [\![k]\!]\qquad\text{-- match syn values}\\
&[\![_{\text{r}}\ p\ e']\!]_k && \rightsquigarrow [\![_{\text{ep}}\ e']\!]_p^k\qquad\text{-- translation for attr def rule}\\
&[\![_{\text{ep}}\ \underline{\text{with}}\ e\ \overline{p}\ e']\!]_p^k\rightsquigarrow \underline{\text{with}}\ e\quad\dots\ |\ [\![p]\!]\ [\![_{\text{r}}\ p\ e']\!]_k && \qquad\text{-- rule RHS is with-constr}\\
&[\![_{\text{ep}}=e]\!]_p^k && \rightsquigarrow \underline{\text{with}}\ e\quad\dots\ |\ [\![p]\!]\ k\qquad\text{-- rule RHS is expr}\\
\end{aligned}
$$

$atref\ inh.c.x = c_i x$	$atname\ inh.x = inh_a x$	-- naming conventions
$atref\ syn.c.x = c_s x$	$atname\ syn.x = syn_a x$	-- *atref*: ref to attr value
$atref\ loc.x\ \ = loc_l x$	$atname\ x\ \ \ = x$	-- *atname*: ref to attr in type
$vis\ I\ x = vis\ lhs\ x$	$sig\ I\ \ = T'I$	-- *vis*: name of visit function
$vis\ c\ x = c_v x$	$sig\ I\ x = T'I'x$	-- *sig*: itf types

Fig. 2. Translation of AG_{DA}^X to Agda

We generate types for coroutines and for the individual visit functions that make up such a coroutine. These types are derived from the interface. For each visit (e.g. *translate* of *Source*), we generate a type that represents a function type from the attribute types of the inherited attributes for that visit, to a dependent product (Σ) of the types of the synthesized attributes and the type of the next visit function. These types are parameterized with the attributes of earlier visits (e.g. T' *Source'translate* $syn_a gathEnv$). The type of the coroutine itself is the type of the first visit.

$T'Source$ $= T'Source'analyze$
$T'Source'analyze$ $= \Sigma\ Env\ T'Source'translate$
$T'Source'translate\ syn_agathEnv =$
$(inh_afinEnv\ :\ Env)\ \rightarrow\ (inh_agathInFin\ :\ syn_agathEnv \sqsubseteq inh_afinEnv)\ \rightarrow$
$\Sigma\ (Errs\ inh_afinEnv \uplus Target\ inh_afinEnv)$
$(T'Source'\square\ syn_agathEnv\ inh_afinEnv\ inh_agathInFin)$
$T'Source'\square\ syn_agathEnv\ inh_afinEnv\ inh_agathInFin\ syn_aoutcome\ = \square$

The restrictions on attribute order in the interface ensure that referenced attributes are in scope. The scheme for $[\![iv\ v]\!]^I_{g,\tau}$ formalizes this translation, where g is the list of preceding attribute declarations, and τ the type for I. The *typrod* function mentioned in the scheme constructs a right-nested dependent product.

The coroutine itself consists of nested continuation functions (one for each visit). Each continuation takes the visit's inherited attributes as parameter, and consists of a tree of with-constructs that represent intermediate computations for computations of attributes and invocations of visits to children. Each leaf ends in a dependent product of the visit's synthesized attributes and the continuation function for the next visit[6].

$sem\diamond\ :T'Source \rightarrow T'Source \rightarrow T'Source$ -- example translation for $\diamond$
$sem\diamond\ loc_cleft\ loc_cright = lhs_vanalyze$ **where**   -- delegates to first visit function
$\quad lhs_vanalyze : T'Source'analyze$ -- signature of first visit function
$\quad lhs_vanalyze$ **with** ...   -- computations for *analyze* here
$\quad ... = (lhs_sgathEnv, lhs_vtranslate)$ *ahwere*   -- result of first visit function
$\quad\quad lhs_vtranslate : T'Source'translate\ lhs_sgathEnv$ -- last visit function
$\quad\quad lhs_vtranslate\ lhs_ifinEnv\ lhs_igathInFin$ **with** ...   -- computations for *translate* here
$\quad\quad ... = (lhs_soutcome, lhs_v\square)$ **where**   -- result of second visit function
$\quad\quad\quad lhs_v\square : T'Source'\square\ lhs_sgathEnv\ lhs_ifinEnv\ lhs_igathInFin\ lhs_soutcome$
$\quad\quad\quad lhs_v\square = \square$ -- explicit terminator value

The scheme $[\![ev\ v]\!]^{\bar{e},\bar{g}}_I$ formalizes this translation for a visit v of interface I, where $\bar{e}$ are type arguments to the interface (empty in the example), and $\bar{g}$ are the attributes of previous visits.

The with-tree for a visit-function consists of the translation of child-rules, invoke-rules and evaluation rules. Each rule plugs into this tree. For example, the translation for $[\![$**child** $left : Source = loc_sleft]\!]$ is:

$\quad ...$ **with** loc_sleft -- evaluate RHS to get first visit fun
$\quad ...\ |\ left_vanalyze$ **with** ...   -- give it a name + proceed with remainder

For $[\![$**invoke** *translate* **of** $left]\!]$ the translation is:

$\quad ...$ **with** $left_vtranslate\ left_ifinEnv\ left_igathInFin$ -- visit fun takes inh attrs
$\quad ...\ |\ (left_soutcome, left_vsentinel)$ **with** ...   -- returns product of syn attrs

For $[\![lhs.gathEnv = left.gathEnv \mathbin{+\!\!\!+} right.gathEnv]\!]$:

---

[6] As a technical detail, a leaf of the with-tree may also be an *absurd pattern*. These are used in Agda to indicate an alternative that is never satisfiable. A body for such an alternative cannot be given.

... with $left_s gathEnv$ ++ $right_s gathEnv$ -- translation for RHS
... | $lhs_s gathEnv$ with ...   -- LHS + remainder

For $[\![lhs.outcome$ with$...]\!]$ (where the RHS is a with-construct), we duplicate the remaining with-tree for each alternative of the RHS:

... with $left_s outcome$ -- translation for RHS
... | $inj_1\ es$ with $right_s outcome$
... | $inj_1\ es_1$ | $inj_1\ es_2$ with $inj_1\ (es_1$ ++ $es_2)$ -- alternative one of four
... | $inj_1\ es_1$ | $inj_1\ es$ | $lhs_s outcome$ with ...   -- LHS + remainder
... | $inj_1\ es_1$ | $inj_2\ \_$ with $inj_1\ es_1$ -- alternative two of four
... | $inj_1\ es_1$ | $inj_2\ \_$ | $lhs_s outcome$ with ...   -- LHS + remainder
... | inj_2 ...   -- remaining two alternatives

The scheme $[\![_r\ r]\!]_k$ formalizes this translation, where r is a rule and k the translation of the rules that follow r.

The size of the translated code may be exponential in the number of rules with with-constructs as RHS. It is not obvious how to treat such rules otherwise. Agda does not allow a with-construct as a subexpression. Neither can we easily factor out the RHS of a rule to a separate function, because the conclusions drawn from the evaluation of preceding rules are not in scope of this function. Fortunately, for rules that would otherwise cause a lot of needless duplication, the programmer can perform this process manually.

When dependent pattern matching brings assumptions in scope that are needed *across* rules, the code duplication is a necessity. To facilitate that pattern matching effects are visible across rules, we need to ensure that the rule that performs the match is ordered before a rule that needs the assumption. We showed in previous work how such non-attribute dependencies can be captured [4].

The translated code has attractive operational properties. Each attribute is only computed once, and each node is at most traversed k times.

6   Partially Defined Attributes

A fine granularity of attributes is important to use an AG effectively. In the mini-compiler of Section 3, we could replace the attribute *outcome* with an attribute *code* and a separate attribute *errors*. This would be more convenient, since it would not require a pattern match against the *output* attribute to collect errors. However, we cannot produce a target term in the presence of errors, thus *code* would not have a total definition. Therefore, we were forced to combine these two aspects into a single attribute *outcome*. It is common to use partially defined attributes in an AG. This holds especially when the attribute's value (e.g. *errors*) determines if another attribute is defined (e.g. *code*). We present a solution that uses the partitioning of attributes over visits.

The idea is to make the availability of visits dependent on the value of a preceding attribute. We split up the *translate* visit in a visit *report* and a visit *generate*. The visit *report* has *errors* as synthesized attribute, and *generate* has *code*. Furthermore, we enforce that *generate* may only be invoked (by the parent in the AST) when the list of errors reported in the previous visit is empty. We accomplish this with an additional attribute *noErrors* on *generate* that gives evidence that the list of errors is empty. With this evidence, we can give a total definition for *code*.

```
itf Source     -- Root's visit needs to be split up in a similar way
   visit report      syn errors    : Errs inh.finEnv     -- parent can inspect errors
   visit generate  inh noErrors : syn.errors ≡ [ ]      -- enforces invariant
                    syn code      : Target inh.finEnv   -- only when errors is empty
datasem Source prod use    -- example for production use
   loc.testInEnv = loc.ι ∈? lhs.finEnv        -- scheduled in visit report
   lhs.code with loc.testIn | lhs.noErrors    -- scheduled in visit generate
     | inj₁ _    | ()                         -- cannot happen, hence an absurd pattern
     | inj₂ isIn | refl = use loc.ι isIn      -- extract the evidence needed for the code term
datasem Source prod ⋄     -- leftNil : (α : Env) → (β : Env) → (α ⧺ β ≡ [ ]) → (α ≡ [ ])
   left.noErrors = leftNil left.errors right.errors lhs.noErrors    -- right.noErrors similar
   lhs.code      = left.code ⋄ right.code    -- scheduled in visit generate
```

For this approach to work, it is essential that visits are scheduled as late as possible, and only those that are needed.

We can generalize the presented approach by defining a fixed number of alternative sets of attributes for a visit, and use the value of a preceding attribute to select one of these sets [6].

7   Related Work

Dependent types originate in Martin-Löf's Type Theory. A variety of dependently typed programming languages are gaining popularity, including Agda [7], Epigram, and Coq. We present the ideas in this paper with Agda as host language, because it has a concept of a dependent pattern match, to which we straightforwardly map the left-hand sides of AG rules. Also, in Coq and Epigram, a program is written via interactive theorem proving with tactics or commands. The preprocessor-based approach of this paper, however, suits a declarative approach more.

Attribute grammars [3] are considered to be a promising implementation for compiler construction. Recently, many Attribute Grammar systems arose for mainstream languages, such as the systems JastAdd and Silver for Java, and UUAG [10] for Haskell. These approaches may benefit from the stronger type discipline as presented in this paper; however, it would require an encoding of dependent types in the host language.

AGs have a straightforward translation to cyclic functions in a lazy functional programming language [9]. To prove that cyclic functions are total and terminating is a non-trivial exercise. Kastens [2] presented Ordered Attribute Grammars (OAGs). In OAGs, the evaluation order of attribute computations as well as attribute lifetime can be determined statically. Saraiva [8] described how to generate (noncyclic) functional coroutines from OAGs. The coroutines we generate are based on these ideas.

8   Conclusion

We presented AG_{DA}, a language for ordered AGs with dependently typed attributes: the type of an attribute may refer to the value of another attribute. This feature allows us to conveniently encode invariants in the type of attributes, and pass proofs of these invariants around as attributes. With a dependently typed AG, we write algebras for catamorphisms in a dependently typed language in a composable way. Each attribute describes a separate aspect of the catamorphism.

The approach we presented is lightweight, which means that we encode AGs as an embedded language (via a preprocessor), such that type checking is deferred to the host language. To facilitate termination checking, we translate the AG to a coroutine that encodes a terminating, multi-visit traversal, under the restriction that the AG is ordered and definitions for attributes are total.

The preprocessor approach fits nicely with the interactive Emacs mode of Agda. Type errors in the generated program are traceable back to the source: in a statically checked AG_{DA} program these can only occur in Agda blocks. These Agda blocks are literally preserved; due to unicode, even attribute references can stay the same. Also, the Emacs mode implements interactive features via markers, which are also preserved by the translation. The AG preprocessor is merely an additional preprocessing step.

With some generalizations, the work we have presented is a proposal for a more flexible termination checker for Agda that accepts k-orderable cyclic functions, if the function can be written as a non-cyclic k-visit coroutine.

Acknowledgments. This work was supported by Microsoft Research through its European PhD Scholarship Programme. We thank the anonymous reviewers of IFL'10 for their extensive comments and suggestions during the post-refereeing process.

References

1. Bove, A., Dybjer, P.: Dependent Types at Work. In: Bove, A., Barbosa, L.S., Pardo, A., Pinto, J.S. (eds.) Language Engineering and Rigorous Software Development. LNCS, vol. 5520, pp. 57–99. Springer, Heidelberg (2009)
2. Kastens, U.: Ordered Attributed Grammars. Acta Informatica 13, 229–256 (1980)
3. Knuth, D.E.: Semantics of Context-Free Languages. Mathematical Systems Theory 2(2), 127–145 (1968)
4. Middelkoop, A., Dijkstra, A., Swierstra, S.D.: Attribute Grammars with Side Effect. In: HOSC (2010), http://people.cs.uu.nl/ariem/wgt10-journal.pdf
5. Middelkoop, A., Dijkstra, A., Swierstra, S.D.: Iterative Type Inference with Attribute Grammars. In: GPCE 2010, pp. 43–52 (2010)
6. Middelkoop, A., Dijkstra, A., Swierstra, S.D.: Visit Functions for the Semantics of Programming Languages. In: WGT 2010 (2010), http://people.cs.uu.nl/ariem/wgt10-visit.pdf
7. Norell, U.: Dependently-typed Programming in Agda. In: TLDI 2009, pp. 1–2 (2009)
8. Saraiva, J., Swierstra, S.D.: Purely Functional Implementation of Attribute Grammars. Tech. rep., Universiteit Utrecht (1999)
9. Swierstra, S.D., Alcocer, P.R.A.: Attribute Grammars in the Functional Style. In: Systems Implementation 2000, pp. 180–193 (1998)
10. Universiteit Utrecht: Homepage of the Universiteit Utrecht Attribute Grammar System (1998), http://www.cs.uu.nl/wiki/HUT/AttributeGrammarSystem

The Design and Implementation of Feldspar
An Embedded Language for Digital Signal Processing

Emil Axelsson[1], Koen Claessen[1], Mary Sheeran[1], Josef Svenningsson[1],
David Engdal[2], and Anders Persson[1,2]

[1] Chalmers University of Technology
{emax,koen,ms,josefs,anders.persson}@chalmers.se
[2] Ericsson
david.engdal@ericsson.com

Abstract. Feldspar is a domain specific language, embedded in Haskell, for programming digital signal processing algorithms. The final aim of a Feldspar program is to generate low level code with good performance. Still, we chose to provide the user with a purely functional DSL. The language is implemented as a minimal, deeply embedded core language, with shallow extensions built upon it. This paper presents full details of the essential parts of the implementation. Our initial conclusion is that this approach works well in our domain, although much work remains.

1 Introduction

The Feldspar project[1] aims to raise the level of abstraction at which Digital Signal Processing (DSP) algorithms are programmed [1]. Today, such algorithms are typically implemented in low level C, which is a poor match for the mathematical notations and concepts used in designing and specifying the algorithms. C is used because performance is critical in applications such as baseband processing in radio base stations. Feldspar is a Domain Specific Language (DSL) embedded in Haskell and generating C. It is designed to raise the level of abstraction at which the programmer works, without sacrificing vital performance.

Feldspar's roots in the DSP domain are reflected in the fact that it is an array programming language. Its design is deliberately minimal, so that it does not contain other DSP-specific features in its core. However, its architecture permits the addition of higher level interfaces built upon the minimal core. The intention to provide a compositional approach to expressing algorithms led to the choice of a purely functional embedded language, and indeed an early design decision was to have Feldspar programs look as much like Haskell as possible. The user works at the GHCi prompt, and the experience is very much like ordinary Haskell programming.

The following example is a Feldspar program that closely resembles the corresponding Haskell function. It computes the bitwise *and* of a mask with each integer in the range 0 to n.

---

[1] The Feldspar project was initiated by Ericsson. Feldspar is available open source [5].

J. Hage, M.T. Morazán (Eds.): IFL 2010, LNCS 6647, pp. 121–136, 2011.
© Springer-Verlag Berlin Heidelberg 2011

```
mask :: Data Int → Data Int → DVector Int
mask m n = map (m .&.) (0...n)
```

The close resemblance between Feldspar and Haskell programs remains, even in larger examples. However, Feldspar is restricted, to enable the generation of code with reasonable and *predictable* performance. It is the restrictiveness that allows us to find a sweet spot in which modular, reusable high level code still permits the user to control important low level details such as when memory allocation should occur or which loops in the generated code are to be fused. A major restriction is the absence of recursion over C data structures. All operations on arrays must be expressed using higher order functions like map and fold.

This paper provides full details (including all code) of how to design and implement an embedded language in Haskell that itself resembles Haskell. Combining a minimal core language with an API that gives the user the feeling of writing in a higher level language was fruitful, and the paper documents a (simplified) implementation of an embedded DSL that follows this pattern. A novel combination of implementation techniques is presented, including mixing of deep and shallow language constructs, typed representation of expressions via GADTs [10], and smart constructors that perform optimizations on the fly.

2   Language Architecture

A convenient way to implement a language is to *embed* it within an existing language. The constructs of the embedded language are then represented as functions (or similar) in the host language. In a *shallow* embedding, the language constructs themselves perform the interpretation of the language. In a *deep* embedding, the language constructs produce an intermediate representation of the program. This representation can then be interpreted in different ways.

In general, shallow languages are more modular, allowing new constructs to be added independently of each other. In a deep implementation, each construct has to be represented in the intermediate data structure, making it much harder to extend the language. Embedded languages (both deep and shallow) can usually be interpreted directly in the host language. This is, however, rather inefficient. If performance is an issue, code generation can be employed, and this typically requires a deep embedding.

The design of Feldspar tries to combine the advantages of shallow and deep implementations. We wanted the language to have the modularity and extensibility of a shallow embedding, but we also wanted to use a deep embedding in order to be able to generate high-performance code. A nice combination was achieved by using a deeply embedded core language and building high-level interfaces as shallow extensions on top of the core. The low-level core language is purely functional, but with a small semantic gap to machine oriented languages, such as C. Its intention is to be a suitable interface to the backend code generator, while being flexible enough to support any high-level interfaces.

The architecture of Feldspar is shown in Figure 1. The user interface (the "API" box) exposes the low-level core language as well as some more convenient

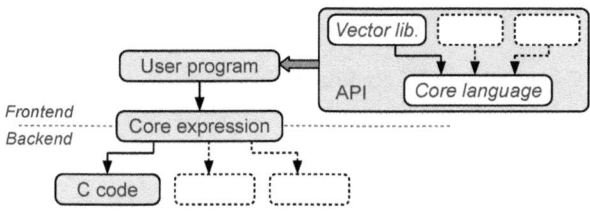

Fig. 1. Feldspar architecture

high-level interfaces. The most prominent of the high level interfaces is the Vector library. But the generality of the core language makes it very easy to implement other interfaces, and this is something we are currently working on. The user's program generates a *core expression*, the internal data structure used as interface to the backends. At the moment, there are two backends: one for producing C code, and one for pretty printing the core expression as Haskell syntax.

3   Core Language

The core language revolves around the type constructor Data. For example, a Feldspar program that computes an integer has type Data Int. Simple expressions can be formed using the interface of Haskell's Num class:

```
numExpr = 3*4+5 :: Data Int
```

This expression can be interpreted directly in Haskell:

```
*Main> eval numExpr
17
```

Since the core language is deeply embedded, it is possible to reify the structure of the program, using the function printCore:[2]

```
*Main> printCore numExpr
program = v2
  where
    v1 = 3 * 4
    v2 = v1 + 5
```

In addition to the functions of the Num class, the core language provides its own versions of many basic Haskell functions; for example

```
not :: Data Bool → Data Bool
div :: Data Int → Data Int → Data Int
```

These functions override the corresponding Prelude definitions, and we will use them without further notice throughout the examples in this paper.

More interesting programs can be built using the constructs in Listing 1. The Computable class generalizes the Data type by allowing various Haskell structures

---

[2] In this example, we have turned off constant folding, which would otherwise have reduced the program to the single value 17.

```
value :: Storable a ⇒ a → Data a

ifThenElse :: (Computable a, Computable b) ⇒
    Data Bool → (a → b) → (a → b) → (a → b)

while :: Computable st ⇒ (st → Data Bool) → (st → st) → (st → st)

parallel :: Storable a ⇒ Data Int → (Data Int → Data a) → Data [a]
```

Listing 1. Basic core language constructs

to be treated as programs. This will be further explained in Section 4.1; for now, it suffices to know that Data a is a member of Computable (for certain types a).

The construct value turns a Haskell value into a core language literal (a program that computes a constant value). For numeric literals, this constructor is inserted implicitly (by fromInteger). This allowed us to use numeric literals directly in the numExpr example.

The conditional construct, ifThenElse, chooses between two functions based on a boolean condition. The reason for operating on functions rather than values is that this lets the user control what expression should go into each branch of the conditional.

The while loop, while, operates on a state of type st. The first argument is a function that computes the *continue condition* based on the current state. The second argument is the *body*, which computes the next state from the current state. The result is a function from initial state to final state. Note that this while loop is a *pure* function with no side-effects. For example, modulus division can be computed by repeated subtraction as follows (assuming a, b > 0):

```
modulus :: Data Int → Data Int → Data Int
modulus a b = while (≥b) (subtract b) a
```

The parallel construct computes an array from a length and a function that maps each index to its element. Arrays are denoted by the type Data [a] (where [a] can be arbitrarily nested). Reusing Haskell's list type for arrays results in compact and readable types. Using parallel, a program that computes the first 10 powers of two is defined as follows:

```
powersOfTwo = parallel 10 (λi → 2^i)
```

```
*Main> eval powersOfTwo
[1,2,4,8,16,32,64,128,256,512]
```

The purpose of parallel is to capture the fact that the array elements are *independent*. This means that they can be computed in any order, or even in parallel. However, our C backend does not yet generate parallel code.

Feldspar's expressiveness comes from the fact that we can use the host language, Haskell, to program powerful abstractions on top of this rather low-level

```
data Expr a where
  Value        :: Storable a ⇒ a → Expr a
  Function     :: String → (a → b) → Expr (a → b)
  Application  :: Expr (a → b) → Data a → Expr b
  Variable     :: Expr a
  IfThenElse   :: Data Bool → (a :→ b) → (a :→ b) → (Data a → Expr b)
  While        :: (a :→ Bool) → (a :→ a) → (Data a → Expr a)
  Parallel     :: Storable a ⇒ Data Int → (Int :→ a) → Expr [a]
```

Listing 2. Core Language Representation

```
data Data a = Typeable a ⇒ Data (Ref (Expr a))

toData :: Typeable a ⇒ Expr a → Data a
toData = Data ∘ ref

fromData :: Data a → Expr a
fromData (Data a) = deref a
```

Listing 3. Wrapper type for expression nodes

core language. In Section 5, we introduce one such language extension: the vector library. This is a substantial extension that more or less eliminates the need for low-level looping constructs in the user's code.

4   Core Language Implementation

Core expressions (see Figure 1) are represented by the generalized algebraic data type (GADT) [10] shown in Listing 2. There is a clear correspondence between the constructs in Listing 1 and those of the Expr type, but also some differences. Expr is mutually recursive through the types Data (see Listing 3) and (:→). The latter type is a representation of functions that supports easy introspection and inlining (see Listing 7).

Each node in an expression tree is wrapped by the Data type, tagging it with a unique reference and enabling observable sharing [3]. References are handled through the interface in Listing 4. In this particular implementation, a reference is just a unique tag attached to a value (rather than a *mutable* reference). Observable sharing is further discussed in Section 4.2.

Another purpose of Data is to make sure that each node in an expression tree stays within the set of types supported by Feldspar. Listing 5 summarizes the two classes that define two sets of supported types (not to be confused with the standard Haskell classes of the same name). Storable is the set of zero- or higher-dimensional arrays of primitive types. These are the types with which the user works; when the user has a value of type Data a, a is generally a Storable type. The Typeable class is the set of nested tuples of Storable types. These types

```
data Ref a
instance Eq (Ref a)
ref   :: a → Ref a
deref :: Ref a → a
```

Listing 4. Interface to observable sharing

```
instance Storable Bool
instance Storable Int
  — Etc. for other primitive types
instance Storable a ⇒ Storable [a]

instance Storable a ⇒ Typeable a
instance (Typeable a, Typeable b) ⇒ Typeable (a,b)
  — Similarly for larger tuples
```

Listing 5. Supported core language types

are only used internally. That is, the user is not allowed to work with types like Data (a,b), but should use (Data a, Data b) instead (see Section 4.1). The methods of the Storable and Typeable classes are for internal use when generating code.

We can now give a simple definition of the value function from Listing 1, which introduces a value from the Storable set of Haskell values (meta level) into Feldspar (object level).

```
value :: Storable a ⇒ a → Data a
value = toData ∘ Value
```

Primitive functions are constructed by the Function constructor of the Expr type. The String argument identifies the function (for use by backends), and the function argument gives the evaluation semantics. The only way to use a Function node is to apply it using the Application constructor. The other constructors use the Data wrapper for their arguments, and the Typeable constraint for Data rules out function types. The separate application operator enables nested application of curried functions. Listing 6 gives handy combinators for defining primitive functions of one and two arguments. Note the nested use of the application operator (|$|) in function2. Now, defining new primitive functions is trivial:

```
not :: Data Bool → Data Bool
not = function "not" Prelude.not

mod :: Data Int → Data Int → Data Int
mod = function2 "mod" Prelude.mod
```

So far, we can define simple values and primitive functions. The remaining core language constructs deal with embedded functions. It is convenient to be able to treat Haskell functions of the form Data a → Data b as functions in the embedded language. This view is supported by the :→ type, defined in Listing 7.

```
( |$| ) :: Expr (a → b) → Data a → Expr b
f |$| a = Application f a

function :: Typeable b ⇒ String → (a → b) → Data a → Data b
function fun f a = toData $ Function fun f |$| a

function2 :: Typeable c ⇒
            String → (a → b → c) → Data a → Data b → Data c
function2 fun f a b = toData $ Function fun f |$| a |$| b
```

Listing 6. Primitive function constructors

```
data a :→ b = Lambda (Data a → Data b) (Data a) (Data b)

freshVar :: Typeable a ⇒ () → Data a
freshVar _ = toData Variable

lambda :: Typeable a ⇒ (Data a → Data b) → (a :→ b)
lambda f = Lambda f var (f var) where var = freshVar ()

apply :: (a :→ b) → Data a → Data b
apply (Lambda f _ _) = f
```

Listing 7. Representation of embedded functions

This type is used to represent the sub-functions of the higher-order constructs of the Expr type (for example, the body of the while loop).

Inspecting a function of type Data a → Data b demands that a suitable argument be conjured up. The function freshVar creates a fresh variable represented by the Variable constructor. Observable sharing makes it possible to uniquely identify each such variable.[3] An embedded function is constructed by lambda, which applies a function to a fresh variable, and stores the original function with the variable and the applied expression. Thus, a term Lambda subst a b can be seen as a lambda expression, where b is an expression in which the bound variable a occurs free. The original function subst gives an effective way of substituting a different expression for the free variable, as done by the apply function.

We now have the building blocks to give simplified definitions of the remaining core constructs. For example, a kind of while loop can be defined as follows:

```
whileData :: Typeable st ⇒
    (Data st → Data Bool) → (Data st → Data st) → (Data st → Data st)
whileData cont body = toData ∘ While (lambda cont) (lambda body)
```

---

[3] This use of observable sharing is arguably dangerous. We have to be careful to prevent different uses of freshVar from being accidentally shared. We are currently investigating safer techniques for handling variable binding.

```
evalE :: Expr a → a
evalE (Value a)        = a
evalE (Function _ f)   = f
evalE (Application f a) = evalE f (evalD a)

evalE (IfThenElse c t e a) | evalD c   = evalD (apply t a)
                            | otherwise = evalD (apply e a)

evalE (While cont body init) = evalD $ head
    $ dropWhile (evalD ∘ apply cont)
    $ iterate (apply body) init

evalE (Parallel l ixf) = map (evalD ∘ apply ixf ∘ value) [0 .. n−1]
    where n = evalD l

evalD :: Data a → a
evalD = evalE ∘ fromData
```

Listing 8. Semantics of expressions

```
tup2 :: Typeable (a,b) ⇒ Data a → Data b → Data (a,b)
tup2 = function2 "tup2" (,)

get21 :: Typeable a ⇒ Data (a,b) → Data a
get22 :: Typeable b ⇒ Data (a,b) → Data b
get21 = function "get21" fst
get22 = function "get22" snd
```

— Similarly for larger tuples: tup3, get31, get32, get33, tup4, etc.

Listing 9. Tuple operations

The semantics of core expressions is given in Listing 8. This is generalized in Section 4.1.

4.1   Extended Interface

The simple loop whileData has only a single value Data st in its state. We may often require more values in the state, for example to accumulate a sum while increasing an index. One way to use multiple state variables is to make a compound state using the tuple operations in Listing 9. However, it is very inconvenient for the user to have to insert those operations explicitly in the code. Luckily, it turns out that the tupling/untupling can be automated. Listing 10 introduces the Computable class. Generally speaking, this class provides an interface between the Data type and an open set of other, more convenient types. For example, it is much more convenient to work with (Data Int, Data Bool) than Data (Int, Bool),

```
class Typeable (Internal a) ⇒ Computable a where
  type Internal a
  internalize :: a → Data (Internal a)
  externalize :: Data (Internal a) → a

instance Storable a ⇒ Computable (Data a) where
  type Internal (Data a) = a
  internalize = id
  externalize = id

instance (Computable a, Computable b) ⇒ Computable (a,b) where
  type Internal (a,b) = (Internal a, Internal b)
  internalize (a,b)   = tup2 (internalize a) (internalize b)
  externalize ab      = (externalize (get21 ab), externalize (get22 ab))

— Similarly for larger tuples

lowerFun :: (Computable a, Computable b) ⇒
    (a → b) → (Data (Internal a) → Data (Internal b))
lowerFun f = internalize ∘ f ∘ externalize

liftFun :: (Computable a, Computable b) ⇒
    (Data (Internal a) → Data (Internal b)) → (a → b)
liftFun f = externalize ∘ f ∘ internalize
```

Listing 10. Computable class

since the former can be constructed and decomposed using Haskell's ordinary tuple syntax. Computable allows us to convert easily between the two types using the internalize / externalize functions. It is possible to automate the insertion of internalize / externalize so that the user will never see a type like Data (Int, Bool). For example, here is the general definition of the while loop, and an example of its use:

```
while :: Computable st ⇒ (st → Data Bool) → (st → st) → (st → st)
while cont body = liftFun (toData ∘ While contL bodyL)
  where contL = lambda (lowerFun cont)
        bodyL = lambda (lowerFun body)

gcd :: Data Int → Data Int → Data Int
gcd a b = fst $ while cont body (a,b)
  where cont (_,b) = b > 0
        body (a,b) = (b,a 'mod' b)
```

For the system to remain sound, the functions internalize and externalize are not allowed to change the semantics of the program, as formalized by the rule:

evalD ∘ internalize ∘ externalize $==$ evalD

```
eval :: Computable a ⇒ a → Internal a
eval = evalD ∘ internalize

ifThenElse :: (Computable a, Computable b) ⇒
    Data Bool → (a → b) → (a → b) → (a → b)
ifThenElse cond t e = liftFun (toData ∘ IfThenElse cond thenSub elseSub)
  where thenSub = lambda (lowerFun t)
        elseSub = lambda (lowerFun e)

parallel :: Storable a ⇒ Data Int → (Data Int → Data a) → Data [a]
parallel l ixf = toData $ Parallel l (lambda ixf)
```

Listing 11. Remaining core language definitions

Computable is very powerful, as it gives a modular way to extend the language. For example, in Section 5, we extend the language with a new type of vectors (seen in the introductory examples). The remainder of the core language implementation is given in Listing 11.

4.2   Inspecting and Optimizing Expressions

Backends, such as printCore, work by inspecting the Expr data structure produced by core language programs, performing a number of simple but powerful optimizations. To save space, this section can only give a brief summary of the techniques used. The main ideas are described in the work on Pan [4].

At the highest level, the language constructors perform local optimizations on the fly: constant folding, algebraic simplification, etc. Thus, the initial Expr data structure is already optimized to a certain extent. In addition, we have experimental support for range-based partial evaluation. A range is an over-approximation of the set of values a variable might take on. This information can be used to fold even non-constant expressions. For example, if the ranges of a and b are known to be disjoint, the comparison a==b can be statically replaced by value False. This kind of partial evaluation is also performed "on the fly."

Code duplication can be avoided by the use of the reference equality provided by observable sharing. Essentially, observable sharing allows us to view the Expr structure as a directed graph rather than a tree. Once this graph has been generated, a global transformation pass performs hoisting of loop-invariant code. The resulting graph can relatively easily be translated to reasonable C code. While the original motivation behind observable sharing was to reify potentially cyclic graphs, we use it mainly as a means to make an efficient implementation of common sub-expression elimination (CSE). However, since there may exist equal expressions that are not shared, our implementation of CSE is not complete. A complete CSE can be implemented (less efficiently) by using structural equality instead of observable sharing.

4.3   Arrays

Core language arrays are denoted by the type Data [a]. Constant arrays are constructed using the value function, as in value   [[1,2,3],[4]]   :: Data [[Int]], which creates a constant 2×3 matrix with the first row initialized to [1,2,3] and the second to [4]. Arrays are always rectangular, so the above constant has two uninitialized values at the end of the second row.

There are a few more functions that deal with arrays. We have already seen parallel which constructs an array from an index function. In addition, we have the two primitive functions

```
getIx :: Storable a ⇒ Data [a] → Data Int → Data a
setIx :: Storable a ⇒ Data [a] → Data Int → Data a → Data [a]
```

The expression getIx arr i returns the element at index i in the array arr. Similarly, setIx arr i a returns a modified version of arr where the element at index i has been replaced by a.

5   Vector Library

Many algorithms in the DSP domain operate on ordered collections of data, which is why we have added special support for vectors. A vector in Feldspar is much like an array, with one important difference: a vector is guaranteed *not to be represented in memory* at runtime, unless it is explicitly converted into a core-level array. This difference is why we sometimes call vectors *virtual*.

The support for Vectors in Feldspar is implemented as a shallow embedding on top of the core language. Implementing vectors as a shallow embedding has had the benefit of allowing us to experiment with various different vector implementations easily, without having to change any other aspect of the language and its implementation. Furthermore the backend need not be aware of vectors and can therefore be simpler.

The vector library provides a set of functions inspired by standard list processing functions found in Haskell and other functional languages. This allows the programmer to write very high level code that is typically rather close to the mathematical specification of the algorithm. Some example vector functions are shown in Listing 12. Vector is the type of our virtual vectors and its argument is the type of its elements. It is very common that the elements of vectors are of type Data. We often use the abbreviation DVector in those cases.

An example of how to program with the vector library is the function to compute the moving average of a vector, specified as $s_i = \frac{1}{n} \Sigma_{j=i}^{i+n-1} a_j$.

```
movingAvg :: Data Int → DVector Int → DVector Int
movingAvg n = map (('div' n) ∘ sum ∘ take n) ∘ tails
```

The function tails produces a vector of all the suffixes of the input vector. The use of take in the argument of map creates a window into the original vector of a fixed size. The average of a window is computed using summation and division.

```
data Vector  a = Indexed { length :: Data Int, index :: Data Int → a }
type DVector a = Vector (Data a)

instance Storable a ⇒ Computable (Vector (Data a))
  where type Internal (Vector (Data a)) = (Int, [Internal (Data a)])

map :: (a → b) → Vector a → Vector b
map f (Indexed l ixf) = Indexed l (f ∘ ixf)

take :: Data Int → Vector a → Vector a
take n (Indexed l ixf) = Indexed (min n l) ixf

drop :: Data Int → Vector a → Vector a
drop n (Indexed l ixf) = Indexed (max 0 (l − n)) (λx → ixf (x + n))

tails :: Vector a → Vector (Vector a)
tails vec = Indexed (length vec + 1) (λn → drop n vec)

(...) :: Data Int → Data Int → Vector (Data Int)
(...) m n = Indexed (n − m + 1) (+ m)

memorize :: Storable a ⇒ Vector (Data a) → Vector (Data a)
memorize (Indexed l ixf) = Indexed l (getIx (parallel l ixf))
```

Listing 12. Implementation of Vector with some smart constructors

The implementation of the vector type in Feldspar is shown in Listing 12. A vector, which is zero-indexed, is represented by a pair containing the length and an index function, as in the core arrays constructed by parallel. This particular representation has the advantage that all elements in the vector are computed independently and can therefore possibly be computed in parallel. Listing 12 shows examples of functions that use this representation. The Computable instances enable vectors to work seamlessly together with the Core language as explained in Section 4.1.

The chosen representation also allows for a very lightweight yet powerful implementation of vector fusion. Indeed, fusion comes as a byproduct of the way we have chosen to represent vectors. It is best illustrated by an example. Consider the following toy function:

```
squares :: Data Int → DVector Int
squares n = map square (1...n) where square x = x * x
```

When given an argument m, squares reduces as follows:

```
map square (1...m) ⇒ map square (Indexed m (+1)) ⇒ Indexed m (square ∘ (+1))
```

The vector computation is reduced to a single vector. No intermediate vector is used in the computation. This style of fusion has a significant advantage: vectors are guaranteed to be fused away and take up no memory during runtime. This is a very strong guarantee and by far exceeds the kinds of guarantees a typical optimizing compiler gives. If the programmer wishes to avoid fusing a vector and store the vector in memory, it is a simple matter of inserting a call to the function memorize, the effect of which is to store a vector in memory. This function is useful when elements of a vector are used more than once. If the vector is not written to memory, then the elements are recomputed each time they are accessed. Such recomputations can in some cases be very costly, in particular when they consist of looping over other vectors or arrays. In such cases, using memorize will often improve the runtime complexity of the function.

In the Computable instance for vectors, the internalize function introduces memory allocation, similarly to memorize. This means that memory is allocated in two situations: (1) explicitly by the memorize function, and (2) implicitly by functions overloaded using Computable when operating on vectors. This scheme provides a simple and easy to remember contract to the programmer which offers both *predictability* and *control*. It is predictable because fusion will always happen, except in the above mentioned situations, and the programmer can control memory allocation and prevent fusion using memorize.

6   Related Work

Embedded Domain Specific Languages are growing in popularity, and are used in many different domains. We cannot survey the entire field, but will restrict our attention to work that has influenced ours, or has aspects in common. Feldspar is compiled, rather than interpreted or used as a library in the host language. An early forerunner is Pan [4] which is similar to Feldspar in many respects. In particular, Pan's treatment of images is similar to Feldspar's vectors, with their associated combinator-based style of programming. However, Feldspar is more general and can handle a larger domain. In implementation, Feldspar differs from Pan in that it uses observable sharing to control intermediate code size, and supports fusion of vectors as an optimization.

Several embedded languages support vector programming in the style of Feldspar. Obsidian [11] is an embedded language for GPU programming that is in many ways similar to Feldspar. Feldspar's vectors were inspired by a similar construct in Obsidian. The main differences arise because Obsidian is specifically targeted to graphics processors. So, for example, loops are unrolled in Obsidian, and the programmer has greater control over the location of data in memory than is currently the case in Feldspar. Repa [6] is a library for array programming in Haskell that shares many similarities with Feldspar's vectors; the two approaches were developed independently. Repa uses the same model of fusion as Feldspar, and also offers programmer controlled memory allocation. It provides greater reusability through a notion of shape polymorphism, which allows functions to work over vectors with different shapes. We intend to adopt this approach in Feldspar.

Other projects aimed at the DSP domain include Spiral [8], Single Assignment C (SAC) [9], and Embedded MATLAB [7]. Spiral automates the production of high performance libraries for DSP applications (among others). To that end, it has a high-level language, SPL, for specifying transforms. SPL has no notion of time or space usage; instead search is used to try to find the best implementation. SAC is a language aimed at efficient array programming and is similar to Feldspar in many respects, including the fact that the array programming model is implemented modularly as a library. However, SAC inherits from C in the sense that it is a sequential, first-order language; thus, the programming experience is rather different, and in particular less modular, than in Feldspar. Embedded MATLAB is an effort to compile MATLAB to C suitable for running on embedded hardware. Of necessity, Embedded MATLAB is a subset of full MATLAB. Since it is common to develop and prototype DSP algorithms in MATLAB, it makes sense to compile these prototypes directly. The compiler is developed using standard methods, and, as with many optimizing compilers, it can be difficult to predict the results when many optimizations are combined.

Several methods exist to aid the embedding of a language in Haskell. The finally tagless technique [2] provides a very powerful and compositional way of embedding languages. We chose not to use it for two reasons. First, the types become more awkward; the (result-) type of an embedded program is simply a qualified type variable. We find it hard to motivate this for Feldspar beginners. Also, it exposes details of the implementation to the user. Second, we have found finally tagless to be incompatible with our use of observable sharing. Since language constructs in finally tagless are overloaded, they are typically implemented as projection functions on dictionaries. When the type is known at compile time, optimization might remove the dictionary. However, this optimization will influence whether the term will be shared under observable sharing or not.

7 Discussion and Future Work

The language presented in this paper has some good sides and some sides that need more work. Our main impression, based on case studies, is that it actually works! Case studies have been performed by Ericsson Baseband Research engineers without prior knowledge of functional programming. They successfully and efficiently implemented a set of signal processing functions and compared them with reference implementations in existing C code.

One of the keys to this result was the decision to use a minimalistic low-level core language with a high-level interface implemented as a shallow extension to the core. The minimal core language is quite close to the hardware, making it relatively easy for the backend to produce C code. At the same time, the core is flexible enough to support different kinds of high-level interfaces.

Feldspar aims to offer the Haskell style of programming: pure functions, list-like processing, higher-order functions, etc. It was not obvious that this would be a good fit for the DSP domain. But now, based on the experience of Ericsson research engineers, we can say that pure functional programming appears to be quite well-suited for this task. Admittedly, we need to work on larger examples, and get feedback from more users before we can draw any real conclusions. But the initial results are very promising. We believe that a key to achieving high-level code with good performance is the vector library, which enables powerful code optimization in a predictable and controllable manner.

While our current language shows great potential, we are also aware of some serious problems. Our simple core language has been a success. It supports powerful high-level interfaces, such as the vector library, while enabling decent code generation. However, the current core language fails to produce code of sufficiently high performance in commonly occurring cases. As an example, take the append function ++. When compiled to C, it generates the following loop:

```
for(var2 = 0; var2 < (* out_0); var2 += 1)
{
  var8 = (var2 < var0_0_0);
  if   (var8) { out_1[var2] = var0_0_1[var2]; }
  else        { out_1[var2] = var0_1_1[(var2 − var0_0_0)]; }
}
```

In each iteration, a conditional decides whether to pick elements from the first argument (var0_0_1) or the second (var0_1_1). In general, having a conditional inside a loop can prevent the C compiler from doing crucial optimizations. It would be better to have two loops in sequence, each reading from one of the arguments. The problem with our current core language is that *this desired loop structure cannot be expressed*. There are a large number of useful C code patterns that are out of reach from the core language. To deal with this problem, we are working on improving the core language.

Another limitation is the lack of control over memory, due to referential transparency. The user can control whether or not to use memory for vectors (via the memorize function), but it is not possible to control memory layout and memory reuse. A "system layer" being built on top of current Feldspar will handle memory usage and parallelism. In principle, this system layer will act as Feldspar's "IO monad," but the aim is to have a more declarative interface.

The openness of Feldspar makes it easy to add new domain-specific combinators that capture patterns commonly used in DSP. We are working on combinators for describing streaming computations with feedback, for use, for example, in defining digital filters. We are developing a more extensive library for algebraic description of DSP transforms, heavily inspired by the Spiral project [8].

Given that we have chosen to keep Feldspar very close to Haskell one might wonder why we did not program the DSP algorithms directly in Haskell, and spend our efforts improving the compilation of Haskell programs. Haskell programs need an extensive runtime system in order to run, taking up precious space on embedded platforms where resources are scarce. Furthermore, the cost model of Haskell is complex, both for time and space consumption. One of the key design philosophies of Feldspar was to keep these things predictable and under programmer control.

It remains to be seen how well programmers without functional programming background can cope with the embedded nature of Feldspar. The reactions from Ericsson programmers so far have been encouraging. If this turns out to be a real obstacle, one option might be to implement a stand-alone language instead, perhaps with a high-level Haskell front end.

8 Conclusion

Feldspar is implemented as an embedded language in Haskell, and its implementation makes essential use of advanced Haskell features, such as GADTs and overloading. The implementation is based around a simple, low-level, functional core language, which can be fairly easily translated to C code. The power of the implementation comes from the ability to program high-level interfaces as shallow extensions to the core language. We have presented one such extension–the vector library–which enables list-like processing and powerful fusion of vector traversals.

Acknowledgements. This research is funded by Ericsson, Vetenskapsrådet, and the Swedish Foundation for Strategic Research. The Feldspar project is an initiative of and is partially funded by Ericsson Software Research and is a collaboration between Chalmers, Ericsson, and ELTE University, Budapest. We wish to thank Peter Brauer of Ericsson for working with us on the case studies.

References

[1] Axelsson, E., Dévai, G., Horváth, Z., Keijzer, K., Lyckegård, B., Persson, A., Sheeran, M., Svenningsson, J., Vajda, A.: Feldspar: A Domain Specific Language for Digital Signal Processing algorithms. In: Proc. 8th ACM/IEEE International Conference on Formal Methods and Models for Codesign, IEEE, Los Alamitos (2010)

[2] Carette, J., Kiselyov, O., Shan, C.: Finally tagless, partially evaluated: Tagless staged interpreters for simpler typed languages. J. Func. Prog. 19(05) (2009)

[3] Claessen, K., Sands, D.: Observable sharing for functional circuit description. In: Thiagarajan, P.S., Yap, R.H.C. (eds.) ASIAN 1999. LNCS, vol. 1742, p. 62. Springer, Heidelberg (1999)

[4] Elliott, C., Finne, S., de Moor, O.: Compiling embedded languages. J. Func. Prog. 13(3), 455–481 (2003)

[5] Feldspar: http://feldspar.inf.elte.hu/feldspar/

[6] Keller, G., Chakravarty, M., Leshchinskiy, R., Jones, S.P., Lippmeier, B.: Regular, shape-polymorphic, parallel arrays in Haskell. In: Proc. 15th ACM SIGPLAN international conference on Functional programming, pp. 261–272. ACM, New York (2010)

[7] Martin, G., Zarrinkoub, H.: From MATLAB to Embedded C, The Mathworks (2009), http://www.mathworks.com/company/newsletters/news_notes/2009/matlab-embedded-c.html

[8] Püschel, M., Moura, J.M.F., Johnson, J., Padua, D., Veloso, M., Singer, B., Xiong, J., Franchetti, F., Gacic, A., Voronenko, Y., Chen, K., Johnson, R.W., Rizzolo, N.: SPIRAL: Code generation for DSP transforms. Proc. IEEE 93(2) (2005)

[9] Scholz, S.: Single Assignment C: efficient support for high-level array operations in a functional setting. J. Func. Prog. 13(06), 1005–1059 (2003)

[10] Schrijvers, T., Peyton Jones, S., Sulzmann, M., Vytiniotis, D.: Complete and decidable type inference for GADTs. In: Proc. 14th ACM SIGPLAN international conference on Functional programming, pp. 341–352. ACM, New York (2009)

[11] Svensson, J., Sheeran, M., Claessen, K.: GPGPU Kernel Implementation and Refinement using Obsidian. In: Proc. Seventh International Workshop on Practical Aspects of High-level Parallel Programming. ICCS, Procedia (2010)

Purity in Erlang

Mihalis Pitidis[1] and Konstantinos Sagonas[1,2]

[1] School of Electrical and Computer Engineering,
National Technical University of Athens, Greece
[2] Department of Information Technology, Uppsala University, Sweden
mpitid@gmail.com, kostis@cs.ntua.gr

Abstract. Motivated by a concrete goal, namely to extend Erlang with the ability to employ user-defined guards, we developed a parameterized static analysis tool called PURITY, that classifies functions as referentially transparent (i.e., side-effect free with no dependency on the execution environment and never raising an exception), side-effect free with no dependencies but possibly raising exceptions, or side-effect free but with possible dependencies and possibly raising exceptions. We have applied PURITY on a large corpus of Erlang code bases and report experimental results showing the percentage of functions that the analysis definitely classifies in each category. Moreover, we discuss how our analysis has been incorporated on a development branch of the Erlang/OTP compiler in order to allow extending the language with user-defined guards.

1 Introduction

Purity plays an important role in functional programming languages as it is a cornerstone of *referential transparency*, namely that the same language expression produces the same value when evaluated twice. Referential transparency helps in writing easy to test, robust and comprehensible code, makes equational reasoning possible, and aids program analysis and optimisation. In pure functional languages like Clean or Haskell, any side-effect or dependency on the state is captured by the type system and is reflected in the types of functions. In a language like ERLANG, which has been developed primarily with concurrency in mind, pure functions are not the norm and impure functions can freely be used interchangeably with pure ones. Still, even in these languages, being able to reason about the purity of functions can prove useful in various situations.

This paper discusses properties that functions must satisfy in order to be classified as having a certain level of purity, and describes the design and implementation of a fully automatic parameterized static analyzer, called PURITY, that determines the purity of ERLANG functions. Although the analysis is simple and very conservative, we were able to determine the purity of roughly 90% of the functions in the code bases we tested.

As a practical application, our analysis has been integrated in a development branch of the ERLANG compiler, allowing functions that the analyzer determines as pure to be used in guard expressions, something not previously possible in ERLANG and, for many years now, one of the most frequent user requests for extending the language. Furthermore, our analysis could make way for some types of optimisations in the ERLANG compiler including common subexpression elimination, useless call elimination, deforestation and automatic parallelization.

J. Hage, M.T. Morazán (Eds.): IFL 2010, LNCS 6647, pp. 137–152, 2011.

The contributions of this paper are as follows:

- we present a relatively simple but parameterized static analysis that can determine the purity of ERLANG functions at different levels;
- we give detailed measurements of percentages of functions that our analysis classifies as definitely pure; to the best of our knowledge this is the first time that such numbers are reported in the literature (especially for a dynamically typed language); and
- we discuss how the analysis has served as a basis for allowing the ERLANG language to be extended with the ability to employ user-defined guards.

The next section reviews the ERLANG language and aspects of its evolution and implementation which are relevant to the topic of the paper. Section 3 describes the analyses we employ to determine the purity of ERLANG functions, followed by a Section 4 which presents experiences from running these analyses on a large corpus of ERLANG code bases. Section 5 describes how the analysis information can be used to allow for user-defined guards in ERLANG and the paper ends with reviewing purity in other languages (Section 6) and some concluding remarks.

2   Erlang: The Language and Its Features

ERLANG is a concurrent functional programming language with dynamic types. What sets ERLANG apart from other functional languages is its support for concurrency, fault tolerance and distributed programming. Other notable features include hot-code reloading whereby the code of some module of an executing ERLANG program can be replaced with a newer version of that module without interrupting the program's execution. The language also provides soft real-time guarantees.

The aforementioned features make ERLANG ideal for building highly scalable, reliable and robust systems. While initially conceived to develop software for telecommunication systems, ERLANG has outgrown this particular niche and with the advent of the multi-core era it is being used for the development of a growing number of diverse software applications. This includes web and chat servers, distributed document stores, and network servers.

ERLANG employs a mixture of purely functional programming, in the form of immutable data structures and single assignment variables, combined with a limited set of impure functions and expressions, in order to support concurrency and distribution. In particular, ERLANG implements the *actor* model of concurrency [1]. Its implementation can be summarised as concurrency based on lightweight processes communicating via asynchronous message passing with copying semantics. This helps express complex concurrency schemes in a more natural and declarative manner.

Impurities in ERLANG originate from particular expressions and functions. An example of the former is the `receive` expression which is used to extract messages from the mailbox of a process. For examples of the latter, we first need to mention the general concept of built-in functions, or BIFs as they are usually known in the ERLANG community. BIFs are functions native to the ERLANG virtual machine, implemented in the language the VM is written in, in this case C. Besides some primitive operations which otherwise cannot be expressed in pure ERLANG, BIFs often substitute commonly used functions for optimisation purposes. As it happens, many BIFs are impure, usually because they interface with the runtime system in various ways.

Like many functional languages, ERLANG supports pattern matching, a way of matching a sequence of values against a corresponding sequence of patterns. The result, if successful, is a mapping of variables from the first pattern that matches to the various terms in the sequence of values. Pattern matching plays a central role in expressing control flow in ERLANG. Additional constraints can be placed on pattern matches with the use of guard tests. Guard tests consist of boolean expressions which are evaluated for each pattern matched and only if their result is true will the match be successful. With guards it is possible to extend the expressiveness of pattern matching significantly, e.g. to add support for value ranges for numbers, or tests for abstract values like process identifiers and function objects.

However, ERLANG currently imposes strict limitations on guard tests. Specifically, they must lack side-effects and execute in bounded time, preferably constant. To this end, guards are limited by the ERLANG language to a small predefined set of built-in functions also known as guard BIFs [2, § 6.20, p. 103].

The example in Listing 1 showcases the use of pattern matching in ERLANG and how it is further extended with guard tests. This combination allows for concise and declarative code, offering a significant boost in programmer productivity.

```
area({square, Side}) when is_integer(Side) ->
    Side * Side;
area({circle, Radius}) when is_number(Radius) ->
    3.14 * Radius * Radius;   %% well, almost
area({triangle, A, B, C}) ->
    S = (A + B + C) / 2,
    math:sqrt(S * (S-A) * (S-B) * (S-C)).
```

Listing 1. Examples of pattern matching and guard tests

As mentioned, ERLANG is dynamically typed. Furthermore, the ERLANG compiler currently does not perform any form of type analysis. This has certain implications on PURITY, which are discussed in detail in Section 3.

3   Purity Analysis in Erlang

In order to determine the purity of ERLANG functions we designed and implemented a fully automated static analysis which operates on ERLANG source code (or compiled bytecode files which include debugging information). The analysis is flexible and allows the user to select between different purity criteria, depending on the intended use of the analysis' results.

3.1   Flavours of Purity

We should first clarify what we mean by pure and impure functions. A *pure* function is one that is *referentially transparent*, i.e., calls to the function can be replaced by their return values without changing the semantics of the program in any way in any execution environment. This is the strongest definition of purity that our analysis supports. In addition, it offers a choice between a few progressively weaker criteria, depending on the intended use of the analysis' results.

In general, a function may lose its referential transparency and be classified as impure: a) either due to *modifying* the execution environment in some way other than returning a value, or b) by *depending* on the environment of execution in some way other than its arguments. A function that falls into the first category is said to have side-effects. Such a function will always be considered impure by our analysis. Regarding the second category, certain uses of the analysis may choose to ignore such violations of referential transparency and force the analysis to consider functions which fall in it as pure. We shall elaborate on this design decision in a later section.

Besides the fundamental categories described above, our analysis distinguishes between yet another condition of purity, one that is more specific to ERLANG. This condition concerns *exceptions*, which represent a non-local return out of a function and are somewhat problematic in their classification. First of all, it is not clear whether exceptions break referential transparency. While we can no longer replace the function by its value, we can still replace it by an exception raising expression, preserving the semantics of the program. This is not the whole truth however, since exceptions usually carry context sensitive information, specifically the series of function calls leading up to them, otherwise referred to as a *stack trace*. In the case of ERLANG, exceptions are regular terms that can be pattern matched on. The stack trace may or may not be part of the exception value, depending on the expression used to *catch* it. The older `catch` expression converts exceptions to tuples which often contain this stack trace, so using `catch` will break referential transparency. The newer and more robust `try-catch` construct [4] however, does not directly capture the stack trace, which is otherwise available through a specific ERLANG built-in function, aptly named `get_stacktrace()`. So, in the absence of a call to this function, `try-catch` blocks can be considered pure.

Still, when it comes to certain uses of the analysis' results — such as optimisations like common subexpression elimination — it makes sense to consider all exceptions as impure. This is why our analysis is flexible and parameterized in this respect as well.

A final note regarding exceptions concerns the semantics of process termination in ERLANG. If a process is terminated by an exception which is not a member of the `exit` class, then this event is reported by the ERLANG runtime system to the error logging service [4, § 2.7]. We choose to ignore this potential side-effect since it does not directly influence the execution of the program, but primarily because we wish to maintain a conceptual separation between exceptions and side-effects. This is important, as we will see in Section 5 that exceptions can be safely ignored in certain contexts.

To sum up, the analysis we will describe in the rest of this section will classify functions as impure based on three progressively stronger criteria of impurity, namely considering a function as impure if it:

1. contains side-effects — this is the default;
2. contains no side-effects but has dependencies on the environment; and
3. contains no side-effects, has no dependencies on the environment, but possibly raises exceptions.

3.2   The Core of the Analysis

Our analysis is relatively straightforward. It operates on a set of ERLANG modules which are first compiled to CORE ERLANG [3] (an intermediate, simpler representation of ERLANG source code). The analysis consists of two distinct stages: an information gathering and an information propagation stage.

The first stage collects necessary information by traversing the *Abstract Syntax Tree* of each function and constructs its *dependency set*: the set of other functions it calls somewhere in its body. In our implementation, functions are identified with triples of the form $\{m, f, a\}$ (where m is a module name, f is a function name, and a is its arity). However, for convenience in this section we will use shorter identifiers for functions: $f_0, f_1, \ldots$ for those that are analyzed and $b_0, b_1, \ldots$ for those that are BIFs or previously analyzed and their purity level is *a priori* known to the analysis.

All analysis information is kept in a *lookup table* which is a hash table whose keys are the function identifiers f and contains as values the *purity level* p_f of each f and D_f the *dependency set* of f. Purity levels are elements from the domain $\{s, d, e, p\}$ representing functions which contain side-effects (s), are side-effect free but have a dependency on the environment (d), are side-effect free and independent from the environment but possibly raise exceptions (e), or are pure (p). The analysis domain is thus ordered as: $s > d > e > p$. We will denote by $sup(p_{f_1}, p_{f_2})$ the supremum of purity levels p_{f_1} and p_{f_2} and by $sup(F)$ the supremum of purity levels of a set of functions F. Note that the purity level of a function is fully determined only when its dependency set is empty; for a function with a non empty dependency set D_f, its purity level is still conditional on the functions which appear in D_f. As we will see, during the information propagation stage of the analysis, dependency sets will be decreasing while purity levels will be increasing. If a function's purity level ever reaches the maximal value (s), its dependency set is not needed anymore and is removed by the algorithm.

Let us see the analysis on an example; cf. Figure 1(a). In the first stage, the analysis has scanned the code of five functions $f_0 \ldots f_4$ and has constructed their dependency sets. In our example, function f_2 depends on the built-in function b_1, while f_4 depends on functions f_1 and f_2 which will be analyzed and on function f_5 which was not given to the analysis. The purity level of all built-in functions is *a priori* known to the analysis; see the bottom part of the tables in Fig. 1. The purity level of all functions that will be analyzed is initialized to p. The analysis maintains as its working set the functions whose purity level is fully determined (i.e. those with empty dependency sets). For each of them it propagates its purity level to functions that depend on it, "contaminating" them with their (im)purity level in the process. After having done so, it also removes the function from the dependency set or completely removes the dependency set if the function it contaminated has reached the highest level of impurity (s). In our example, functions with known purity level are the two BIFs and by propagating their information we end up with the table of Fig. 1(b). Note that D_{f_3} has been set to empty because it has reached the highest level of impurity. Functions f_2 and f_3 join the working set and their use by the information propagation stage results in the table of Fig. 1(c). At this point the working set of the analysis is empty, but there are still some functions whose purity level is still conditional on functions which are part of the analysis. To achieve further progress the analysis finds an independent strongly connected component (SCC), i.e.,

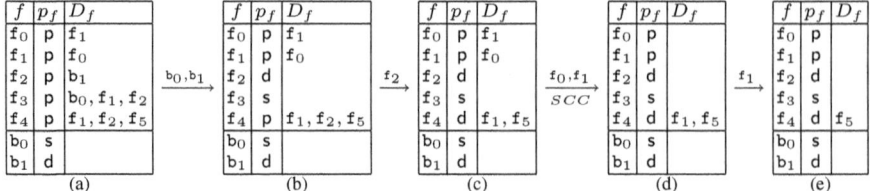

Fig. 1. Illustration of the analysis algorithm on an abstract example

a set of functions mutually dependent on each other, but on no other functions outside the SCC, sets their purity level to the supremum of their purity levels, and simplifies the dependency sets of these functions. In our example, functions f_0 and f_1 form such an SCC. (If functions in the SCC had different purity levels, which is not the case here, they would all collapse to their supremum at this point.) Simplifying their dependency sets results in the table of Fig. 1(d) and adds f_0 and f_1 to the analysis' working set. After a further simplification using f_1 (f_0 has no effect here), the final result of the analysis on our example is shown in Fig. 1(e).

We can now present the information propagation stage of the analysis in more detail. Algorithm 1 shows its pseudocode which is self-explanatory. What is not shown in that pseudocode is that, for efficiency reasons, the actual implementation maintains a *working set*. Whenever a function's dependency set becomes empty, the function is added to this working set. Another data structure maintained by the analysis is the *active function dependency graph*: its nodes are functions with non-empty dependency sets and its edges are formed by the elements in these dependency sets. This graph is used to find independent SCCs whenever needed.

Algorithm 1. The information propagation stage of the analysis

---

repeat
    for each function e in the lookup table with $D_e = \emptyset$
        for each function f where $e \in D_f$
            $p_f := \sup(p_f, p_e)$
            if $p_f = s$ **then** $D_f := \emptyset$ **else** $D_f := D_f \setminus \{e\}$
    $F :=$ an independent strongly connected component
    for each f in F
        $p_f := \sup(F)$
        $D_f := D_f \setminus F$
until there are no more changes to the lookup table

The result of the analysis is left in the lookup table where the purity level of some functions may still be conditional; i.e. their dependency sets may still contain some elements, like the dependency list of function f_4 in Fig. 1(e). Note that in this way the analysis is also able to handle incomplete programs. Subsequent uses of the analysis' results must typically consider this information in a conservative way: all functions with unknown dependencies are viewed as belonging to the highest level of impurity.

3.3   Higher Order Functions

Higher order functions, i.e. functions that return other functions or accept functions as arguments, are common in functional programming languages. Considering the latter type of higher order functions, if a call is made to one of the arguments in the body of the higher order function, it follows that its purity depends on that argument, and cannot be resolved to a fixed value. The only exception to this is when the function depends on other *impure* functions as well.

Let us consider the example of a higher order function, h, which just makes a call to its first argument. Clearly this has an unfixed purity. But what can be said about a function g, which depends on h? This function would either be a higher order function itself, taking another function as argument, and passing it along to h, or it would pass a *concrete* function f, as argument to h. It is thus possible in the second case —assuming the purity of f is known— to resolve the purity of this specific instance of h and consequently that of g. Listing 2 shows such an example; the comments in the code provide the necessary explanations.

```
%% A higher order function which depends on its first argument.
fold(_Fun, Acc, []) -> Acc;
fold(Fun, Acc, [H|T]) -> fold(Fun, Fun(H, Acc), T).

%% A pure closure is passed to a higher order function
%% so function g1/0 will be determined pure by the analysis.
g1() -> fold(fun erlang:'*'/2, 1, [2, 3, 7]).

%% An impure closure is passed to a higher order function
%% so function g2/0 is classified as impure.
g2() -> fold(fun erlang:put/2, computer, [ok, error]).
```

Listing 2. An example showing the treatment of higher order functions

This is a fairly simple example, but it manages to capture the most common use of higher order functions in ERLANG. To handle higher order functions the implementation extends the dependency sets to also contain information about argument positions that may contain function closures that will be called. Another important case, albeit a less frequent one, has to do with higher order functions which do not call their arguments directly, passing them instead to other higher order functions. This way, multiple levels of indirection are present between a call with a concrete function as argument and the actual higher order function which will end up using it. This is better illustrated by way of an example, like the one in Listing 3. To detect such cases and analyse them correctly in the absence of type information, we employ dataflow analysis. The current dataflow analysis we use is pretty simple and therefore not so accurate. Its details are beyond the scope of this paper. We note however that such cases account for less than 10% of the functions in the code bases we examined (cf. Sect. 4).

Another limiting factor is the fact that functions may be passed as parts of more complex data structures instead of directly as arguments. Common cases include, but

```
%% One level of indirection: it is not apparent this is a higher
%% order function since no direct call to its argument is made.
fold1(Fun, Acc, Lst) ->
  fold(Fun, Acc, Lst).

%% Two levels of indirection. The function argument has also
%% changed position.
fold2(Lst, Fun) ->
  fold1(Fun, 1, Lst).

g3() -> fold1(fun erlang:put/2, ok, [computer, error]).

g4() -> fold2([2, 3, 7], fun erlang:'*'/2).
```

Listing 3. An example of indirect higher order functions

are not limited to lists, tuples and records. In fact, most of these cases require runtime information in order to be properly resolved.

3.4   Implementation Aspects

Some aspects relating to the implementation of PURITY deserve further elaboration. The most important is the way the analysis is bootstrapped, in other words, the way we obtain the initial set of functions whose purity is predefined. This set includes all functions built-in to the ERLANG runtime system. Since these are implemented in C instead of ERLANG, they cannot be analysed. Therefore, it was necessary to extract them from the ERLANG runtime system and hard-code their purity. The values assigned were derived from their semantics, not the actual implementation.

Beyond this, it is possible to bootstrap the analysis with a more generalised mechanism, the *persistent lookup table* or PLT for short. The PLT is used to store all the information necessary to repeat the analysis as well as cached versions of the analysis' results for a given set of modules. This way, the user does not have to re-analyse every library his application depends on. The PLT also plays an important role in contexts were only one module can be analysed at a time but information regarding functions in other modules is necessary.

4   Experiences

In the course of testing our implementation diverse code bases were analysed providing some insight as to the current practices of ERLANG programmers. The applications analysed (Table 1) were primarily high profile open source projects.

Table 2 includes further information about each application. Table 3 presents the results of the analysis with the default options. Tables 4 and 5 present alternate runs of the analysis with progressively stronger purity criteria.

The columns of Table 3 labeled Pure and Impure are self-explanatory. The column labeled Undetectable represents the percentage of functions which cannot be analysed statically. These include functions like erlang:apply(M, F, Args) which applies function

Table 1. Brief description of the applications which were analysed

Erlang/OTP	The latest open source ERLANG distribution; among other things, it includes the bytecode and native code compilers, the standard library, static analysis tools like DIALYZER, an XML parsing library, and the Open Telecom Platform with its various networking applications
Wings3D	A subdivision modeler, used for generation of polygon models in computer graphics
CouchDB	A distributed, fault-tolerant and schema-free document oriented distributed database system
ejabberd	A server for the Extensible Messaging and Presence Protocol (XMPP), an open standard used primarily for instant messaging
Yaws	A high performance HTTP 1.1 server
ibrowse	An HTTP 1.1 client, also a dependency of Yaws
erlssom	Another XML parsing library and dependency of Yaws
purity	The analyzer described in this paper

Table 2. Details of analysed applications

Application	Version	Modules	Functions	LOC
Erlang/OTP	R14A	1,900	120,982	742,681
Wings3D	1.2	168	9,523	78,996
ejabberd	2.1.4	149	5,186	53,881
CouchDB	0.11.0	97	2,509	22,938
Yaws	1.88	42	1,563	19,438
Erlsom	1.2.1	18	568	9,562
ibrowse	1.6.1	7	227	2,683
purity	0.2	12	517	3,208

F in module M to some argument list of terms `Args`. Since this list can be of any length we cannot know the exact arity of the function being called at compile time. The percentage also includes functions which depend on such functions or on functions whose source code was not available during the analysis. The Limited column represents the percentage of functions which could not be conclusively analysed because of limitations in our implementation. Finally, the last column shows the CPU time required to analyse each application (in minutes/seconds), as reported by the `erlang:statistics/0` function. The tests were run on a GNU/Linux system, equipped with an Intel Core 2 Duo processor clocked at 1.6GHz and 2 GBs of RAM. Currently, our analysis only takes advantage of the second core during the information gathering stage by spawning a separate process (up to the number of available cores) for each module which is analyzed.

To better interpret the above results one should keep the following in mind. First of all, ERLANG is primarily a concurrent language and is thus expected of most applications to make extended use of concurrency primitives which render the corresponding functions impure. Furthermore, it only takes one impure function call to characterise all dependent functions as impure. Finally, although purity may initially seem as something easy to detect, reasoning about the purity of functions is not always straightforward — at least not as easy as the average programmer naïvely expects — according to our

Table 3. Analysis results with side-effects impure

Application	Pure	Impure	Undetectable	Limited	Time
Erlang/OTP	44.0%	41.4%	1.1%	13.6%	2:43
Wings3D	54.3%	34.9%	1.2%	9.6%	0:12
ejabberd	39.1%	51.2%	5.8%	4.0%	0:06
CouchDB	44.4%	44.7%	1.2%	9.7%	0:03
Yaws	44.6%	46.9%	1.1%	7.4%	0:03
Erlsom	46.0%	9.2%	0.5%	44.4%	0:02
ibrowse	44.1%	55.9%	0.0%	0.0%	0:01
purity	68.5%	20.1%	1.9%	9.5%	0:01

Table 4. Analysis results with side-effects and non-determinism impure

Application	Pure	Impure	Undetectable	Limited	Time
Erlang/OTP	37.3%	58.2%	0.6%	4.0%	2:35
Wings3D	44.6%	47.4%	1.0%	7.0%	0:10
ejabberd	33.9%	63.2%	1.6%	1.3%	0:06
CouchDB	41.8%	48.9%	0.5%	8.8%	0:03
Yaws	40.8%	52.0%	0.9%	6.3%	0:03
Erlsom	38.4%	41.5%	0.5%	19.5%	0:01
ibrowse	39.2%	60.8%	0.0%	0.0%	0:01
purity	64.4%	24.8%	1.9%	8.9%	0:01

experience. Consider for example a function like `filename:basename/1` which is part of the ERLANG standard library. This function takes a filename and returns it with the leading path component removed, e.g., `filename:basename("/usr/bin/purity")` will return `"purity"`. This function is obviously used for the value it returns and, since strings are lists in ERLANG, one would expect that this function merely performs some simple list manipulation operations. This is verified by taking a quick look at the actual source code. Most programmers would therefore consider its use consistent with programming in a purely functional style. The function is however impure as our analysis — and some more careful consideration — demonstrates. The reason has to do with portability. In order for this function to be useful across different operating systems, its behaviour needs to vary according to the character used to separate paths in each OS. It is thus dependent on the execution environment and is not referentially transparent.

The results of Table 5 in particular may appear disheartening at first. If one wishes to use the results of the analysis in contexts were exceptions cannot be regarded as pure, there is little one can gain from it. All hope is not lost however, since some of these results may be misleading. The reason so many functions appear to potentially raise exceptions is that the ERLANG compiler adds extra clauses at function definitions and `case` expressions, which raise the corresponding clause failure exception if no pattern is matched. Later optimisation passes try to remove any such clauses which are redundant, when a function is total for instance, or when it takes no arguments. Without some form of type analysis however, it is not possible to safely remove such clauses in more complex cases. An example of an ERLANG function which warrants such a clause is that of Listing 1. It is apparent from its definition that the `area` function does not cover

Table 5. Analysis results with side-effects, non-determinism and exceptions impure

Application	Pure	Impure	Undetectable	Limited	Time
Erlang/OTP	5.3%	94.6%	0.0%	0.1%	2:16
Wings3D	5.7%	94.0%	0.3%	0.1%	0:10
ejabberd	9.4%	89.8%	0.5%	0.3%	0:06
CouchDB	6.3%	92.8%	0.2%	0.7%	0:03
Yaws	7.2%	92.5%	0.1%	0.3%	0:03
Erlsom	3.9%	96.1%	0.0%	0.0%	0:01
ibrowse	6.2%	93.8%	0.0%	0.0%	0:01
purity	7.4%	91.5%	0.8%	0.4%	0:01

```
foo(42) -> ok;
foo(N) when is_integer(N) ->
  {error, N}.


bar(N) ->
  case foo(N) of
    ok -> ok;
    {error, _} -> error
  end.
```

(a) Code as written by the programmer

```
foo(42) -> ok;
foo(N) when is_integer(N) ->
  {error, N};
foo(_) -> erlang:error(badarg).

bar(N) ->
  case foo(N) of
    ok -> ok;
    {error, _} -> error;
    _ -> erlang:error(case_clause)
  end.
```

(b) Code with exceptions inserted

Fig. 2. An example where the compiler fails to remove the redundant exception raising clauses that it has inserted due to lack of type information

all possible arguments it might be called with. On the other hand the exception raising clauses will not be removed for function bar in the example of Figure 2. The reason is that the ERLANG compiler currently cannot determine that the pattern matching on the return value of the call to foo is complete, since it does not keep any information regarding foo's return value.

Furthermore, these percentages do not account for the masking of exceptions by other functions. Consider the example in Listing 4 where an exception is raised by one function but is later masked in the body of another. With a more sophisticated analysis it is possible that some of these cases can be detected.

```
foo(X) ->
  throw(X).

bar() ->
  try foo(42) of
    Val -> {ok, Val}
  catch
    throw:E -> {error, E}
  end.
```

Listing 4. An example of exception masking

Table 6. Analysis results with side-effects impure and termination analysis

Application	Pure	Impure	Undetectable	Limited
Erlang/OTP	23.1%	74.8%	0.5%	1.7%
Wings3D	30.5%	67.6%	0.8%	1.1%
ejabberd	26.6%	69.3%	2.3%	1.7%
CouchDB	30.2%	65.0%	0.4%	4.4%
Yaws	36.0%	61.3%	0.7%	2.0%
Erlsom	29.2%	57.4%	0.4%	13.0%
ibrowse	36.1%	63.9%	0.0%	0.0%
purity	50.9%	45.8%	1.4%	1.9%

For completeness we include one more table. Table 6 presents the results of Table 3 when these are combined with a simple termination analysis we have also developed (whose details are beyond the scope of this paper). In effect, the first column of the table shows how many functions are found both pure and terminating. Why this information is interesting is described in the next section.

5   Extending Erlang with User-Defined Guards

The original motivation for our analysis was to extend the ERLANG language with support for user-defined guards. Besides being a very popular request by users, such an extension is important since it increases the language's expressiveness and allows for more compact and descriptive code.

We mentioned in Section 2 that guard expressions are currently limited to a pre-defined set of built-in functions. The reason for this is that the ERLANG specification requires that guard expressions are an extension of pattern matching. As such, functions used in guards should have no observable side-effects and should complete in bounded time. Notice that these prerequisites do not mention determinism. In fact, valid ERLANG guard expressions include the `erlang:node/0` and `erlang:node/1` BIFs, which depend on the execution environment. Specifically, the former returns the name of the current ERLANG node,[1] while the latter returns the name of the node a specific process belongs to. It is possible to change this node name from within the ERLANG runtime system by calling functions `start/1` and `stop/0` of the `net_kernel` module. The example in Figure 3 shows an excerpt from a session in the ERLANG shell, illustrating how a guard expression might succeed on one call and fail on another.

Another aspect of ERLANG guards which has not been discussed yet, is that any exceptions which may be raised as part of a guard test are caught and silently converted to the value `false`. That is to say that functions that raise an exception during normal execution, will not do so when used in a guard context.

With these issues in mind, it should now be clear why we chose to support multiple criteria of purity in our analysis. The guard in the previous example is not a referentially transparent function and a more strict analysis would reject it. Other valid guard tests,

---

[1] Taken from the ERLANG manual "A node is an executing Erlang runtime system which has been given a name"[5, Chapter 12].

```
1> F = fun () when node() =:= nonode@nohost -> error;
         () -> {ok, node()}
      end.
#Fun<erl_eval.6.13229925>
2> F().
error
3> net_kernel:start([test@localhost]).
{ok,<0.36.0>}
(test@localhost)4> F().
{ok,test@localhost}
(test@localhost)5> net_kernel:stop().
ok
6> F().
error
```

Fig. 3. Example of a non-deterministic guard expression

e.g., functions like `erlang:node/1` and `erlang:length/1`, raise exceptions when called with invalid arguments outside of guard contexts. Obviously, we did not want to break any existing code with our extension. As can be seen from Table 6, there is a fair number of functions in existing ERLANG programs that our analyses classify as both pure and terminating and therefore it could enable their employment as a guard.

In our opinion, one of the biggest advantages that such a language extension has to offer, is the fact that it enables user-defined tests for abstract data types in guards. The problem with ADTs in ERLANG is that their structural information is exposed, as the language allows inspection through pattern matching and primitive type tests. Allowing arbitrary type tests as guards can help make code cleaner and could even discourage programmers from breaking ADT contracts. The example in Figure 4 illustrates the benefits of such an approach.

Prototype Implementation. To this end, we developed a proof of concept implementation on top of the ERLANG compiler. Two distinct aspects of the compilation process have been altered, while a third modification has been identified in the runtime system of Erlang/OTP. First of all, a compiler pass performing purity and termination analysis is placed in the compiler front-end, just after the pass which converts ERLANG source to CORE ERLANG. Additionally, errors regarding illegal guard expressions are silenced until the purity of the functions in question can be verified by looking up their values. Second, the compiler back-end needs to be changed, specifically the code generation stage up to the point where bytecode is produced. This was the trickiest part, since this compiler phase heavily relied on the assumption that only built-in functions might be called from within guard expressions. BIFs differ significantly from a regular ERLANG function call with respect to the bytecode that needs to be generated.

A third aspect we identified but have not implemented yet has to do with the ERLANG loader. As mentioned earlier, ERLANG is unique in that it supports loading new code while the system is still running. It should be evident that a check must be placed at this stage, to verify that the same properties hold for the newly loaded code as the code which was previously analyzed, specifically with regard to its purity and termination

```
foo(Set) ->
  case gb_sets:is_set(Set) of
    true ->
      handle_gb_set(Set);
    false ->
      case sets:is_set(Set) of
        true ->
          handle_set(Set);
        false ->
          error
      end
  end.
```

```
foo(Set) when gb_sets:is_set(Set) ->
  handle_gb_set(Set);
foo(Set) when sets:is_set(Set) ->
  handle_set(Set);
foo(_) ->
  error.
```

(a) Custom tests not allowed as guards   (b) When user-defined guards are allowed

Fig. 4. Two ways of writing a function that operates on different term representations when user-defined tests are forbidden as guards 4(a) and when they are allowed 4(b). The code is not only more succinct, but it is also significantly more clear. Writing the code of Figure 4(b) is something currently not possible in ERLANG.

characteristics, and take some appropriate action (e.g. refuse the re-loading or re-compilation of modules that depend on this code) if there is a difference. Other engineering issues not addressed in our current prototype have to do with optional user annotations of pure functions. Such annotations would make the programmer's intentions more explicit and could be further used by the code loader.

6   Related Work

Purity is a fundamental property of programming components, regardless of language. In this respect, it is a bit surprising that in the literature it is hard to locate descriptions of analyses that detect purity or papers that report statistical data about the purity aspects of programs. In particular, we are not aware of any published such works in the context of dynamically typed functional languages. Still, being able to determine side-effect freeness is important for optimisation, automatic parallelization, and for program transformation tools such as refactoring editors. No doubt many such systems probably contain analysis components that determine purity properties of programs of different degrees.

Statically typed languages on the other hand, usually encode purity information in their type system. One approach which may be employed in languages with imperative features is a *type and effect system* (see, e.g., Lucassen and Gifford's paper [6] or Chapter 3 in Pierce's book [8]). Such a system extends a traditional type system with information about how values are computed and the possible effects that expressions can have (such as their side-effects or the set of memory regions that may be modified as a result of their evaluation).

Conversely, practical constraints — such as efficient I/O operations — compel many purely functional programming languages to allow for impure operations, without violating their pure semantics. Different approaches have been explored, the most notable of which are the uniqueness type system of Clean and the monadic approach of Haskell. The equivalence between monads and effect systems has also been ascertained [12].

Clean is a general purpose, strongly typed, pure and lazy functional programming language. Clean handles side-effects and non-determinism by means of a *uniqueness typing* system [9, ch. 9]. This extends a traditional type system by allowing the user to specify that a given argument to a function is unique. Such an annotation guarantees the function will have private access to the argument, therefore destructively updating it will not violate the semantics of the function during the execution of the program. Besides side-effects, uniqueness typing can be used to convert pure operations to mutable state transformations without violating the pure semantics of the operation. With a uniqueness guarantee it is trivial to verify referential transparency, as the function will never be called with the same argument. Furthermore, any side-effects of the function will never influence another function in an unforeseen manner [11].

Haskell is similar to Clean in many respects. It is purely functional, strongly typed and also features non-strict evaluation. However, Haskell takes a different approach with respect to purity, utilizing the more general concept of *monads*. Like Clean, this information is reflected in the type system and can be automatically inferred by way of a type inference scheme. Besides side-effects, monads can be used to express more general, and not necessarily impure, computations [7].

BitC was developed as a systems programming language with the goal of supporting formal verification. Unlike the languages previously mentioned, BitC is not purely functional. It does however support user level type annotations regarding the purity of functions, by means of an effect type system [10, ch. 10]. Such annotations associate expressions with an effect type variable which can have a value of *pure*, *impure* or *unfixed*. By verifying that certain parts of a program are pure, the BitC compiler can safely perform certain kinds of optimisations, like automatic parallelization.

7   Concluding Remarks

In this paper, having presented the defining properties of impure functions according to three independent and progressively weaker criteria (presence of side-effects, dependency on the environment of execution and possibility of raising an exception), we described the design and implementation of a parameterized static analysis for determining such properties in the context of ERLANG. Our analysis is relatively simple, but it has very important consequences both for the optimisation and, more importantly, for the expressivity of ERLANG programs. As a direct result of the existence of our analysis, we are currently enhancing the ERLANG language with user-defined guards and have already developed a suitable patch to the compiler which can form the basis of the final implementation in Erlang/OTP.

In the course of testing our implementation, we have analyzed diverse code bases of significant size, providing concrete data regarding the current practices of ERLANG programmers with respect to purity. The percentage of functions classified as pure by our analysis ranges on average between 30% and 50% for the applications we examined. This percentage is significant considering that ERLANG is primarily a concurrent language. To the best of our knowledge, this is the first time that such data is reported in the literature, not only for ERLANG, but for any functional language where purity of functions is not captured by the type system.

Acknowledgements. We thank Patrick Maier and Phil Trinder for their detailed suggestion on how to show a run of the analysis on an example, which has clearly improved the presentation aspects of our work.

References

1. Agha, G.: Actors: A Model of Concurrent Computation in Distributed Systems. MIT Press, Cambridge (1986)
2. Barklund, J., Virding, R.: Erlang 4.7.3 reference manual (February 1999), `http://www.csd.uu.se/ftp/mirror/erlang/download/erl_spec47.ps.gz`
3. Carlsson, R., Gustavsson, B., Johansson, E., Lindgren, T., Nyström, S.O., Pettersson, M., Virding, R.: Core Erlang 1.0 language specification. Tech. Rep. 030, Information Technology Department, Uppsala University (November 2000)
4. Carlsson, R., Gustavsson, B., Nyblom, P.: Erlangs exception handling revisited. In: Proceedings of the ACM SIGPLAN Workshop on Erlang, pp. 16–26. ACM (2004)
5. Ericsson, A.B.: Erlang Reference Manual Users Guide, version 5.8 (June 2010), `http://www.erlang.org/doc/reference_manual/users_guide.html`
6. Lucassen, J.M., Gifford, D.K.: Polymorphic effect systems. In: Conference Record of the Fifteenth Annual ACM Symposium on Principles of Programming Languages, pp. 47–57. ACM, New York (January 1988)
7. Newbern, J.: All about monads, `http://www.haskell.org/all_about_monads/`
8. Pierce, B.C. (ed.): Advanced Topics in Types and Programming Languages. MIT Press, Cambridge (2005)
9. Plasmeijer, R., van Eekelen, M.: Clean Language Report, version 2.1 (November 2002), `http://clean.cs.ru.nl/download/Clean20/doc/CleanLangRep.2.1.pdf`
10. Shapiro, J., Sridhar, S., Doerrie, M.S.: The origins of the BitC programming language (April 2008), `http://www.bitc-lang.org/docs/bitc/bitc-origins.html`
11. de Vries, E., Plasmeijer, R., Abrahamson, D.M.: Uniqueness typing simplified. In: Chitil, O., Horváth, Z., Zsók, V. (eds.) IFL 2007. LNCS, vol. 5083, pp. 201–218. Springer, Heidelberg (2008)
12. Wadler, P.: The marriage of effects and monads. ACM SIGPLAN Notices 34(1), 63–74 (1999)

iTask as a New Paradigm
for Building GUI Applications

Steffen Michels, Rinus Plasmeijer, and Peter Achten

Institute for Computing and Information Sciences
Radboud University Nijmegen, P.O. Box 9010,
6500 GL Nijmegen, The Netherlands
s.michels@science.ru.nl, {rinus,p.achten}@cs.ru.nl

Abstract. The *iTask* system is a combinator library written in Clean offering a declarative, domain-specific language for defining workflows. From a declarative specification, a complete multi-user, web-enabled, workflow management system (WFMS) is generated. In the *iTask* paradigm, a workflow is a definition in which interactive elements are defined by editors on model values (abstracting from concrete GUI implementation details). The order of their appearance is calculated dynamically using combinator functions (abstracting from concrete synchronisation details). Defining interactive elements and the order of their appearance are also major concerns when programming GUI applications. For this reason, the *iTask* paradigm is potentially suited to program GUI applications as well. However, the *iTask* system was designed for a different application domain and lacks a number of key features to make it suited for programming GUI applications. In this paper, we identify these key features and show how they can be added to the *iTask* system in an orthogonal way, thus creating a new paradigm for programming GUI applications.

1 Introduction

Workflow management systems (WFMS) are software systems that coordinate, generate, and monitor tasks performed by human workers and computers. The *iTask* system [10] is a combinator library written in *Clean*, which offers a high-level, declarative, domain specific language for defining web-based workflows. Tasks are defined by typed, pure functions, and are dynamically calculated: the actual work to do can depend on the outcome of previous tasks. One can sequence tasks, create parallel tasks in all kinds of flavors, tasks can be defined recursively and can be higher order. User interaction points are editors on model values.

Due to the use of generic programming techniques, an *iTask* programmer does not need to worry about boilerplate programming, such as the handling of the communication between client and server, and the form rendering and handling of form updates on the browser. Thus, the *iTask* paradigm allows the programmer of a workflow to fully concentrate on its logic: the description of tasks and the dependencies between them.

J. Hage, M.T. Morazán (Eds.): IFL 2010, LNCS 6647, pp. 153–168, 2011.
© Springer-Verlag Berlin Heidelberg 2011

Programming GUI applications shares many concerns with programming work-flows: user interaction points need to be defined and their order of appearance needs to be controlled as well. However, existing approaches for programming GUI applications are very different from the *iTask* paradigm (see Section 5). Earlier ex-perience in using the *iTask* system to create an interactive application to explore extended state machine specifications [7] suggested that the *iTask* paradigm is suited to define GUI applications. However, essential features for defining GUIs are lacking in the current *iTask* system. Those shortcomings emerge from the dif-ferent nature of normal workflows and GUI applications. Typically, when the user fills in some form in the *iTask* system, she works on local data in a browser, and by pushing a button a value of required type is returned to the server. An average GUI application offers many more options for the user to choose from, using GUI elements like buttons, menus, and dialogs. It offers multiple interactive windows one can work on simultaneously. Information being modified is no longer local, because doing something in one window might affect the contents of another.

In this paper we identify the missing key features for GUI programming in the *iTask* system and show how they can be added orthogonally, thereby making the *iTask* paradigm fit for defining GUI applications. To obtain a GUI specification which is as declarative as possible, we realised that we had to restrict ourselves as well. We do not provide the programmer with fine-grained control over the layout of forms, dialogs, menus, and windows. Such information has to be defined separately, e.g. in style sheets. We also do not offer primitives for drawing on canvas but stick to handling forms with generically generated layouts and the like. The contributions of this paper are:

- We show that the *iTask* system can be extended to support programming GUI applications. The result is a new paradigm for programming GUI ap-plications in a declarative way, i.e., **only** data and processes (tasks) need to be defined.
- The extensions are fundamental GUI elements: windows that can be dynam-ically opened and closed, and user actions that are (dynamically) organized in buttons and menus.
- In the new system stand-alone web-based GUI applications can be created. The extensions are orthogonal to the *iTask* system, i.e. they do not alter existing workflow applications.
- *iTask* users can now work simultaneously on GUI tasks which share infor-mation. A change made by one worker is made visible to others, enabling new kinds of tasks such as chat or dashboard applications.

The remainder of this paper is organized as follows. First, in Section 2, the *iTask* system is introduced using a running example of a text editor. This is a somewhat unconventional example of a workflow. However, the goal is to illustrate both that the *iTask* system is potentially sufficiently powerful to express such kinds of GUI applications as well as pin-pointing its current shortcomings for that do-main. We introduce the required extensions to the iTask system step-by-step in Section 3 and apply them in the running example. In Section 4, we demonstrate that the extensions are orthogonal to *iTask* and create a multi-user workflow application that uses the GUI features. Related work is discussed in Section 5. We conclude and discuss future work in Section 6.

2 Introducing the iTask System

The *iTask* system is a monadic combinator library for specifying workflows. In Section 2.1 we give a concise overview of the library. We present in Section 2.2 the running example of a simple text editor. Further, we discuss what kind of functionality is missing in *iTask* for programming GUI applications.

2.1 Library Overview

The *iTask* library consists of *basic tasks*, representing the atomic actions the user can take, which can be composed to build complex workflows using *combinators*. Basic tasks that are used in the running example are:

```
updateInformation :: String String  a  → Task a | iTask a
enterInformation  :: String String     → Task a | iTask a
enterChoice       :: String String [a] → Task a | iTask a
```

Note that in *Clean* the arity of functions is shown explicitly by separating argument types by spaces instead of →. Every task in the system returns a value of abstract type `Task a` where `a` is some concrete type. The basic task `updateInformation` generates a form for a value of type `a`. The form is an editor: the user can inspect and alter the value arbitrarily many times. The programmer provides a short title and description to inform the user about the purpose of this editor. When the form is completed in the editor, the information committed by the user is turned into a value of type `a`. The *iTask* system automatically performs the necessary conversions, using generic functions for serialisation, generating user interfaces, updating and verifying values included in the type class `iTask`. The function `enterInformation` is the same except that the system generates a form with blank fields for entering a value of type `a`. The function `enterChoice` lets the user choose a value from a list of options.

Other basic tasks that we need are concerned with reading and writing values of type `a` in a database, using typed references of type `DBId a`:

```
createDB :: a              → Task (DBId a) | iTask a
readDB   :: (DBId a)       → Task a        | iTask a
writeDB  :: (DBId a) a     → Task a        | iTask a
```

iTask uses the monadic combinators `return`, `>>=`, and `>>|` to combine tasks:

```
return          :: a                        → Task a | iTask a
(>>=) infixl 1 :: (Task a) (a → Task b)    → Task b | iTask a & iTask b
(>>|) infixl 1 :: (Task a) (Task b)        → Task b | iTask a & iTask b
```

Finally, we need a combinator to compose tasks in parallel: `-&&-` performs both tasks and returns their combined result when both are terminated. The operator `@:` assigns a task to the indicated user:

```
(-&&-) infixr 4 :: (Task a) (Task b) → Task (a,b) | iTask a & iTask b
(@:)   infix  3 :: User     (Task a) → Task a      | iTask a
```

The *iTask* paradigm lets the programmer concentrate on defining the workflow processes and the data involved. The generic machinery takes care of building and handling forms, storing intermediate results, and keeping track of the application state.

2.2   Running Example: A Simple Text Editor

In order to investigate the suitability of the *iTask* paradigm for programming GUI applications, we perform a case study of a typical GUI application, viz. a single-user text editor. Although *iTask* was not designed for such a purpose, it is possible to create such an application. The case study pin-points the shortcomings of the *iTask* system for programming GUI applications.

First, we define the "global" state of the editor. Since we are dealing with a pure functional language, this state is explicitly passed from one task to another. The state consists of the current text and in which file it is stored, if at all:

```
:: State    =   State Note FileInfo
:: Note     =   Note String
:: FileInfo =   NotStored | StoredFile FileName
:: FileName :== String
derive class iTask State, FileInfo

initState   = State (Note "") NotStored
```

The current content is of type `Note` which contains a string. Type `Note` is predefined and represented in a browser by a multi-line text-area. To keep the example simple, only one file can be opened at a time. The current content is either stored in a file with given name or it is not yet stored. For any user defined type used in the iTask system, such as `State` and `FileInfo`, an instantiation of the generic iTask type class is needed. The compiler can derive them automatically. Initially the application starts with empty content that is not stored yet.

There are a number of different operations the user can perform on the state. Examples are: editing the content, replacing substrings, or saving the content. To let the user choose which action to perform, the task `enterChoice` (see Section 2.1) is used. The different actions are straightforwardly represented by string constants:

```
Edit :== "Edit Content"
New  :== "New"
...
allActions = [ Edit, New, Open, Save, SaveAs, ... ]
```

To actually perform those actions, `enterChoice` has to be put in sequence with a task performing the selected operation:

```
1 textEditorApplication = performAction initState
2
```

```
3  performAction :: State → Task Void
4  performAction state =
5    enterChoice "Choose Action" "Which action to perform?" allActions >>= λaction →
6    case action of
7      New      →                       performAction initState
8      Edit     → edit    state >>= performAction
9      Open     → openFile        >>= performAction
10     Save     → save    state >>= performAction
11     SaveAs   → saveAs  state >>= performAction
12     Replace  → replace state >>= performAction
13     Quit     →                       return Void
```

First, the user chooses an action (line 5). The resulting GUI is given in Figure 1a. When finished, the result **action** is inspected to dynamically determine how to proceed. If Quit is chosen, **performAction** terminates and returns Void (line 13). If the user requests editing a new file (New), **performAction** is called recursively with the initial state (line 7). Tasks for other purposes return an updated state which is used for the next recursion (lines 8–12). Hereafter the user can choose another action. The file operations are implemented using Clean's **StdFile** operations. Due to space limitations, we do not discuss their implementation, but restrict ourselves in the remainder of this paper to the **edit** and **replace** tasks.

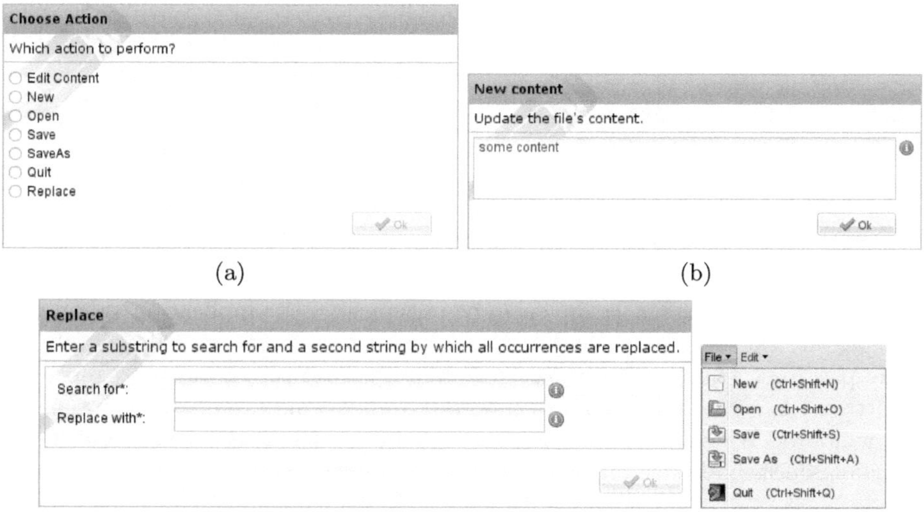

(a)   (b)

(c)   (d)

Fig. 1. Screenshots of the text editor example and the file menu

The task **edit** lets the user modify the current content stored inside the state:

```
edit :: State → Task State
edit (State content file) =
  updateInformation "New content" "Update the ..." content >>= λnewContent →
  return (State newContent file)
```

The current content is updated by the user, using the `updateInformation` task. The new content is returned in the new state. Figure 1b shows the corresponding GUI. In order to replace substrings, we need to know the search string and the replacement string. We derive a GUI for the appropriate type (see Figure 1c for a screenshot):

```
:: Replace = { searchFor :: String, replaceWith :: String }
derive class iTask Replace
```

Given a desired replacement, we can replace substrings in a `String`, `Note`, and `State` in a straightforward way:

```
class    replSubStr a :: Replace a → a
instance replSubStr String, Note, State
```

The task to replace substrings first asks the desired parameters, and applies the replacement function on the current note content of the state:

```
replace :: State → Task State
replace state =
  enterInformation "Replace" "Enter a substring to search for and..." >>= λr →
  return (replSubStr r state)
```

One might want to define conditions under which a certain action is possible. For instance, choosing `Replace` only makes sense for non-empty content. Because the task is dynamically generated at each recursion, this is easily achieved by making the list of actions depend on the current state:

```
allActions :: State → [String]
allActions (State (Note cont) _) =
    [Edit, New, Open, Save, SaveAs, Quit]
  ++ if (cont ≠ "") [Replace] []
```

The case study demonstrates that the *iTask* language is, in principle, powerful enough to describe all the functionality of this typical GUI application. However, the resulting application is an entirely untypical GUI application. Turn and turn about, the user must select an operation and must complete it fully to make progress. The user interface (selecting operations, editing text, replacing substrings) is scattered instead of integrated and being organized using menus and windows. We want to add menus and windows to *iTask* without sacrificing the conciseness and declarative nature of the above specification.

3 Extending the iTask System

We saw in the previous section that in *iTask* the user interface is scattered along the application instead of integrated and organized using common GUI elements such as menus and windows. In this section we show how to glue the scattered pieces together in order to obtain a system that is fit for GUI programming. These extensions are illustrated with the running text editor example to show their effect. The extensions are a significant design and implementation effort.

For this reason, we break down their discussion into smaller units. We start with adding the concept of actions, from which the user can choose, to the *iTask* editor concept (Section 3.1). The next step is to associate and organize editor actions with menus (Section 3.2). Before we can introduce multiple windows, we need to enable editors to listen to each other (Section 3.3). Once this has been done, we can introduce windows that can be added and closed dynamically (Section 3.4). The final step is to make menus also dynamic (Section 3.5).

3.1 Giving the User More Choices

The control flow of the text editor in Section 2.2 allowed the user to edit the text only after invoking a command to do so. It is more natural to regard the task for editing the content as a central task that offers a number of optional actions to complete this task. So, instead of offering only the standard 'commit' button to an editor, we extend the editing combinators with a list of optional actions to terminate the editor and commit its value. Here we give the variant of updateInformation:

```
updateInformationActions :: String String [TaskAction a] a → Task (Action, a)
                                                         | iTask a
```

A list of *task actions* of type TaskAction a is included. Besides the updated value of type a, the selected *action* of type Action is returned. (Note that if the list is empty, the user has no way to terminate the editor and can only edit the value. This will prove to be useful after we have taught editors to listen to each other in Section 3.3.) Before we explain the roles of these new types, we show the improved text editor:

```
1  textEditorApplication = performAction initState
2
3  performAction (State content file) =
4     edit content          >>= λ(action, nContent) →
5     let state = State nContent file
6     in case action of
7       ActionNew         →                 performAction initState
8       ActionOpen        → openFile    >>= performAction
9       ActionSave        → save    state >>= performAction
10      ActionSaveAs      → saveAs  state >>= performAction
11      Action "replace" _ → replace state >>= performAction
12      ActionQuit        →                 return Void
13 where edit            = updateInformationActions "Text Editor" "..." allActions
```

The structure is very similar to the structure of the text editor defined in Section 2.2. The available action options are now a parameter of the editing task (line 4 and 14). This emphasizes the central role of the editor. The result of the editor task is a tuple of the chosen termination action and updated content (line 4).

Each time an action is performed, the task is called recursively which generates an entire new user interface. However, the user interface is rendered as a form inside a browser and can be updated without producing a flickering window. Starting the same task recursively many times can be avoided by using grouped tasks running in parallel (see Section 3.4).

The type `TaskAction a` is defined in the library:

```
:: TaskAction a :== (Action, Selectable a)
:: Action        =    Action ActionID ActionLabel | ActionOk | ActionCancel | ...
:: ActionID      :== String
:: ActionLabel   :== String
:: Selectable a :== (Verified a) → Bool
:: Verified   a =    Invalid | Valid a
```

Instead of using only text labels, a list of task actions given to the editor task `updateInformationActions` adds an identification (`ActionID`) and a predicate (`Selectable a`) to each label. For convenience, we include a number of frequently used actions (`ActionOk`, `ActionCancel`, ...). Their appearance is dictated by the client platform. For custom defined actions, the text label appears in the user interface, and the action ID is used to identify the selected action. The selected `Action` is returned. The `Selectable a` predicate is a condition that determines whether an action is enabled or disabled. The condition is checked each time the value being edited is updated. The library contains a number of predefined conditions, such as `always`, `ifvalid` and `ifinvalid`. An editor can be in an invalid state if no value has been provided. The condition commonly depends on the state of the editor, hence it is parameterized with the value if valid. For instance, the replace-action is applicable only if the text is not empty. The editor actions can now be defined as:

```
allActions :: [TaskAction Note]
allActions = [ (ActionNew,     always), (ActionOpen, always), (ActionSave, always)
             , (ActionSaveAs, always), (ActionQuit, always)
             , (Action "replace" "Replace", notEmpty) ]
notEmpty (Valid (Note txt)) = txt ≠ ""
notEmpty _                  = False
```

The result of this step is that optional actions are integrated with the editor concept without reducing the declarative nature compared to the original specification.

3.2 Structuring Choices Using Menus

Instead of presenting a long list of buttons representing the optional actions, a more user-friendly and common solution is to use menus to organize the commands. Conceptually, they act just like buttons. We separate the definition of optional actions in a particular context from the way they are presented to the user: either in the shape of a button or as a menu item. The programmer can define the desired menu layout in a task annotation. By default, a button is generated for actions in the task not mentioned in the menu declaration. Actions mentioned in the menu annotation which are not defined in the task, are ignored.

Before explaining the extension, we show how to extend the running example with menus (Figure 1d illustrates the corresponding menus):

```
textEditorApplication = performAction initState <<@ StaticMenus menus
```

```
menus :: Menus
menus = [ Menu "File" [ MenuItem ActionNew    (hotkey N)
                      , MenuItem ActionOpen   (hotkey O)
                      , MenuItem ActionSave   (hotkey S)
                      , MenuItem ActionSaveAs (hotkey A)
                      , MenuSeparator
                      , MenuItem ActionQuit   (hotkey Q)
                      ]
        , Menu "Edit" [ MenuItem "replace"    (hotkey R) ]
        ]
hotkey key = Just {ctrl = True, alt = False, shift = True, key = key}
```

The overloaded *iTask* tuning combinator <<@ can be used to annotate arbitrary tasks, for example to change the initial worker or the priority. It is extended with an instance for menu annotations, defined as:

```
:: MenuAnnotation = NoMenus | StaticMenus Menus
```

The constructor NoMenus is added as a more readable way of using StaticMenus []. The menu structure is inherited by all children of that task, but can always be overridden with another annotation. For example, if a subtask should have no menus, it can be annotated with NoMenus.

The types available for defining menus are:

```
:: Menus     :== [Menu]
:: Menu      =   Menu MenuLabel [MenuItem]
:: MenuItem  =   ∃action: MenuItem action (Maybe Hotkey) & menuAction action
             |   SubMenu MenuLabel [MenuItem]
             |   MenuSeparator
:: MenuLabel :== String
:: Hotkey    =   { key :: Key, ctrl :: Bool, alt :: Bool, shift :: Bool }
:: Key       =   A | B | C | D | E | F | G | H | I | J | K | L | M | N | O | ...
```

The type variable action in the MenuItem data constructor is existentially quantified. The notation & menuAction action means that instances for a class menuAction are required and available within the data constructor for the existentially quantified action type. In this way, the programmer can choose to use the default Actions (ActionOk, ActionCancel, ...), ActionIDs, or a combination of ActionID and ActionLabel. For this purpose, instances have been defined for menuAction to map these items to their corresponding Action:

```
class menuAction :: a → (ActionID,ActionLabel)
instance menuAction Action, ActionID, (ActionID,ActionLabel)
```

In the first two cases the label shown in the menu is determined by the action given to the actual task the menu is built for. The last case is used to define another label. In this way items generating actions with the same ID but different

labels can be added to the menu. An example how this can be used is given in
Section 3.5.

3.3   A View on Shared State

In this section we discuss how parallel tasks can mutually influence each other.
This is required when constructing applications that handle a dynamic number
of windows. The actual creation of such tasks is discussed in Section 3.4. We illustrate mutual influence by means of the running example: instead of switching
between atomically editing the text and atomically replacing substrings in the
same text, we want both actions available at the same time and in an interleaved
way. While the edit task is running, any update of the text performed by invocations of the replace task (and also any other action) should update the text
within the edit task as well. Hence, these tasks need to *share* the same state.
Shared state is readily available in *iTask* by creating a database to the state,
obtaining a typed reference DBId State, and updating this with the derived task
updateDB[1]. The result is that all editor actions are parameterized with the shared
state instead of the state. In this way, replace can simply update the shared state:

```
replace :: (DBId State) → Task Void
replace ref =
  enterInformationActions "Replace" "Enter..." actions >>= λ(action, r) →
  case action of
    Action "replaceAll" _ → updateDB ref (replSubStr r) >>| return Void
    ActionClose           → return Void
where
  actions = [ (ActionClose, always)
            , (Action "replaceAll" "Replace All", ifvalid) ]
```

```
updateDB :: (DBId a) (a → a) → Task a | iTask a
updateDB ref f = readDB ref >>= λa → writeDB ref (f a)
```

To keep the edit task informed of updates to the shared state, we add the well-
known *model-view-controller* (MVC) concept [8] to *iTask*. In the case study, the
model is the state, and edit is a view (it is only interested in the text of the
state) on the state. The edit task registers itself as a view on this model in the
following way:

```
edit :: (DBId State) → Task Void
edit ref = updateShared "Text Editor" "..." [ActionQuit] ref view >>| return Void
where
  view :: Bimap State (Display String,Note)
  view = ( λ(State content info)       → (Display (title info),content)
         , λ(_,newContent) (State _ info) → State newContent info
         )
  title NotStore         = "New Text Document"
  title (StoreFile name) = name
```

---

[1] The *iTask* system ensures that all tasks a derived task is composed of is performed
as one atomic operation.

The difference with the previous version is that it is applied to a reference of the state, instead of the state value, and that it describes its view on the state with a separate bimap, defined by **view**. Here only the content part of the state is given as view to the user. Additionally a title is shown, wrapped by the special constructor **Display** to make it not editable.

Views are closely related to the theoretical concept of lenses [3]. The type class **SharedVariable** contains a new generic function that takes care of the automatic update of registered views whenever a shared value is modified. This generic function applies a merging algorithm in case of conflicting values. The signature of the function to register a viewer to a shared model value is an extension of the signature of **updateInformationActions** (Section 3.1):

```
updateShared :: String String [TaskAction a] (DBId a) (Bimap a v)
                        → Task (Event, a) | iTask a & iTask v & SharedVariable a
:: Bimap m v :== (m → v, v m → m )
```

We have shown how the tasks **replace** and **edit** can mutually influence each other. We have deliberately ignored the issue of creating these tasks in parallel. This is discussed in the next section.

3.4   Dynamic Task Groups

In general, a GUI application controls zero or more windows, which are dynamically created during the life-cycle of the application. Therefore, we need a means to identify a *group* of (windowed) tasks, the number of which can vary during execution. It is convenient to attach a set of global actions to a group which can be chosen even if no window is opened, in addition to the local actions which can be attached to each task individually. Before we discuss the details, we first adapt the running example to use this feature to dynamically create tasks:

```
 1 textEditorApplication =
 2   createDB initState >>= λref →
 3   dynamicGroup [edit ref] (allActions ref) (doAction ref) <<@ StaticMenus menus
 4
 5 allActions :: (DBId State) → [GroupAction Void]
 6 allActions ref = [ (ActionNew,    Always), (ActionOpen, Always), (ActionSave, Always)
 7                 , (ActionSaveAs, Always), (ActionQuit, Always)
 8                 , (Action "replace" "Replace", SharedPredicate ref notEmpty) ]
 9
10 doAction :: (DBId State) Action → DynAction
11 doAction ref action = case action of
12   ActionNew          → Extend [new      ref]
13   ActionOpen         → Extend [openFile ref]
14   ActionSave         → Extend [save     ref]
15   ActionSaveAs       → Extend [saveAs   ref]
16   ActionQuit         → Stop
17   Action "replace" _ → Extend [replace  ref]
```

The editor application starts initially with one task, the text editing task `edit` as presented in Section 3.3, that registers itself as a view on the current state (line 3). The list of editor actions, `allActions`, is now promoted to group actions because they are always available. Because the availability predicate for the `replace` task depends on a shared state, this function is parameterised with the proper reference. The group behaviour is defined with the function `doAction`. It is very similar to the case distinction in the earlier examples: the difference is that the list of chosen tasks given to `Extend` are dynamically added to the group. A separate window is created for every task thus created, such that one can work on all tasks simultaneously. The group, and all tasks in it, *terminate* when `Stop` is chosen. These are all alternatives of the `DynAction` type. A group is created with the `dynamicGroup` combinator:

```
:: DynAction = Extend [Task Void] | Stop
```

```
dynamicGroup :: [Task Void] [GroupAction Void] (Action → DynAction) → Task Void
```

It is applied to the tasks that initially belong to the group, the group actions, and the function that handles an action event. The group actions are similar to task actions, except that conditions on group actions do not depend on an edited value. Instead, they are either always possible, or when a predicate on the shared state is valid. In the GUI there is a menu bar for the entire group for triggering those group actions. Optionally, there is also a toolbar for buttons triggering actions not included in the menu. So group actions are handled in the same way as task actions.

The final part to discuss is to decide the rendering of the tasks `replace` and `edit`. For this purpose we introduce a new instance for the task annotation operator `<<@`:

```
:: GroupedBehaviour = Fixed | Floating | Modal
```

By annotating a task as `Fixed`, it displays its content in a fixed window; `Floating` tasks can be moved around by the user, and `Modal` tasks are shown in a modal dialog, forcing the user the finish this task before any other. Floating tasks inside the group have their own menu bar and buttons which are generated as usual. Fixed tasks have no menu bar of their own. Therefore, buttons are generated for all task actions. A screenshot illustrating a fixed editor task and a floating replace dialog is given in Figure 2.

3.5   Dynamic Menus

Sometimes one wants to dynamically extend a menu structure. An example is to extend the text editor with a menu for re-opening recently opened files. We model such a dynamic menu structure as a view on a state. The menu annotation (see Section 3.2) is extended with a third alternative. In this way the entire structure of the menu is determined dynamically:

```
:: MenuAnnotation = ... | ∃m: DynamicMenus (DBId m) (m → Menus) & iTask m
```

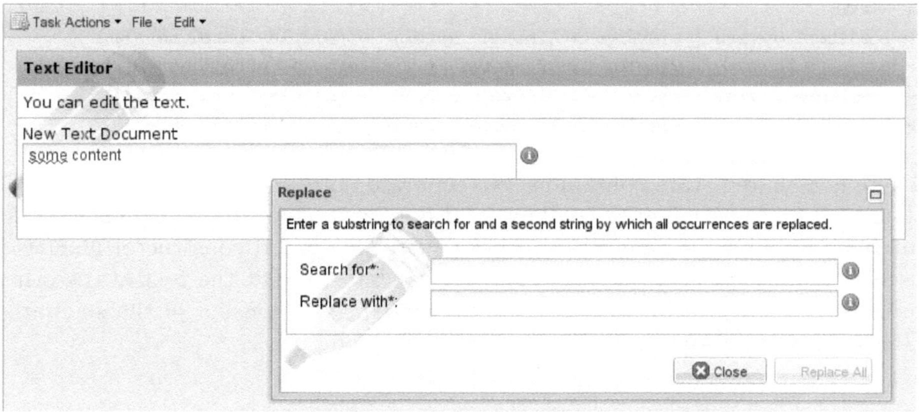

Fig. 2. A screenshot of the text editor GUI application

As an example, we extend the text editor with the above mentioned menu. We first extend the state with a history of recently opened file names:

```
:: State = State Note FileInfo [FileName]
```

We deploy the (ActionID,ActionLabel) instance of the menuAction class to pass the correct file name to be opened with an action with ID "openFile":

```
dynamicMenus ref (λ(State _ _ history) →
   [ Menu "File"  [ MenuItem ActionNew  (hotkey N)
                  , MenuItem ActionOpen (hotkey O)
                  , SubMenu "Recently opened" (recentItems history)
                  , ...
   ])
recentItems hs = [MenuItem ("openFile", fname) Nothing \\ fname ← hs]
```

4   Mixing Workflow and GUI

In the previous section we have presented the new features of *iTask* that are concerned with programming GUI applications. We emphasize that this has been done in an orthogonal way: existing *iTask* workflow definitions do not change because of these extensions. However, it is now possible for workflows to use the extended functionality. For instance, tasks providing views on the same shared state can be assigned to different users. This approach gives multi-user functionality for free. To illustrate this, we give an example of a simple chat program:

```
1 chat = createDB (Note "", Note "") >>= λref →
2   (NamedUser "user1" @: updateShared "Chat" "" [(ActionQuit,always)] ref [editor1])
3   -&&-
4   (NamedUser "user2" @: updateShared "Chat" "" [(ActionQuit,always)] ref [editor2])
```

```
5 where
6    editor1 = view { viewFrom = λ(note1, note2) → (Display note2,note1)
7                   , viewTo   = λ(_,note1) (_, note2) → (note1, note2) }
8    editor2 = view { viewFrom = λ(note1, note2) → (Display note1,note2)
9                   , viewTo   = λ(_,note2) (note1, _) → (note1, note2) }
```

There is a shared state containing two separate notes, one for each user to edit (line 1). Two tasks assigned to different users are started (line 2, 4). Those tasks provide views on the same state (lines 6–9). The special constructor **Display** is used to make sure that one user can only see but not edit the text of the other user. In this way editing conflicts are prevented. A screenshot of the generated GUI is given in Figure 3.

Fig. 3. A screenshot of the chat example

5   Related Work

There already exist many proposals and libraries for defining GUIs in a functional language. A detailed comparison is out of scope of this paper. Instead we choose, for each of the different paradigms, a number of representative approaches.

A large number of approaches have adopted the traditional widget-callback GUI paradigm (e.g., *Object I/O* [1] and *wxHaskell* [9]). Here, the programmer is responsible for the entire life-cycle of the GUI elements: creation, management, event handling, and destruction. This style of programming mixes up the visualisation, the program logic, the processed data, and the current state of the application. Comparing to the enhanced *iTask* approach, we find that the code of the former approaches is harder to understand and maintain.

Other approaches make better use of the level of abstraction provided by functional languages. Programmers compose the user interface in a declarative way using basic elements and are freed from explicitly managing them. There are different approaches for realizing interaction between different components. In *Haggis* [6] each component is treated as a virtual I/O device. User events are represented by messages generated by components, e.g., buttons. Additionally, a separation between the user interface and the application, i.e., between the representation and the actual value or interaction with the user, is made. *Fudgets* [4] uses the model of *stream processors* to represent GUI elements. They pass messages and are hierarchically combined to build up the application. There is no explicitly shared state. State is realised by routing messages between components. An even more formal model of continuous time-varying *signals* transformed by pure *signal transformers* is used by *Fruit* [5]. A drawback of the formal model used by *Fruit* is that all kinds of I/O must explicitly be added to the input and output signal. The *iData toolkit* [11] models web-applications as interconnected forms. *Generic programming* techniques [2] are used to automatically generate forms for editing values for any type. This allows for a way of modelling applications which abstracts from the visualisation.

In all these approaches the programmer has to handle the application's execution state manually. Having the possibility to define the control flow in a declarative way is a unique advantage of the *iTask* paradigm.

6   Conclusions and Future Work

We have shown that the workflow-based *iTask* system can be used as a paradigm for building GUI applications. Because the *iTask* system was originally designed for managing workflows, this involved a significant implementation effort to add the required features. One reason is that dealing with tasks sharing data generates extra dependencies between them which required changing the way tasks are calculated. Also the way the state of parallel tasks is handled had to be changed since tasks can be added dynamically. A last point is that on each change not the entire GUI is replaced but update instructions generated by the server are used to adapt only changed parts (details are explained in [10]). Form fields being changed by the underlying data model and dynamically added forms also required extending this mechanism.

One design goal was to retain the level of abstraction as offered by the *iTask* system. When defining GUI applications, programmers only have to define the processed data and the application's control flow in the same spirit as with the 'original' *iTask* system. They are freed from manually handling the application's execution state. Dependencies between the application's state and the user interface are declaratively defined using predicates and views. The system automatically creates proper GUIs, stores intermediate results, and keeps track of the execution state.

Another advantage is that applications are embedded in the web-based *iTask* WFMS. All work the user performs is synchronised with a server. The user can stop working at any moment and continue on any (other) computer. Also, applications can be used as part of a workflow, and, vice versa, workflow functionality can be used by GUI applications. In this way implementing multi-user GUI applications comes for free.

Although generically generated GUIs are very powerful, for some applications one might want to influence the layout more precisely. One direction for future work is to develop a way to influence the layout with more fine-grained annotations in the same spirit as done for menus.

We want to conduct more case studies. Examples are sophisticated GUI components, and applications that use huge amounts of data such as spreadsheet applications. Also, multi-user applications are good candidates since one gets much functionality from the WFMS for free. Multi-user applications more easily lead to editing conflicts. A good error reporting and recovery system has to be explored.

Acknowledgements. We would like to thank the anonymous referees and Bas Lijnse and Thomas van Noort for their valuable comments.

References

1. Achten, P., Plasmeijer, R.: Interactive functional objects in Clean. In: Clack, C., Hammond, K., Davie, T. (eds.) IFL 1997. LNCS, vol. 1467, pp. 304–321. Springer, Heidelberg (1998)
2. Alimarine, A.: Generic Functional Programming - Conceptual Design, Implementation and Applications. PhD thesis. Radboud University Nijmegen (2005)
3. Bohannon, A., Pierce, B.C., Vaughan, J.A.: Relational lenses: a language for updatable views. In: PODS 2006: Proceedings of the twenty-fifth ACM SIGMOD-SIGACT-SIGART symposium on Principles of database systems, pp. 338–347. ACM, New York (2006)
4. Carlsson, M., Hallgren, T.: FUDGETS - A Graphical User Interface in a Lazy Functional Language. In: FPCA 1993 - Conference on Functional Programming Languages and Computer Architecture, pp. 321–330. ACM Press, New York (June 1993)
5. Courtney, A., Elliott, C.: Genuinely functional user interfaces. In: Haskell Workshop, pp. 41–69 (September 2001)
6. Finne, S., Jones, S.P.: Composing the user interface with Haggis. In: Launchbury, J., Sheard, T., Meijer, E. (eds.) AFP 1996. LNCS, vol. 1129, pp. 26–30. Springer, Heidelberg (1996)
7. Koopman, P., Achten, P., Plasmeijer, R.: Validating specifications for model-based testing. In: Arabnia, H., Reza, H. (eds.) Proceedings of the International Conference on Software Research and Practice, SERP 2008, Las Vegas, NV, USA, July 14-17, pp. 231–237. CSREA Press (2008)
8. Krasner, G.E., Pope, S.T.: A cookbook for using the model view controller user interface paradigm in Smalltalk-80. Journal of Object-Oriented Programming 1(3), 26–49 (1988)
9. Leijen, D.: wxHaskell: a portable and concise gui library for Haskell. In: Haskell 2004: Proceedings of the 2004 ACM SIGPLAN workshop on Haskell, pp. 57–68. ACM, New York (2004)
10. Lijnse, B., Plasmeijer, R.: iTasks 2: iTasks for End-users. In: Morazán, M., Scholz, S.-B. (eds.) IFL 2009. LNCS, vol. 6041, pp. 36–54. Springer, Heidelberg (2010)
11. Plasmeijer, R., Achten, P.: iData for the world wide web - programming interconnected web forms. In: Hagiya, M. (ed.) FLOPS 2006. LNCS, vol. 3945, pp. 242–258. Springer, Heidelberg (2006)

Improving Your CASH Flow:
The *C*omputer *A*lgebra *SH*ell

Christopher Brown[1], Hans-Wolfgang Loidl[2], Jost Berthold[3],
and Kevin Hammond[1]

[1] School of Computer Science, University of St. Andrews, UK
{chrisb,kh}@cs.st-andrews.ac.uk
[2] School of Mathematical and Computer Sciences, Heriot-Watt University, UK
hwloidl@macs.hw.ac.uk
[3] DIKU Department of Computer Science, University of Copenhagen, Denmark
berthold@diku.dk

Abstract. This paper describes CASH (the Computer Algebra SHell),
a new interface that allows Haskell programmers to access the complete
functionality of a number of computer algebra systems directly and interactively. Using CASH, Haskell programmers can access previously-
unavailable mathematical software. Additionally, users of computer algebra systems can exploit the rapidly growing Haskell code base and its
rich set of libraries. In particular, CASH provides a simple and effective interface for users of computer algebra systems to parallelise their
algorithms using domain-specific *skeletons* written in Haskell.

1   Introduction

Users of functional programming languages can often feel as if they are in a
ghetto. While foreign-function interfaces (FFIs) often exist to, e.g., C, they can,
indeed, feel foreign to use, especially where complex data structures are involved.
And while library developers work hard to provide new functionality to functional programmers, this hard-won capability often bit-rots faster than it can
be used effectively. As part of an EU-funded project[1], we have been working to
address some of these issues (and, incidentally, to provide a new user base for
functional languages). In this way, we hope to open the gates to the ghetto of
functional programming, and break some of the barriers preventing wider use.

This paper describes a new way to link Haskell [1] with computer algebra
systems, avoiding the FFI route. CASH (the Computer Algebra SHell) provides
a two-way interface to a number of widely-used computer algebra systems, including GAP [2], KANT [3], MuPAD[4], Maple [5], and Macaulay [6]. In order
to achieve this, it exploits the generic SCSCP [7] protocol that has been implemented for all these systems. This, in turn, uses the *OpenMath* [8] standard
format to describe the structure of mathematical objects.

---

[1] SCIEnce: Symbolic Computation Infrastructure in Europe, RII3-CT-2005-026133.

J. Hage, M.T. Morazán (Eds.): IFL 2010, LNCS 6647, pp. 169–184, 2011.
© Springer-Verlag Berlin Heidelberg 2011

Interfacing between (an interactive shell for) Haskell and computer algebra systems has several advantages. First, these systems are *domain-specific environments* that provide a large number of specialised data-types and that build on decades of expert experience. For instance, the open source system GAP [2] comes with a library of complex computer algebra algorithms that have been contributed by hundreds or thousands of domain experts. Exploiting existing optimised environments such as GAP from within Haskell increases programmer productivity since the Haskell programmer does not have to learn the mathematics behind the code. Providing an interface to Haskell from within a computer algebra system allows advanced features to be accessed, such as Haskell's parallelisation capabilities. The domain expert does not have to learn about parallel programming: they can use their favourite computer algebra system.

Contributions. The main technical contributions of this paper are as follows:

1. we show how CASH can be used to integrate Haskell and computer algebra code using SCSCP and OpenMath, giving examples that show how CASH can be used to call computer algebra systems from Haskell and vice-versa;
2. we show how to define *domain-specific* parallel skeletons for computer algebra in the Eden [9] dialect of Haskell, in particular, we describe a new *multiple homomorphic images skeleton*; and
3. we expose these parallel skeletons as SymGrid-Par [10] services, that can be called directly both from the CASH shell and from within the shell of any SCSCP-enabled computer algebra client.

The idea of interfacing functional languages and computer algebra systems is, of course, not new. For example, GHC-Maple [11] and Eden-Maple [12] provide dedicated sequential and parallel interfaces, respectively, to the commercial Maple system. However, CASH goes beyond these earlier approaches in terms of both usability and generality: CASH uses a Haskell implementation of the standardised OpenMath-based SCSCP [7] interface, which means that it can interact with *any* computer algebra system that implements the SCSCP standard; moreover, it also allows *any* SCSCP-compliant system to interact with Haskell.

2   Linking Haskell and Computer Algebra Systems

CASH uses the GHCi interpreter to provide a Haskell-side shell for accessing computer algebra systems via SCSCP. The underlying libraries provide data structures and conversion functions targeted at computer algebra, plus a "command line API" for an interactive front end, that is used to establish a connection to, and interact with, an SCSCP-enabled system. To show how powerful, expressive, and useful the CASH system can be, we will consider a simple example involving matrix groups over *finite fields*. We first define two matrices, m1 and m2 over the finite field $\mathbb{Z}_3 = \{0, 1, 2\}$, interactively, using the CASH shell

```
*Cash> let m1 = [[Z(3)^0, Z(3)^0],[Z(3),0*Z(3)]]
*Cash> let m2 = [[Z(3),  Z(3)],[Z(3),0*Z(3)]]
```

Here we have used the GAP-like syntax Z(3) for the element which generates the multiplicative group in the finite field $\mathbb{Z}_3$, 0*Z(3) for the 0-element and Z(3)^0 for the 1-element. Using CASH, we can directly exploit any of the GAP functions on group algebra. Here we compute the multiplicative matrix groups generated by each of these two matrices and then determine their intersection.

```
*Cash> group(m1)
Group([ [ [ Z(3)^0, Z(3)^0 ], [ Z(3), 0*Z(3) ] ] ])
*Cash> group(m2)
Group([ [ [ Z(3), Z(3) ], [ Z(3), 0*Z(3) ] ] ])
*Cash> intersection(group(m1), group(m2))
Group([ [ [ Z(3), 0*Z(3) ], [ 0*Z(3), Z(3) ] ] ])
```

The generator of the intersection is the unit matrix multiplied by the scalar Z(3). Note that the result of each group operation is simply a symbolic representation of the result in terms of one or more generators, rather than an enumeration of all possible elements of the group. This is important, because the number of elements in a group can be huge and the user is usually only interested in some specific properties of the group. We can often determine these properties without needing to generate all the elements of the group. This dramatically reduces the amount of computation that is required.

2.1   The SCSCP Interface

The interface between a client and a server is defined by the SCSCP communication protocol [7], which itself builds on the existing OpenMath standard [8] for data representation of mathematical objects. The SCSCP communication protocol defines how messages are exchanged between client and server processes. Its main functionality is to support (remote) calls of SCSCP server-side services and to deliver results to the SCSCP client. In order to support automatic service discovery, the protocol also specifies how to obtain a list of all the available services that are supported by the SCSCP server, including their types.

Figure 1 shows a CASH session interacting with a GAP server using SCSCP. The CASH session first connects to GAP with a **Procedure Call** message, containing information such as the *Procedure name*, any *Arguments* and any *Options/Attributes*, encoded in OpenMath. Alternatively, the user may **interrupt** the interaction at any time between the computer algebra system and the server. In this case the computation terminates and no result is returned. The GAP server responds to the CASH client by sending a **Procedure Completed** message: an OpenMath encoding containing the information about the result of the procedure. This message contains the (OpenMath) *Result value*; any *Mandatory Additional Information*, such as the internal SCSCP call identifier; and any *Optional additional information*, such as the procedure runtime/memory usage. Alternatively, the GAP server may instead return a **Procedure Terminated** message containing an *Error* message. The CASH user-level interface is provided by the callSCSCP function, which takes a service name and a list of *OpenMath* objects as arguments and issues an SCSCP call to the server. To simplify this

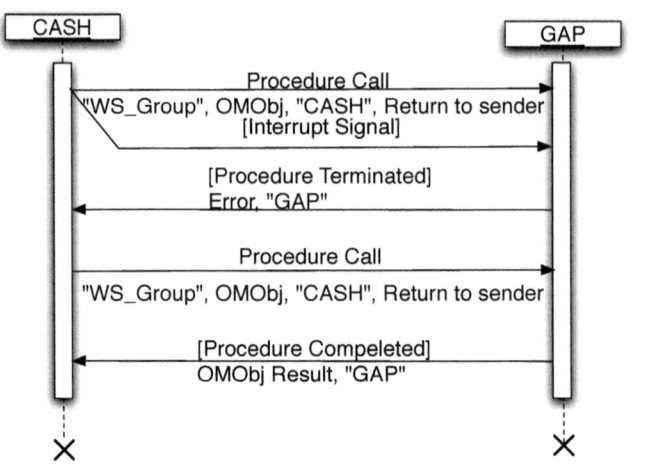

Fig. 1. An example interaction between CASH and GAP using SCSCP

interface, a family of functions `call1`, `call2` etc. are defined, which hide the
(un)marshalling of the data-structures. Specifically, `call1` is used to connect
with SCSCP functions that take one argument, `call2` is used to SCSCP functions
taking two arguments, and so forth. These functions differ only in their arity,
and could be automatically generated using tools such as Template Haskell.

2.2   The OpenMath Data Format

The OpenMath [8] data format is an XML-based representation of mathematical objects such as polynomials, finite field elements, or permutations. Formally,
an OpenMath object is a labelled tree whose leaves form typical computer algebra type representations. These include integers, unicode strings, variables,
or symbols, where *symbols* consist of a name and a *content dictionary*. For instance, a vector of finite field elements `[[Z(3)^0,Z(3)^0]]` can be encoded in
the OpenMath representation shown in Figure 2. This uses the `linalg2` content
dictionary to define `matrix` and `matrixrow`.

3   Calling GAP from Haskell and Vice-Versa

We now give two examples of using CASH that show the usefulness of being
able to call computer algebra functionality from a Haskell environment without
having to step out of the functional paradigm.

3.1   Greatest Common Divisor

Our first, simple, example shows how to implement a generic greatest common
divisor (GCD) function by first calling existing factorisation functions in the

```
<OMOBJ>
    <OMA> <OMS cd="linalg2" name="matrix"/>
         <OMA> <OMS cd="linalg2" name="matrixrow"/>
              <OMA> <OMS cd="arith1" name="power"/>
                   <OMA> <OMS cd="finfield1" name="primitive_element"/>
                        <OMI>3</OMI>
                   </OMA>
                   <OMI>0</OMI>
              </OMA>
              <OMA> <OMS cd="arith1" name="power"/>
                   <OMA> <OMS cd="finfield1" name="primitive_element"/>
                        <OMI>3</OMI>
                   </OMA>
                   <OMI>0</OMI>
              </OMA>
         </OMA>
    </OMA>
</OMOBJ>
```

Fig. 2. An example of an OpenMath encoding for finite field elements

computer algebra system (here, GAP) and by then combining the results in Haskell. Although this operation is fairly trivial in itself, it highlights some important design features: first, we use Haskell's overloading mechanism to define a generic GCD implementation; and second, the compute-intensive parts (that is, the factorisation and polynomial operations) are all delegated to the computer algebra system using SCSCP services. The myGcd algorithm first factors the inputs x and y. It then perfoms a bag-intersection on the Haskell side, to identify all the common factors. Finally, the GCD is computed by performing the product over the list of common factors.

```
-- intersection on multi-sets (bags)
bagInter :: (Eq a) => [a] -> [a] -> [a]
bagInter [] _ = []
bagInter (x:xs) ys | elem x ys = x:(bagInter xs (delete x ys))
                   | otherwise = bagInter xs ys

-- generic GCD computation
myGcd :: (Num a, Factorisable a) => a -> a -> a
myGcd x y = let  xs = factors x
                 ys = factors y
                 zs = xs `bagInter` ys
            in product zs
```

Marshalling and UnMarshalling Polynomials In order to use the algorithm on polynomials in the computer algebra system, we need to define their OpenMath representation, as part of the `OMType` type. We currently implement `Polynomials` as Haskell `Strings`, since it is usually easy to convert strings to polynomials in the computer algebra system.

```
data OMType = List [OMType]  | Rational [OMType] | Matrix [OMType]
            | MatrixRow [OMType] | Mul FiniteField Int
            | Power FiniteField Int | Num Integer
            | Polynomial String
            | ...
data FiniteField = PrimEl Int
```

Basic operations on polynomials are implemented via SCSCP calls to the corresponding SCSCP services. These calls use the `call2` wrapper function, which implicitly applies `toOM`/`fromOM` to convert data to/from values of type `OMType`.

```
instance  Num (OMType) where
  (*) p1@(Polynomial _) p2@(Polynomial _) = call2 scscp_WS_ProdPoly p1 p2
  (*) ...
  (+) p1@(Polynomial _) p2@(Polynomial _) = call2 scscp_WS_SumPoly p1 p2
  (+) ...
```

Factorising Polynomials We can now write Haskell code that calls computer algebra functions to factorise polynomials. The `Factorisable` class contains a single function `factors` that returns a list of all the factors of a given argument.

```
class Factorisable a where
  factors :: a -> [a]
```

We can easily define an instance of this class for polynomials that invokes the corresponding computer algebra service, as follows:

```
instance Factorisable (OMType) where
  factors = call1 scscp_WS_Factors
```

An Example CASH Session The trace below shows how CASH can be used with our GCD implementation. We define two simple input polynomials `p1` and `p2` and compute their GCD in Haskell using GAP polynomial operations.

```
*Cash> let p1 = polyFromString "x_1^3-x_1"
*Cash> factors p1
[x_1-1,x_1,x_1+1]
*Cash> let p2 = polyFromString "x_1^2+x_1"
*Cash> factors p2
[x_1,x_1+1]
*Cash> myGcd p1 p2
x_1^2+x_1
```

3.2   A Linear System Solver

We now show how CASH can connect to GAP to run more serious computer algebra computations. Given a linear system of equations over arbitrary precision integers, represented as a matrix $A \in \mathbb{Z}^{n \times n}$ and a vector $b \in \mathbb{Z}^n$, $n \in \mathbb{N}$, we want to find a vector $x \in \mathbb{Z}^n$ such that $Ax = b$. As is common for symbolic computations, and in contrast to the more usually encountered numerical algorithms, we need to produce an *exact* solution for arbitrary precision integers.

Multiple Homomorphic Images. A potential problem in solving a system of linear equations is that the values in the matrix tend to become very large, meaning that even simple arithmetic operations can become expensive to compute. A common way to avoid this is to use a technique known as Multiple Homomorphic Images [13]. In order to control the size of the matrix elements, a solver based on homomorphic images will use a list of prime numbers, generate new matrices modulo each prime, find the solutions to these smaller problems, and finally combine these solutions using the Chinese Remainder algorithm (CRA). The general *multiple homomorphic images* approach [13] consists of the following three stages, where the names in parentheses refer to the Haskell skeleton below:

1. map the input data into several homomorphic images (`fwd`);
2. compute the solution in each of these images (`sol`); and
3. combine the results of all images to a result in the original domain (`comb`).

In this case the original domain is $\mathbb{Z}$, the set of (arbitrary precision) integer values, and the homomorphic images are $\mathbb{Z}$ modulo p, written $\mathbb{Z}_p$, with p being a prime number. If suitably large prime numbers are chosen, then cheap fixed-precision arithmetic can be used for each of the homomorphic images. It is only necessary to use expensive arbitrary precision arithmetic in the combination phase, when applying the Chinese Remainder Algorithm [14] in Step (3). Thus, this is already a very efficient sequential algorithm. It also has many uses. For example, it allows us to solve a wide class of problems over Euclidean domains and can be used to compute multivariate resultants.

A Multiple Homomorphic Images skeleton. It is straightforward to define a skeleton in Haskell to compute multiple homomorphic images:

```
multHomImg :: (Integer    -> OMType -> OMType) ->
              (Integer    -> OMType -> OMType) ->
              ([Integer] -> OMType -> OMType) ->
              [Integer] -> OMType -> OMType
multHomImg fwd sol comb ps x = res
  where xList   = zipWith fwd ps (repeat x)
        resList = zipWith sol ps xList
        res     = comb ps (toOMMatrix resList)
```

The local definitions are each the result of one of the three steps above. The lists of inputs, `xList`, and solutions in the homomorphic images, `resList`, are both (potentially infinite) lists. The combiner, `comb` is allowed to ignore the tail of the possibly infinite list ps. This design uses Haskell's laziness to avoid hard-coding a bound on the list lengths into the skeleton itself. Since data marshalling in SCSCP is eager, however, these lists have to be finite when using SCSCP calls in a concrete instance of the skeleton. Only data structures that remain on the Haskell side can be infinite.

The Linear Solver. We can use this skeleton to define a linear system solver:

```
linearSolver :: [ Integer ] -> [ [Integer] ] -> [ Integer ] -> OMType
linearSolver ps ms vs
  = multHomImg (call2 scscp_WS_Mod) (call2 scscp_WS_Sol)
              (call2 scscp_WS_CRA) ps
              (toOMList ((toMatrix ms):[toOMList (map toNum vs)]))
```

The functions scscp_WS_Mod, scscp_WS_Sol and scscp_WS_CRA are *SCSCP* calls to the GAP functions ModMat, SolMat and CRAMat, respectively. ModMat takes a prime number, a matrix and a vector and returns the matrix and the vector modulo the prime number.

```
ModMat:=function(p, x)
    return([x[1] mod p, x[2] mod p]);
end;
```

Here, x is a GAP list containing both the matrix and the vector, so x[1] accesses the matrix and x[2] accesses the vector. SolMat computes the solution for a matrix and vector modulo a prime number. The interesting thing here is that the GAP code computes the modulus by transforming the vector and matrix to an element in a finite field of p elements, where p is a prime number. The function checks that the determinant of the matrix is not 0 and returns the empty list if so, since there would be no solution otherwise. To compute the solution for a matrix and a vector in GAP we use the builtin library function SolutionMat.

```
SolMat:=function(p, x)
  local e, r;
  e:=One(GF(p));
  if Determinant(x[1]*e) = 0*Z(p) then
    return([]);
  fi;
  r:=SolutionMat(TransposedMat(x[1]*e),x[2]*e);
  return(List(r, Int));
end;
```

Finally, CRAMat combines the result vectors using GAP's built-in Chinese Remainder algorithm which works over (finite) lists. We also need to eliminate any empty matrices that were generated by 0-determinants in the SolMat stage:

```
CRAMat:=function(ps, r)
  local i, pris, vecs, res;
  i:=0;
  vecs:=[];
  while ( i < Length(r) ) do
    if not r[i] =  [] then
       pris:=Concatenation(pris, ps[i]);
       vecs:=Concatenation(vecs, r[i]);
    fi;
    i:=i+1;
  od;
  res:=ChineseRem(pris, vecs);
  return res;
end;
```

Testing the solver in CASH. For the purposes of this example, we will generate a random 1000 x 1000 matrix, together with a 1000 element vector of solutions.

```
*Cash> let m = generateMatrix(1000)
*Cash> let v = generateVector(1000)
```

We can then compute $m \times v$ to form b, and test the solution in CASH:

```
*Cash> let b = m * v
*Cash> (linearSolver [1009, 10007, 100003, 1000003] m b) == v
True
```

We note that the operator (*) is *overloaded* here so that it actually calls the GAP (*) operator on matrices.

4   Using CASH to Enhance Parallelism

Using one of the several available parallel Haskell implementations, such as the one that is provided with GHC, it is easy to parallelise the multiple homomorphic images skeleton from Section 3.2. We can then make this available to computer algebra users through the CASH interface. Hitherto most computer algebra systems have limited, if any, support for parallelism. Therefore, a Haskell-side parallel skeleton which is accessible to the computer algebra user in this way is a major advantage of our design. Here we use the Eden parallel dialect of Haskell which targets parallel clusters. Using Eden, we can simply transform the original skeleton, which called the sequential `zipWith` function, into an equivalent parallel version that uses `parZipWith` instead.

```
multHomImg fwd sol comb ps x = res
   where xList = zipWith fwd ps (repeat x)
         resL  = parZipWith sol ps xList
         res   = comb ps (toOMMatrix resL)
```

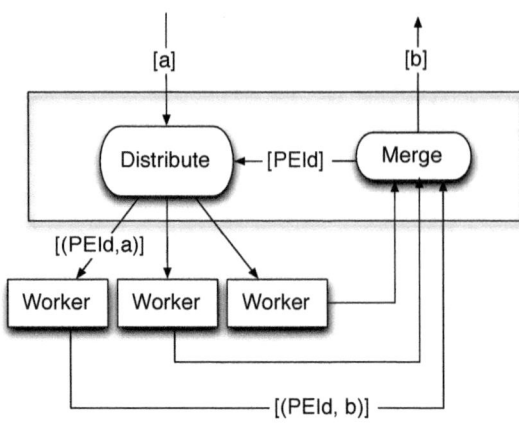

Fig. 3. The workpool skeleton

A parallel zipWith skeleton The `parZipWith` skeleton uses a *workpool* [15] approach (see Figure 3). Workpools are commonly used where tasks have varying granularities, to dynamically balance the allocation of tasks to processors.

```
parZipWith f l1 l2 = newTasks
  where
    (newReqs, newTasks) = ...
    workerProcs = [process (zip [pe,pe..].(worker f))| pe <- [1..noPe]]
    worker f [] = []
    worker f ((v1, v2) : ts) = (f v1 v2) : worker f ts
```

The `parZipWith` skeleton creates one `worker` process for each available processor (PE), where each worker process applies `f` to a pair of two arguments in a curried way. Each of these processes is executed in parallel using the Eden `process` construct. The identifier `workerProcs` defines this set of worker processes and pairs each result with the id of the PE, `pe`, that produced it. This is used by the skeleton to determine which PEs have surplus capacity.

```
(newReqs, newTasks) = (unzip . merge) (zipWith ( # ) workerProcs
                            (distributeLists (l1, l2) requests))
requests = (concat (replicate 2 [1..noPe])) ++ newReqs
```

The skeleton pairs the input tasks (the pairs of arguments to the worker function `f`) with a list of *requests*. The `requests` value is a list of process ids that is used to map tasks to processes. Each task is paired with a process id using the `distributeLists` function and these ids are then used to assign the task to the corresponding Eden process. The results of the Eden processes executing the tasks can be merged using Eden's non-deterministic `merge` operation and then unzipped to give the lists of new requests, `newReq`, and new tasks, `newTasks`.

The distributeLists function simply accumulates the tasks for each PE in an ordered list so that these can be passed on to the correct worker process.

```
distributeLists tasks reqs = [taskList reqs tasks n | n <- [1..noPe]]
   where taskList (r:rs) (v1:vs1, v2:vs2) pe
              | pe == r   =   (v1, v2) : (taskList rs (vs1, vs2) pe)
              | otherwise =   taskList rs (vs1, vs2) pe
           taskList _ _ _ = []
```

Modifying the GAP functions. For the linear solver, the results need to be ordered so that they can be combined correctly. Since not all instances of the multiple homomorphic pattern will require this ordering, we offload it to the relevant GAP functions. We therefore also need to modify the GAP function ModMat so that it returns a pair of the solution vector and the prime. This pair is implicitly passed through the skeleton so that in the combination phase the CRAMat function first sorts the pairs by their prime numbers before computing the Chinese Remainder algorithm. The modified GAP functions are as follows:

```
SolMat:=function(p, x)
 ...
 return([List(r, Int), p]);
end;

CRAMat:=function(ps, r)
local x, pris, vecs, res;
pris:=[];
vecs:=[];
for x in r do
 if not x = [] then
    pris:=Concatenation(pris,[x[2]]);
    vecs:=Concatenation(vecs,[x[1]]);
 fi;
od;
res:=ChineseRem(pris, vecs);
return(res);
end;
```

Performance. In order to demonstrate the effectiveness of the parallel performance of the skeleton, we tested it on several sample matrices of 200 x 200 17-digit elements. Experimentation shows a 1.795 speedup on 2 cores over the original sequential version of the skeleton discussed in Section 3.2. Clearly, these early results show that the skeleton can be used to increase the performance of the linear solver and, more importantly, the speedup shows that parallel skeletons can be an effective way of increasing the performance of computer algebra systems. Indeed, our domain-specific *orbit* skeleton has previously shown a maximum speedup of 8.295 on eight cores [16].

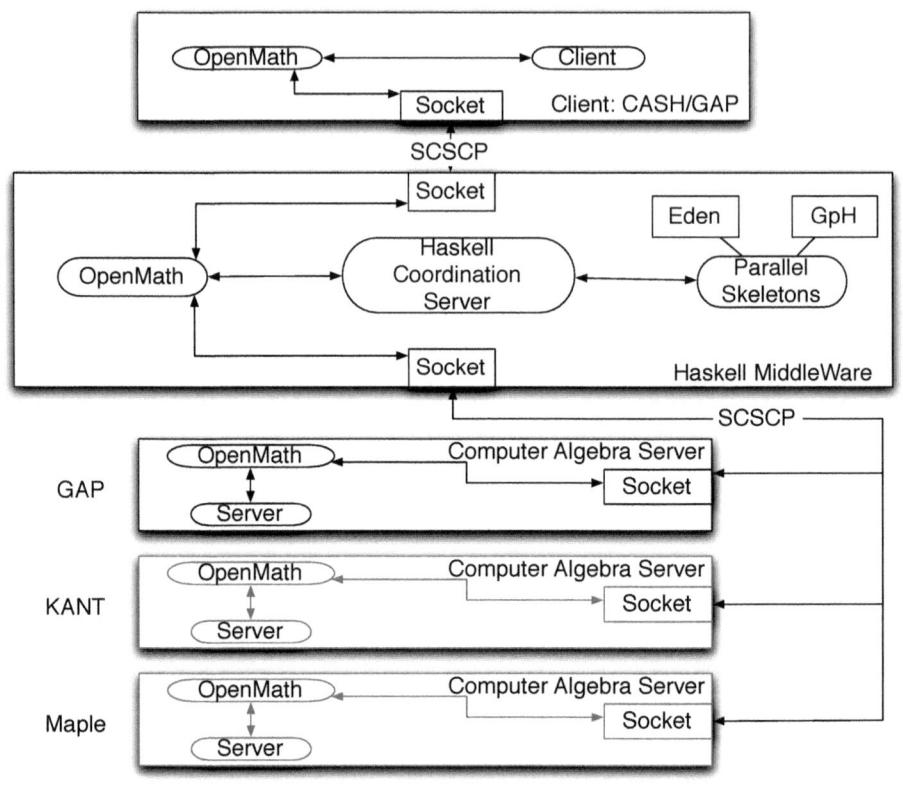

Fig. 4. SymGrid-Par System Architecture

4.1 SymGrid-Par

While this paper focuses on the interface between Haskell and computer algebra systems, the full power of Haskell as a coordination language only becomes apparent when we consider how large-scale symbolic computations can be coordinated. SymGrid-Par (Figure 4) has been designed to achieve a high degree of flexibility in constructing a platform for high-performance, distributed symbolic computation, including computer algebra systems. It has three main components:

- **The Client.** The end user works in his/her own familiar programming environment, so avoiding needing to learn a new computer algebra system or a new language to exploit parallelism. We can imagine here the client being CASH which connects through the Haskell middleware coordination layer to the computer algebra systems. The coordination layer is completely hidden from the CASH end users and they work exactly as they would dealing directly with computer algebra systems. For example, the CASH client could send an SCSCP request to the coordination server to use the multiple homomorphic images skeleton.

- **The Coordination Server.** This middleware provides parallelised services and parallel skeletons to the client. The client may invoke these skeletons as standard higher-order functions. The Coordination Server then delegates work (usually calls to expensive computational algebra routines) to the Computation Server, which is another SCSCP-compliant computer algebra system. Currently the Coordination Server is implemented in Haskell, allowing the user to exploit polymorphism, purity, and higher-order functions for effective implementation of high-performance parallelism. In this example, the Coordination Server executes the Eden multiple homomorphic images skeleton to create GAP instances as separate worker processes.
- **The Computation Server.** This component is typically a dedicated computer algebra system, e.g. GAP. Each server handles the requests that are sent to it and sends the results back to the coordination layer for processing. Finally, the coordination layer returns the result to the client.

Currently, all communication between the components uses the SCSCP interface to maximise flexibility and interoperability. In the future, we could adapt this to call computer algebra functions directly to avoid the marshalling and communication overhead. This could be useful on multi-core machines, whereas the generic interface is better suited for large-scale distribution. Such a design is discussed in [17].

4.2   Calling Haskell from GAP

Using the SymGrid-Par architecture, which provides an SCSCP server with a collection of parallel skeletons, we can now use our interface to call parallel Haskell code from a GAP client. In order to call the Multiple Homomorphic Images skeleton from GAP, we first install it as an SCSCP service called CS_MHI. We then create a GAP wrapper that calls this parallel SCSCP service:

```
ParMHI:=function( mod_fct, sol_fct, cra_fct, primes, matvec )
local res;
res:=EvaluateBySCSCP("CS_MHI",
                     [mod_fct, sol_fct, cra_fct, primes, matvec],
                     SCSCPclientHost, SCSCPclientPort);
return res.object;
end;
```

In the GAP shell, we can then simply call this SCSCP wrapper as follows:

```
gap> ParMHI("WS_Mod", "WS_Sol", WS_CRA", Primes, [m,v])
```

Here, **Primes** is the list of prime numbers passed to the algorithm and m and v are GAP representations of a matrix and a vector that need to be solved. This is only an example of the power of the approach, of course. In addition to *domain-specific skeletons* such as this, we also provide a number of general-purpose skeletons such as parallel maps and folds that can be freely used by the computer algebra user.

5   Related Work

We are aware of two previous attempts to link computer algebra systems with a general-purpose functional language. The GHC-Maple [11] system provides a bespoke interface between sequential Haskell and the Maple heap, using an internal, string-based representation of mathematical objects in Maple. The Eden-Maple system [12] builds on this interface, using Haskell's foreign function interface (FFI) to link Maple with the parallel Eden system. The main difference to CASH is that both these systems are restricted to one computer algebra system using an interface that is specific to that system. They are therefore fragile to change. In the wider arena, one early system that used a declarative language to coordinate parallel Maple programs was ||MAPLE|| [18]. This used the guarded horn clause language Strand to coordinate parallel Maple computations, executing on networks of workstations. Another system enabling parallelism for Maple is Distributed Maple [19] which provides primitives for explicit thread creation and synchronisation, as well as non-determinism and speculation. Compared to the above approaches, it provides a lower level of coordination with explicit threads. In contrast to the approach we have taken here, of *offloading* computer algebra to dedicated systems, DoCON, the Algebraic Domain Constructor [20] aims to provide a full computer algebra system for students using a Haskell implementation. At present, DoCON provides only a small subset of the functionality of computer algebra systems such as GAP. It mainly provides support for linear algebra, polynomial GCD, and Gröbner bases.

GAP itself has been parallelised with the ParGAP [21] package using the MPI message passing library. To ease parallel programming, it builds higher-level abstractions over the MPI layer, for example a `ParList` skeleton that computes a function in parallel over a list. The latest development in the open source GAP system is to make the GAP kernel itself parallel [2] by providing both high and low levels of parallel abstraction for the end GAP user. However, in contrast to CASH, all these approaches are specific to GAP and cannot exploit the existing large body of work on parallelism in Haskell.

Finally, the recently revised Numeric Prelude [22], is a Haskell library that contains many complex mathematical representations together with those most commonly found in computer algebra systems. For example, it contains support for groups, rings, domains, fields, lattices, monoids, polynomials and basic matrix manipulation. In contrast to our design, the numeric prelude does not offer a full system for computer algebra and tends to focus on numerical rather than symbolic computation.

In the longer term we intend to support the evolving class hierarchy that is being developed as part of the Numeric Prelude to simplify our Haskell-side usage of symbolic computations while maintaining the SCSCP link to computer algebra systems.

6   Conclusions

By connecting SymGrid-Par to the CASH front-end client, using the generic SC-SCP interface, we have allowed computer algebra systems to be easily combined with functional programming. This makes the existing rich repertoire of complex and efficient library functions over mathematical data structures, with all the mathematical knowledge that has been captured in them, easily available to the Haskell programmer. It also makes Haskell available to computer algebra users. One particular advantage of this is that parallelism can be much more easily expressed in Haskell using any of the available parallel Haskell implementations. We have used this in the Coordination Server component of SymGrid-Par, showing here how the Eden distributed memory implementation can be exploited to parallelise the new domain-specific multiple homomorphic images skeleton.

There are several possible avenues for future work for both SymGrid-Par and CASH itself. First, in order to simplify the interface for the CASH user, we intend to build on the evolving Haskell class hierarchies that are being developed as part of the Numeric Prelude [22]. We are also in the process of extending the library of parallel skeletons that are available to the CASH user by implementing more domain-specific skeletons for computer algebra, and, conversely, we are consolidating client-side functionality by defining and revising content dictionaries for particular computer algebra sub-domains [23]. Finally, we are promoting the SCSCP protocol in order to increase the number of computer algebra (and other) systems that can be exploited in this way.

This paper represents a first, but important, step in removing the walls of the ghetto between functional programming and computer algebra systems. We are pleased by our initial results and believe that there are significant benefits to both communities both from this development and from the future cooperation that this will enable.

Acknowledgements. This work has been generously supported by the EU Framework VI SCIEnce project (Symbolic Computation Infrastructure in Europe, RII3-CT-2005-026133), and by the UK's Engineering and Physical Sciences Research Council (HPC-GAP: High Performance Computational Algebra and Discrete Mathematics, EP/G 055181).

Downloading CASH

CASH is available for download from Hackage at `http://hackage.haskell.org` or with the Cabal installer [24] using `cabal install cash`.

References

1. Peyton Jones, S., Hammond, K.: Haskell 98 Language and Libraries, the Revised Report. Cambridge University Press, Cambridge (December 2003)
2. The GAP Group: GAP – Groups, Algorithms, and Programming, Version 4.4.12 (2008), `http://www.gap-system.org`
3. Daberkow, M., Fieker, C., Klüners, J., Pohst, M., Roegner, K., Schörnig, M., Wildanger, K.: KANT V4. J. Symb. Comput. 24(3/4), 267–283 (1997)
4. Morisse, K., Kemper, A.: The Computer Algebra System MuPAD. Euromath Bulletin 1(2), 95–102 (1994)
5. Char, B.W.: Maple V Lang. Ref. Manual. Maple Publ., Waterloo Canada (1991)

6. Grayson, D.R., Stillman, M.E.: Macaulay 2, a Software System for Research in Algebraic Geometry, http://www.math.uiuc.edu/Macaulay2/
7. Freundt, S., Horn, P., Konovalov, A., Linton, S., Roozemond, D.: Symbolic Computation Software Composability. In: Autexier, S., Campbell, J., Rubio, J., Sorge, V., Suzuki, M., Wiedijk, F. (eds.) AISC 2008, Calculemus 2008, and MKM 2008. LNCS (LNAI), vol. 5144, pp. 285–295. Springer, Heidelberg (2008)
8. Abbott, J., Díaz, A., Sutor, R.S.: A Report on OpenMath: a Protocol for the Exchange of Mathematical Information. SIGSAM Bull. 30(1), 21–24 (1996)
9. Loogen, R., Ortega-Mallén, Y., Peña-Marí, R.: Parallel Functional Programming in Eden. J. Func. Prog. 15(3), 431–475 (2005)
10. Zain, A.A., Hammond, K., Trinder, P., Linton, S., Loidl, H.-W., Costanti, M.: SymGrid-Par: Designing a Framework for Executing Computational Algebra Systems on Computational Grids. In: Shi, Y., van Albada, G.D., Dongarra, J., Sloot, P.M.A. (eds.) ICCS 2007. LNCS, vol. 4488, pp. 617–624. Springer, Heidelberg (2007)
11. Schreiner, W., Loidl, H.W.: The GHC-Maple Interface. On-line Documentation (2000), http://www.risc.jku.at/software/ghc-maple/
12. Martínez, R., Pena, R.: Building an Interface Between Eden and Maple. In: Trinder, P., Michaelson, G.J., Peña, R. (eds.) IFL 2003. LNCS, vol. 3145, pp. 135–151. Springer, Heidelberg (2004)
13. Lauer, M.: Computing by Homomorphic Images. In: Computer Algebra — Symbolic and Algebraic Computation, pp. 139–168. Springer, Heidelberg (1982)
14. Lipson, J.D.: Chinese Remainder and Interpolation Algorithms. In: Symp. on Symbolic and Algebraic Manipulation, pp. 372–391. Academic Press, London (1971)
15. Klusik, U., Loogen, R., Priebe, S., Rubio, F.: Implementation Skeletons in Eden: Low-Effort Parallel Programming. In: Mohnen, M., Koopman, P. (eds.) IFL 2000. LNCS, vol. 2011, pp. 71–88. Springer, Heidelberg (2001)
16. Brown, C., Hammond, K.: Ever-Decreasing Circles: a Skeleton for Parallel Orbit Calculations in Eden. In: TFP 2010 – Draft Proceedings, Oklahoma, US (May 2010)
17. SCIEnce Team: SymGrid-Par: Parallel Orchestration of Symbolic Computation Systems. In: ISSAC 2010, Munich, Software Demonstration (July 2010)
18. Siegl, K.: Parallelizing Algorithms for Symbolic Computation Using ||MAPLE||. SIGPLAN Not 28(7), 179–186 (1993)
19. Schreiner, W., Mittermaier, C., Bosa, K.: Distributed Maple: Parallel Computer Algebra in Networked Environments. J. of Symb. Comp. 35(3), 305–347 (2003)
20. Mechveliani, S.D.: The Haskell Functional Language and Computer Algebra. In: Proc. of Program Systems, pp.56–64 (2003)
21. Cooperman, G.: Parallel GAP: Mature Interactive Parallel groups and Computation. Technical report, College of Comp. Sci., Northeastern Univ., (2001)
22. Thurston, D., Thielemann, H., Johansson, M.: Numeric prelude (0.2) (2010), http://www.haskell.org/haskellwiki/Numeric_Prelude
23. Linton, S., Hammond, K., Konovalov, A., Al Zain, A., Trinder, P., Horn, P., Roozemond, D.: Easy Composition of Symbolic Computation Software: A New Lingua Franca for Symbolic Computation. In: ISSAC 2010, pp. 339–346. ACM, New York (2010)
24. Jones, I.: The Haskell Cabal: A Common Architecture for Building Applications and Libraries. In: van Eekelen, M. (ed.) TFP 2005, Intellect, pp. 340–354 (2006)

Concurrent Non-deferred Reference Counting on the Microgrid: First Experiences[*]

Stephan Herhut[1], Carl Joslin[1], Sven-Bodo Scholz[1],
Raphael Poss[2], and Clemens Grelck[2]

[1] University of Hertfordshire, United Kingdom
{s.a.herhut,c.a.joslin,s.scholz}@herts.ac.uk
[2] University of Amsterdam, Netherlands
{r.c.poss,c.grelck}@uva.nl

Abstract. We present a first evaluation of our novel approach for non-deferred reference counting on the Microgrid many-core architecture. Non-deferred reference counting is a fundamental building block of implicit heap management of functional array languages in general and Single Assignment C in particular. Existing lock-free approaches for multi-core and SMP settings do not scale well for large numbers of cores in emerging many-core platforms. We, instead, employ a dedicated core for reference counting and use asynchronous messaging to emit reference counting operations. This novel approach decouples computational workload from reference-counting overhead. Experiments using cycle-accurate simulation of a realistic Microgrid show that, by exploiting asynchronism, we are able to tolerate even worst-case reference counting loads reasonably well. Scalability is essentially limited only by the combined sequential runtime of all reference counting operations, in accordance with Amdahl's law. Even though developed in the context of Single Assignment C and the Microgrid, our approach is applicable to a wide range of languages and platforms.

1 Introduction

Functional programming languages are particularly suitable for concurrent execution due to their side-effect-free nature. However, when run on a conventional von Neumann architecture, side effects can ultimately not be avoided. Values from the functional world need to be manifested in heap memory. Managing this heap brings back some of the challenges that imperative programming faces when it comes to concurrent execution. Fortunately, in the context of functional languages, the added complexity remains confined to the programming language's runtime system. Commonly, heap management is implemented by means of deferred garbage collection: heap usage is monitored, and, whenever a high-water mark is reached, program execution is interrupted and dead objects in the heap are identified and removed. Following Amdahl's law, performing garbage collection sequentially would introduce a serious detriment to scalability. Parallel

---

[*] This research is supported by EU research grant FP7/2007/215216 Apple-CORE.

J. Hage, M.T. Morazán (Eds.): IFL 2010, LNCS 6647, pp. 185–202, 2011.

garbage collectors [16,5] alleviate this problem to some extent, but their scaling is limited by the inevitable locking of heap objects during collection.

The functional array language SaC [17,11] uses a different approach to heap management, namely non-deferred reference counting [4]. Each heap object is accompanied by a counter that maintains the number of live references during the object's life time and de-allocates the heap object as soon as no references are left. While memory management overhead is nicely parallelised alongside an application itself, this technique suffers from a similar problem as deferred garbage collection: updating the reference counter of a heap object requires exclusive access. Unfortunately, locking can quickly over-sequentialise a data parallel program, leaving most threads waiting for some lock to become available. Lock contention has a progressively detrimental effect on runtime performance as concurrency increases. Furthermore, performing reference-counting operations on different cores requires the reference counter to be communicated between cores. Most emerging many-core architectures support only weak memory consistency. Thus, accessing a reference counter from different cores involves explicit invalidation of caches and synchronisation of memory to ensure a consistent global view of reference counters. Both aspects are very costly.

With only a small number of threads, as in current mainstream multicores, locks can be avoided by managing thread-local copies of reference counters [12]. However, the runtime cost for maintaining thread-local reference counters and collating them into a globally consistent view whenever necessary is linear in the number of threads. The same holds for memory overhead. On the Microgrid architecture [3] (or any other many-core system) with its large number of cores and thousands of hardware threads, one reference counter per object per thread is not viable as the inflicted overhead would quickly outgrow the actual workload.

In this paper, we present an alternative approach to lock-free concurrent reference counting that can indeed be efficiently implemented on many-core architectures in general and specifically on the Microgrid. We make use of two specific features: *exclusive places* and *delegation*. An *exclusive place* is a dedicated hardware resource that is guaranteed to run a thread to completion without interleaving. This ensures single-threaded access to heap objects if all such attempts originate from the same exclusive place. *Delegation* allows any thread running on any core to delegate the execution of code to another place, be it exclusive or not. Such delegation requests can be performed synchronous, *i.e.*, the delegating thread waits for completion of the delegated task, or asynchronous, *i.e.*, the delegating thread directly continues execution. The use of exclusive places and delegation for reference counting is based on two observations. Firstly, reference-counting operations of different threads can be interleaved, as long as each thread's reference counting operations remain in order. Secondly, reference counting operations do not need to be executed before a thread can continue; it suffices if they are executed eventually. Thus, on the Microgrid we delegate all reference-counting operations on some heap object to a single exclusive place. Since the delegation mechanism does guarantee the order of requests, all interleavings are safe.

Yet, using just delegation has the same drawbacks as using locks would have: If multiple threads issue a reference-counting request, one thread will be blocked until the other thread is serviced. In contrast to locks, however, delegation can alleviate this effect: as the result of the reference-counting operation is not required for either thread to continue, reference-counting requests can be executed asynchronously with the main computation. Hence, we make use of asynchronous delegation. As first experiments show, asynchronous delegation allows us to hide the latency of reference counting operations for a large range of workloads and varying numbers of processing cores.

The remainder of this paper is structured as follows. The next section gives a brief introduction to SAC and motivates the use of reference counting for heap management. An overview of the Microgrid architecture is given in section 3. Next, we present our distributed approach for non-deferred reference counting in section 4. In section 5 we discuss experimental results. We discuss related work in section 6 before we conclude in section 7.

2   SAC and Non-deferred Reference Counting

Single Assignment C, or SAC for short, is a data-parallel, purely functional programming language with a strong emphasis on processing truly multidimensional arrays. While on the syntactic level SAC very much resembles ANSI C, the semantics of SAC is based on the principle of context-free substitution of expressions rather than the step-wise manipulation of state. This choice facilitates far-reaching compiler-directed program transformations for optimisation [10] and parallelisation [8]. We refer the interested reader mainly to [11] for a thorough introduction to the design rationale of SAC, the ambivalence of functional and imperative interpretation of C-like code and the essence of code transformation in the SAC compiler.

It is a design principle of SAC not to provide aggregate array operations as built-in operations, but rather SAC features a versatile array comprehension construct to define such aggregate operations in SAC itself. Figure 1 shows a

---

with $\{\,(\,lower\_bound_1 \leq idxvec < upper\_bound_1\,)$: $exp_1\,;$

   $\cdots$

   $(\,lower\_bound_n \leq idxvec < upper\_bound_n\,)$: $exp_n\,;$

$\}$: **genarray** ($shape\,,\ default$)

Fig. 1. The WITH-loop: array comprehensions in SAC. Here, *lower_bound* and *upper_bound* denote expressions that must evaluate to integer vectors of equal length. They define a rectangular (generally multidimensional) index set. The identifier *idxvec* represents elements of this set, similar to loop variables in for-loops. However, no order is defined on these index sets, making the WITH-loop a truly data-parallel construct. An index set specification is called a *generator* and it is associated with an arbitrary SAC expression. It creates a mapping between index vectors and values, in other words an array.

```
    int[6,7], int fun (int[6,7] A, int[6,7] B)
2   {
       tmp = foo( A);
4      C = with {
             ([3,0] <= iv < [6,4]) : bar( A, iv );
6            ([0,4] <= iv < [6,7]) : B[iv];
          }: genarray( [6,7], tmp);
8      return( C, foo( C));
    }
```

Fig. 2. Example WITH-loop

simplified form of WITH-loop. Essentially, a WITH-loop maps expressions on a multi-dimensional index space to define the elements of a multi-dimensional array.

Figure 2 shows an example SAC function named **fun** featuring a WITH-loop that defines a 6×7 matrix C using two generators and the default element. Each element of the lower left 3×4 submatrix is defined by the application of function **bar** to the argument array A and the index vector **iv**. The right 6×3 submatrix is "copied" from the corresponding elements of the argument matrix B while all remaining elements, *i.e.* the upper left 3×4 submatrix are defined by the default value **tmp**. Note that the function **fun** has two return values, C and **foo(C)**. We assume that both functions **foo** and **bar** are defined elsewhere in the code. We use a contrived example here to expose most relevant reference counting related features in a relatively short and simple program fragment.

As with any other functional language, automatic memory management is a core feature of SAC. Still, the setting substantially differs from that of most functional languages that are based on algebraic data types. Whereas deeply nested, pointer-interconnected structures made up of large numbers of relatively small entities prevail in main-stream functional languages, SAC programs rather deal with a much smaller number of mostly very large data structures that in turn are either not nested at all or are characterised by a small nesting level. As a consequence, conventional deferred garbage collection techniques are not suitable for SAC, and we use non-deferred reference counting instead. This choice has two essential advantages: Large chunks of memory can be reclaimed as early as possible and not only once heap space is exhausted. Moreover, suitable operations can immediately reuse the memory of argument arrays for storing result arrays. If the elements of a result array are actually identical with those of the reused argument array, any copying of data from argument to result array can be avoided entirely.

Figure 3 shows pseudo C code compiled from the example in Figure 2. We focus on memory management aspects of compiled code and keep the generation of efficiently executable C loop nestings from SAC WITH-loops opaque; the interested reader is referred to [9] for details. The argument arrays A and B carry reference counters that have at least the value 1 as in the calling context of the

```
1   int [6 ,7] , int [6 ,7] fun (int [6 ,7] A, int [6 ,7] B)
    {
3     incrc ( A, 1);

5     tmp = foo ( A);

7     if (getrc (B) == 1) {
        C = B;
9       for (iv = [0 ,0] to [3 ,4]) { C[ iv ] = tmp ;              }
        for (iv = [3 ,0] to [6 ,4]) { incrc ( A, 1);
11                                      C[ iv ] = bar ( A, iv ); }
      }
13    else {
        C = malloc ( ... );
15      for (iv = [0 ,0] to [3 ,4]) { C[ iv ] = tmp ;              }
        for (iv = [3 ,0] to [6 ,4]) { incrc ( A, 1);
17                                      C[ iv ] = bar ( A, iv ); }
        for (iv = [0 ,4] to [6 ,7]) { C[ iv ] = B[ iv ];          }
19    }

21    incrc ( C, 1);
      incrc ( A, −1);
23    incrc ( B, −1);

25    return ( C, foo ( C));
    }
```

Fig. 3. Pseudo C code generated from example in Figure 2

function **fun** the corresponding arrays must appear in argument position. The values can be higher, of course, if the arrays are also referenced elsewhere.

Our reference counting scheme implements a *caller-increments/callee decrements* policy. So, at the end of the computation of **fun** each reference counter must have a value one less than at call time. At compile time we count the number of references of A and B. A appears twice in the body of **fun**, once in the first application of **foo** and again in the WITH-loop. Thus, as **fun** has only received one conceptual reference from the caller (the caller increment), we have to increment the reference counter of A by one to cater for the second reference. This is encoded by means of the pseudo operation **incrc**. B only appears in the WITH-loop, hence we leave the reference counter as is. Following the caller-increments/callee decrements principle, the reference counter of A will be decremented during the evaluation of **foo**.

The SAC compiler generates two code variants for the WITH-loop, one that reuses the argument array B for storing the result array C and one that allocates fresh memory. The decision which code to execute is taken at runtime by querying the value of B's reference counter (**getrc**). Note that this choice can generally not be made at compile time as the number of references to B outside the current function context is unknown and depends among others on the call site of foo. If the reuse is successful, we not only avoid a costly memory allocation, but can also leave out all the code that is merely concerned with copying values from the argument array to the result array. Within the WITH-loop, we need to add code that increments the reference counter of A in each iteration because, following our guiding principle, the function bar will decrease the reference counter of its argument and we must avoid the premature de-allocation of A.

After the reuse conditional, we increment the reference counter of C as we have two occurrences of C in the subsequent code. Note that the reference counter of C initially will be 1. In the reuse case this is obvious, and in the non-reuse case the reference counter is initialised to this value. In contrast, both the reference counters of A and B are decremented since these arrays are no longer needed after completion of the WITH-loop. Whether or not they are also de-allocated solely depends on the existence of further references outside the context of foo. The interested reader is referred to [13] for a more thorough discussion of reference counting in SAC.

3   The Microgrid and the SVP Concurrency Model

The Microgrid is a customisable many-core chip architecture. It is based on single-issue, in-order RISC cores. Cores are hardware multi-threaded and capable of context switching between threads at each pipeline cycle. A context switch is triggered by any long latency instruction such as memory accesses, floating point operations or synchronisations and, thus, hides the instruction's latency and prevents pipeline stalls. Cores are clustered in rings we call *places* to allow for efficient thread mapping and communication of inter-thread dependencies. Figure 4 shows a block diagram of the Microgrid configuration we used in our experiments.

The Microgrid is actually a hardware implementation of a more general fine-grained concurrency model named SVP for *Self-adaptive Virtual Processor* [14].

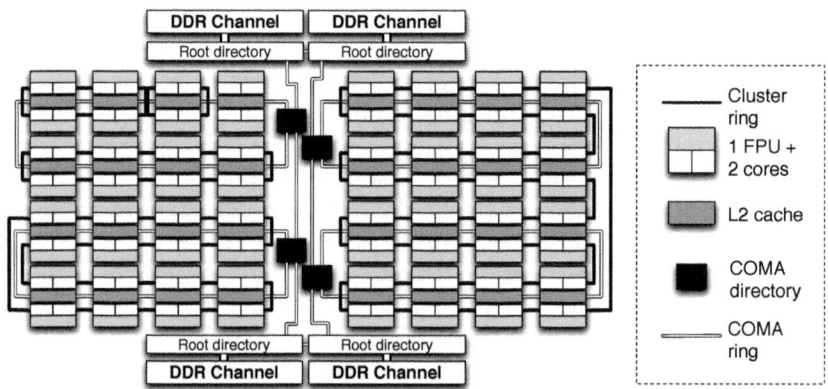

Fig. 4. The layout of a 128 core Microgrid

The SVP model is based on the concept of *thread families*. A family consists of one or more threads that execute the same procedure. Still, each thread has an independent control flow, optionally dependent on a unique index within the family. Any thread can create subordinate families, which take arguments in a similar way as functions do. The arguments to a family of threads are passed on to each thread upon creation and are read-only within the subordinate family. Families of threads can either be created detached or non-detached. In the latter case the parent thread waits for termination of the child family and signals resource reclamation; in the former case the child family terminates independently and resources are released implicitly and immediately.

Furthermore, families of threads can be created at a specific place. This is called *delegation*. The SVP model distinguishes two kinds of places. On *generic places* all families run concurrently up to exhaustion of cores and hardware threads. On *exclusive places* each family runs to completion without interleaving with other families. Cores in the SVP model have access to a distributed memory. While the address space is shared, there is no implicit consistency between memory writes and reads performed by different threads. Consistency is only guaranteed between parent and child threads at the points of creation and synchronisation.

As mentioned before, the Microgrid is effectively a hardware implementation of the SVP concurrency model. On the Microgrid thread family parameters are stored in a hardware family table while information about each individual thread is stored in a hardware thread table. Both are configurable, a typical Microgrid supports up to 32 families and 256 threads per core. If a family of threads is created across multiple cores then a family table entry is allocated on each of the cores. The Microgrid has slightly stronger memory consistency than required by the SVP model. It allows a program to explicitly request system-wide consistency if needed at the expense of increased on-chip network traffic.

The delegation network implements deterministic routing: exclusive families created by a single thread execute in the order they were issued. Similarly, exclusive families issued by a parent thread before a child thread is created are started and complete before any of the child thread's exclusive families. The processing order of exclusive creates issued by unrelated threads is non-deterministic.

Exclusion is negotiated by dedicating a single family context to all exclusive delegations. This way all exclusive delegations are made sequential. A queueing mechanism is required in hardware to avoid having the creating thread wait when the exclusive place is busy.

4   Our Approach: Asynchronous Reference Counting

Our approach for asynchronous non-deferred reference counting is based on two key observations. First, if communicating reference counting state is costly, it may be cheaper to communicate a reference counting operation to the core where the current state of the reference counter resides as opposed to communicating the reference counting state like in classical approaches. On the Microgrid, this can be achieved with minimal overhead using delegation. The idea is to spawn a dedicated thread for the reference counting operation only and delegate that thread to a reference counting core that is statically assigned to the heap object whose reference counter is to be manipulated. By using exclusive creates, we ensure exclusive access to the reference counting state, efficiently managed in hardware, including the queueing of waiting threads.

Second, although it is important to keep the reference counter accurate during program execution, most threads do not actually require knowledge of the current state of the reference counter. That state is only required for reuse operations, which are relatively infrequent during data-parallel operations. This observation motivates us to perform reference counting operations asynchronously. As we already perform reference counting by separate threads, spawning these threads asynchronously is rather simple. Even more, delegation is ordered between cores on the Microgrid. Thus, even though operations are performed asynchronously, they still remain in order, ensuring a valid, yet slightly delayed reference counting state at all times.

For reuse operations, however, a synchronous approach is required. In this case, the issuing thread is actually interested in the current state of a heap object's reference counter. Thus, the issuing thread has to wait for the reference counting operation to finish. Again, as reuse decisions are relatively infrequent with respect to workload connected to the subject of the decision, such delay can be tolerated, in particular as long as other threads are still ready to compute.

We use a fixed assignment of reference counting places to memory addresses. Each heap object's reference counter is created at its corresponding place and remains there until the object is freed. Furthermore, we use only two operations: An asynchronous `incrc` operation and a synchronous `getrc` operation. The former expects a heap object and an offset as arguments; it asynchronously updates the heap object's reference counter by delegating a thread using a detached create to the exclusive place that is assigned to the heap object. That thread, once having gained exclusive access, increments the heap object's reference counter by the given offset (positive or negative).

Apart from updating a heap object's reference counter, the `incrc` operations also takes care of deallocating no longer needed heap objects. As soon as the reference counter drops to zero, the `incrc` operation notifies the heap manager that the object is no longer needed. This operation, as well, is performed asynchronously to ensure that the reference counting place as soon as possible becomes available again for other pending reference counting operations. For the `getrc` operation we use a similar approach. However, instead of a detached create, we use a synchronous create that allows the issuing thread for the reference counting operation to complete. Furthermore, the `getrc` operation only expects a heap object as argument; it yields the current value of the reference counter of that heap object as its result.

Note here that the returned state is accurate with respect to the inquiring thread's timeline. However, there may still be other pending reference counting requests. Thus, the `getrc` operation might produce *false negatives* in that it returns a reference counter greater than one, although the object actually is no longer referenced by any other thread. The opposite, a *false positive* where the `getrc` operation returns a reference counting state of one although other threads still access the object can be excluded. As reference counting operations by a single thread are always processed in order, the returned value is accurate with respect to that thread, *i.e.* the inquiring thread holds only a single reference. All other threads then can no longer hold any references, as their local number of references must have dropped to zero. Otherwise, the global reference counting state would need to be at least two.

5   Evaluation

To evaluate our approach, we have first conducted a study using a synthetic benchmark to characterise the scaling behaviour and to quantify the impact of reference counting on runtime behaviour on many-core architectures. Using a synthetic benchmark rather than some real-world computational kernel allows us to study the behaviour of our approach in a controlled setting. However, to show the applicability of our technology outside of the clean room, we include a two dimensional FFT kernel in our experiments.

We have produced our measurements using revision 4196 of the cycle accurate Microgrid simulator and revision 3.2 of the Microgrid toolchain[1]. Our specific platform illustrated in Figure 4 consists of 128 cores, arranged in 8 places of 1, 1, 2, 4, 8, 16, 32 and 64 cores. Each core has split 8K/8K L1 caches for instructions and data, two cores share an FPU and four cores share a 64K unified L2 cache. These are connected to a cache-only memory architecture (cache lines migrated to point of use), with 4 directories and 4 DDR channels to backing store. Each core supports up to 256 hardware threads. Timings are scaled to simulate 1.2GHz cores and DDR3-2400 channels.

We have recorded full traces of the processor states during simulation and have post-processed these traces to compute pipeline utilisation and resource usage. The benchmark code itself was compiled using the Microgrid back-end of the SAC research compiler `sac2c` revision 17128[2]. For concurrent execution, we have sampled the state of the Microgrid only for the runtime of the relevant data-parallel operation(s). For dedicated sequential execution, we present whole program figures as the standard back-end of the SAC compiler does not support this feature. This difference, however, does not affect the validity of our results.

5.1   Synthetic Kernel

Our synthetic kernel is shown in Figure 5. Given an input vector vect, the WITH-loop computes a new vector of the same length. Each element of the result is

---

[1] The Microgrid simulator and toolchain are available on request from the CSA group at the Institute for Informatics of the University of Amsterdam.
[2] The SAC research compiler `sac2c` is freely available for non-commercial use from http://www.sac-home.org.

```
   int work( int i , int [.] vect)
2  {
     r = 0;
4    for( j=0; j<vect[[i]]; j++) {
       r = r+1;
6    }
     return( r );
8  }

10 result = with {
             ([0] <= [i] <= shape( vect )):  work(i,vect);
12           }: genarray( shape( vect), 0);
```

Fig. 5. Source code of the synthetic benchmark used for evaluating non-deferred reference counting on the Microgrid

computed by concurrently applying the function work to the current index i and the input vector vect. The function work is given in lines 1–8; it encodes a selection of the i-th element from the argument vector vect. In order to model different workloads, selection is implemented by means of a for-loop that consecutively increments a counter, starting at zero, until the value at the i-th position in vect is reached. Thus, the total runtime of work is largely determined by the values in the vector vect.

From a reference counting perspective, the above benchmark encodes a worst case scenario. All threads created due to the WITH-loop first emit two reference counting operations: The caller increment issued before the application of work and the callee decrement issued directly after the read from vect in line 4. Note here that in SAC other than in C there is only a single read operation from vect. Due to the purely functional semantics of SAC, it is a valid optimisation to store the read operation's result in a local variable, which is then used for consecutive checks of the termination condition of the for-loop.

We have designed our synthetic kernel with two tunable parameters: tuning the length of the input vector vect allows us to influence the number of created threads and thus the number of reference counting operations emitted. As each thread contains one call to work with vect as argument, we get two reference counting operations per thread. As the first argument of work, the index i, is a scalar, it is not heap allocated and thus not reference counted.

The second tunable parameter is the value used for the elements of vect. Each thread performs three operations per loop iteration. Thus, the overall workload per thread can be computed as roughly three times the value of the elements of vect. For our experiments, we use a single number for all vector elements, thereby encoding a uniform workload.

In our program, the main computation only results in a single thread family. Hence, the family table can be kept small at the computing place. Due to a current limitation of the architecture, which prevents asynchronous queueing of detached families, we use two-level creates to implement asynchronous creates at exclusive places. In this scheme the work thread detaches a thread at a non-exclusive proxy place; the detached thread in turn issues a synchronous create at an exclusive place. We thus simulate queueing in software by allowing multiple families at the proxy place to wait simultaneously for the exclusive place. This is less efficient than hardware queueing, but offers an advantage for our evaluation: the number of active threads at the proxy place indicates the number of pending requests to the exclusive place. With this scheme, we can easily tune the number of family entries at the proxy place used for reference counting to compensate for contention. To benchmark our program we use 256 family entries per core.

Figures 6 and 7 show the results for a vector of 512 elements and a value of 100. This corresponds to a total of 1024 reference counting operations and a workload of about 150k instructions. The left hand side of both figures presents the results for the executables as produced by the SAC compiler. On the right hand side, we have repeated the same measurements with hand patched executables where all reference counting operations have been removed.

We have first measured runtime and pipeline efficiency for a fully sequential version of the benchmark that does not expose any concurrency. Furthermore, we have used classical reference counting by direct manipulation of a reference counter in memory for these measurements. As direct comparison of Figure 6a and Figure 6b shows, reference counting in the sequential case introduces an overhead of about 200k cycles. Apart from the actual cost of the reference counting operations, we mainly attribute this overhead to the reduced pipeline efficiency. The Microgrid does not feature sophisticated branch predictors or memory pre-fetching stages. Instead, it relies on concurrency to hide the latencies of branches and memory loads.

As expected, adding concurrency and our asynchronous approach to reference counting therefore leads to improved runtime behaviour even on a single core. Figures 6c and 6d both show significant improvement over their sequential counterparts. By offloading reference counting to a dedicated asynchronous core, we have reduced the incurred overhead to less than 50k cycles.

An interesting artefact is the relatively low pipeline utilisation at the beginning of the data-parallel section when reference counting is enabled. We attribute this to queueing effects. Each thread has to successfully enqueue two reference counting operations before it can start computing its workload. It seems that due to the scheduling chosen by the architecture most threads only manage to enqueue their first request before the request queue is full. Thus, threads initially have to wait for reference counting operations to complete.

The version of our benchmark without reference counting exhibits almost linear scaling with increasing numbers of cores as Figures 6f to 7h show. For the runtimes with reference counting enabled, as shown on the left hand side, however, scaling is less favourable and it hits a limit at about 4 cores. Furthermore, we can observe that the number of pending reference counting operations (the dotted lines in the figure) increases with the number of cores. This effect culminates in Figure 7a where for the first time the reference counting queue remains

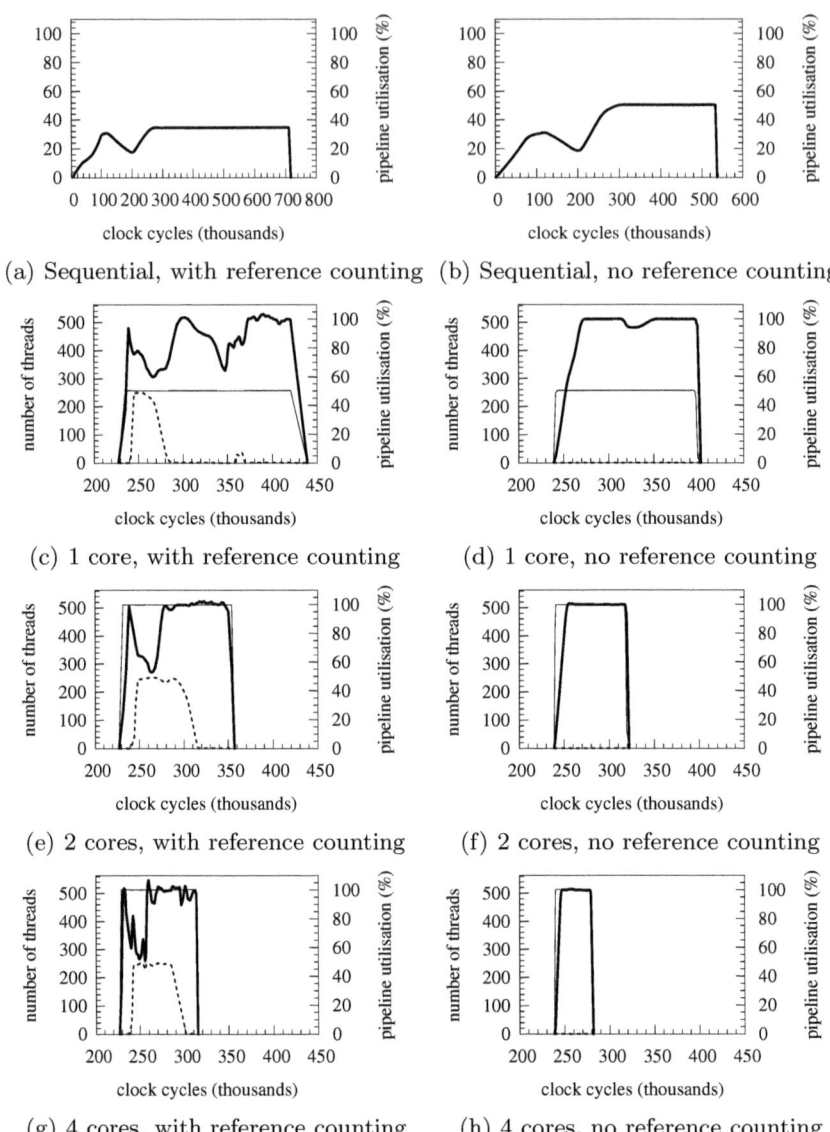

(a) Sequential, with reference counting   (b) Sequential, no reference counting

(c) 1 core, with reference counting   (d) 1 core, no reference counting

(e) 2 cores, with reference counting   (f) 2 cores, no reference counting

(g) 4 cores, with reference counting   (h) 4 cores, no reference counting

Fig. 6. Benchmark results for a vector of 512 elements and a workload of 100 additions. Thin lines show the number of threads computing the actual workload; dotted lines represent the number of pending reference counting operations; thick lines give the average pipeline utilisation across cores that compute the workload. We start with fully sequential code and then continue with parallel code for 1, 2 and 4 cores. In the left column we show results for the code generated by our compiler, in the right column for code where we manually removed all reference counting operations. We continue this in Figure 7 for larger numbers of cores.

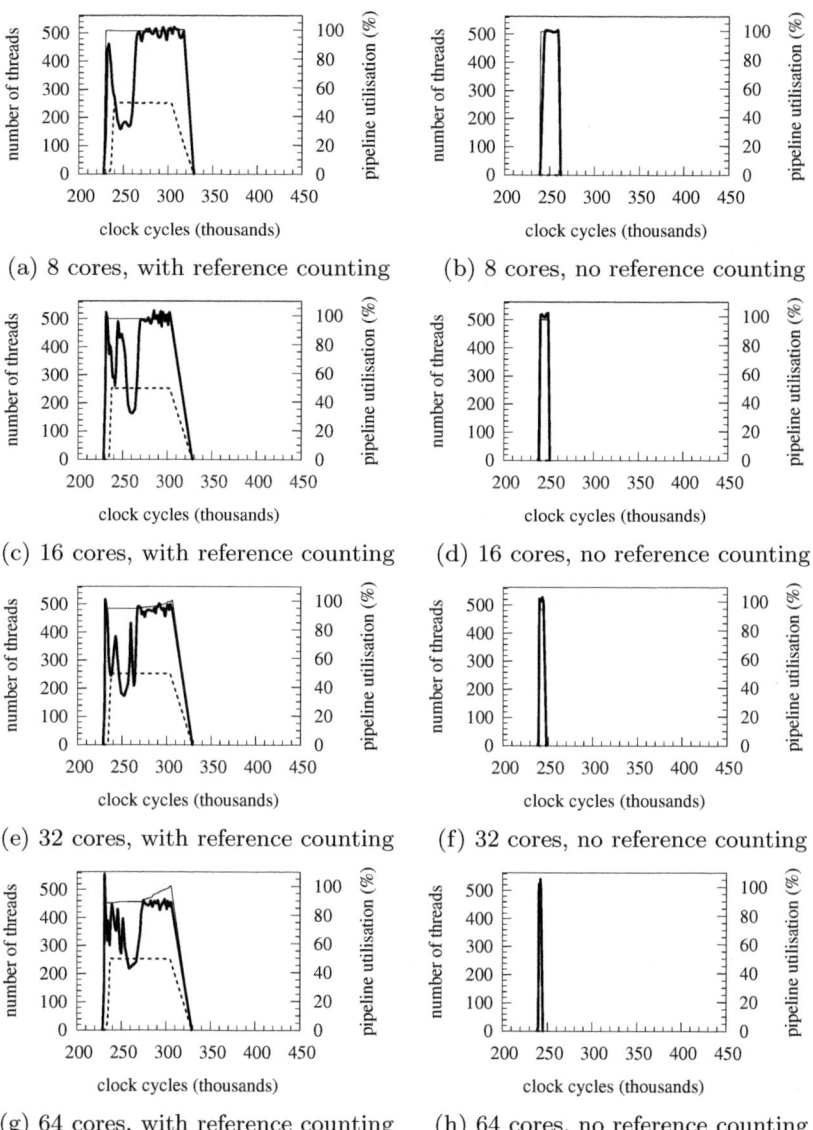

Fig. 7. Benchmark results for a vector of 512 elements and a workload of 100 additions. Thin lines show the number of threads computing the actual workload; dotted lines represent the number of pending reference counting operations; thick lines give the average pipeline utilisation across cores that compute the workload. Continuing from Figure 6 we show results for using 8, 16, 32 and 64 cores. In the left column we show results for the code generated by our compiler, in the right column for code where we manually removed all reference counting operations.

fully loaded during the entire data-parallel section; the reference counting operations dominate the overall execution. This is a consequence of the necessity to perform all reference counting operations sequentially. Our software implementation of the asynchronous reference counting operations requires roughly 100 cycles each leading to 100k cycles in total. This observation enables us to predict the best possible speedup by means of Amdahl's law: it equates to the ratio between workload and reference counting time which, in our example, are 300 and 100 cycles per element, respectively.

This ratio of 1.5 in fact is the limiting factor for the speedups observed as shown in Figure 8. To confirm our explanation, we repeated the same experiment for larger vectors and with varying ratios between workload and reference counting times. Figure 8 shows three different experiments in total. Besides our initial experiment, it also contains an experiment on a 4096-element vector with the same ratio of 1.5, and an experiment with a ratio of 15 (1000 iterations).

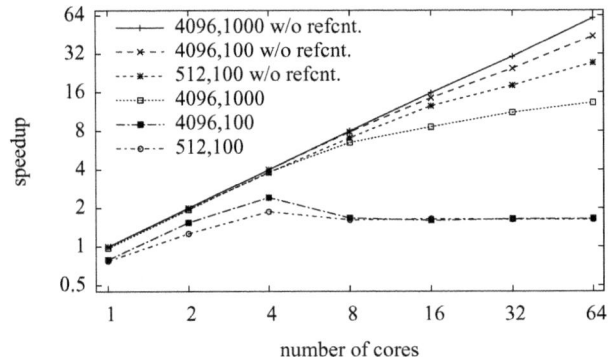

Fig. 8. Observed speed up for varying numbers of threads and workload sizes compared to the runtimes on a single core with reference counting operations removed

A first observation is that increasing the number of elements and, thus, the overall load has no impact on speedups even though it entails an eightfold increase in the number of threads created. Increasing the number of iterations to 1000, and with it the ratio between workload and reference counting time to a factor of roughly 15, directly impacts scaling. Even more, we can see that our predicted speedup factor is reached when using 64 cores. This demonstrates nicely that the architecture is capable of hiding all the workload (roughly 12M cycles) behind the sequential program fragment due to reference counting (roughly 800k cycles). For completeness, we have included the results for running the benchmark with reference counting operations removed, as well. For 100 iterations we observe close to linear scaling while 1000 iterations scale perfectly linear.

5.2   2-Dimensional FFT

As a representative of a real-world computational kernel, we chose 2-dimensional FFT. In fact, our code is a stripped-down version of the NAS benchmark FT [1],

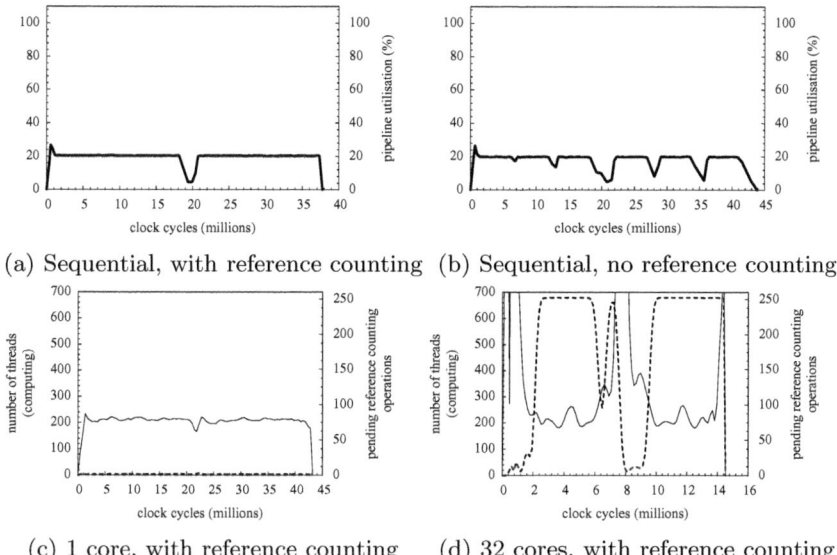

(a) Sequential, with reference counting (b) Sequential, no reference counting

(c) 1 core, with reference counting   (d) 32 cores, with reference counting

Fig. 9. Results for a two dimensional FFT on a 128 × 128 complex matrix

which implements 3-dimensional FFT. We restrict ourselves here to the 2-dimensional case and a relatively small problem size due to the computational complexity of cycle-accurate simulation of the Microgrid. In essence, our kernel transforms a matrix of complex numbers by applying 1-dimensional FFTs to each row vector, then transposing the result matrix and again applying 1-dimensional FFTs to each row vector, i.e. the former column vectors. We implement the 1-dimensional FFTs using the Danielson-Lanczos algorithm, which recursively decomposes the argument vector into the vectors of even- and odd-indexed elements. A detailed discussion of the SAC implementation of this benchmark can be found in [7].

Figure 9 shows our experimental results for running the 2d-FFT kernel on a matrix of 128 × 128 double precision complex numbers. The baseline performance for fully sequential execution with classical reference counting is given in Figure 9a. The three phase nature of our implementation can be nicely observed in the pipeline utilisation graph. During the first phase, the computation of FFT on the rows of the input, we achieve an efficiency of just above 20%. This is followed by a short phase, the transpose operation, with efficiency dropping below 10% before it goes back to 20% for the second round of FFT on the columns. The low pipeline utilisation is to be expected as FFT and to an even larger degree transpose operations are memory bound.

Note here that the fully sequential version without reference counting is actually slower than the version with reference counting. We attribute this to the unexploited memory reuse potential when reference counting is disabled. The same effect can be observed across 2, 4, 8, 16, 32 and 64 cores. An implementation using our concurrent reference counting scheme consistently outperforms the version without any form of reference counting. We omit the details here due to space limitations.

Figure 9c shows the runtime behaviour of a concurrent implementation running on a single core. The observed reference counting behaviour greatly differs from our synthetic benchmark. Instead of a high initial reference counting load that tails off during program runtime, we observe continuous, yet low frequency reference counting throughout the runtime of the benchmark.

The changed pattern relates well to the different reference counting distribution in FFT. Whereas our synthetic benchmark first issues all reference counting operations and then computes the workload, FFT starts with an increment of the argument due to the initial function call but then immediately processes some workload before further reference counting operations are emitted. Thus, reference counting operations and the computation of the actual workload are better interleaved, resulting in a lower pressure on the reference counting queue.

As expected, the pressure on the queue grows with increasing numbers of cores until a maximum is reached at 32 cores, shown in Figure 9d. At this stage, we can observe a constant reference counting load and further scaling becomes constrained by Amdahl's law. This finding matches our previous experience with the synthetic benchmark. As before, the architecture is able to hide the 45 million cycles of workload in 14 million cycles of reference counting operations.

6   Related Work

Although we are aware of recent work on using non-deferred reference counting in the context of object-oriented languages [15], we did not come across any work of non-deferred reference counting in the context of distributed shared memory systems. However, the underlying principles of our approach, *i.e.* shipping computation to data and exploiting asynchronous communication for latency hiding, have been applied to related problems in distributed systems before.

One example in this setting is the multi kernel paradigm adopted by the Barrelfish operating system [2] for multi- and many-core systems. In Barrelfish, instead of using a single global kernel and shared state, the operating system is built around a communicating network of kernels. Each computing resource is managed by its own kernel and state is replicated using message passing. Similar to our approach, operating system services are delegated to responsible cores that hold the corresponding state instead of communicating the state. The motivation here, like for us, is scalability.

Similar, but on a significantly larger scale, distributed file systems have to contend with typically large objects (files) replicated in storage across several applications (clients). Usually, metadata and directories are maintained separately from the data, with tables that keep track of which clients currently hold a copy of each file. Storage reclamation after path deletion can only occur when the last client has dropped its replica of the corresponding file. The Hadoop distributed file system [18] and the Google File System [6] are particular examples of distributed file systems that employ a scheme closely related to our approach. In both, objects are file data blocks and are distributed across a set of *data nodes*. Separate from these, *name nodes* hold the metadata and reference information. When data nodes duplicate data or create new data they must inform the name node of the existence of new copies through *heartbeat messages*. Client applications can enquire through a name node to know how many copies of a data block exist. On each name node, heartbeats are handled in order but asynchronously, except when an application requests a *flush-and-sync* of pending heartbeats. This is similar to our asynchronous updates/synchronous read scheme.

7 Conclusion

We have presented a novel approach for concurrent non-deferred reference counting on many-core architectures. Instead of locks and exclusive regions, we employ exclusive processing units for reference counting. We communicate the reference counting operation to the core where the associated state is stored rather than communicating state between cores. In a many-core setting, this greatly reduces reference counting related overheads. Furthermore, we use asynchronous communication where possible to hide the latencies involved.

As a first evaluation shows, our approach is able to tolerate even worst-case reference counting scenarios. The scaling behaviour of our synthetic benchmark is dominated by the combined sequential runtime of the inflicted reference counting operations. According to Amdahl's law, this is the best possible behaviour we can expect as reference counting operations must be performed sequentially. Nonetheless, there is room for improvement. The current implementation of our approach encodes the asynchronous communication protocol between cores in software. For a purely hardware based solution, we expect the sequential runtimes of reference counting operations to be reduced by at least a factor of 4. This would directly reflect in a four-fold increase in the expected maximum speedups.

Yet, ultimately reference counting remains the bottleneck. In particular for data-parallel operations as investigated here, the bursts of reference counting operations typical for SPMD style code may dominate runtime behaviour. Our future research in this context, therefore, concentrates on further reducing the number of reference counting operations on shared data in data-parallel codes.

We believe our approach is well suited for task-parallelism, as well. The less structured interleaving of reference counting operations and workloads found in task-parallel applications should allow for even better exploitation of asynchronism for hiding reference counting overheads. However, an extension of our approach to support less structured settings remains future work.

Acknowledgements. The authors would like to thank Mike Lankamp, University of Amsterdam, for his contributions to the discussion of experimental results, Nilesh Karavadara, University of Hertfordshire, for his help in running the measurements and producing the figures presented in this paper and the anonymous referees for their helpful comments.

References

1. Bailey, D., et al.: The NAS Parallel Benchmarks. International Journal of Super-computer Applications 5(3), 63–73 (1991)
2. Baumann, A., Barham, P., Dagand, P.E., et al.: The multikernel: a new OS architecture for scalable multicore systems. In: 22nd Symposium on Operating Systems Principles (SOSP 2009), pp. 29–44. ACM, New York (2009)
3. Bousias, K., Guang, L., Jesshope, C., Lankamp, M.: Implementation and Evaluation of a Microthread Architecture. J. Systems Architecture 55(3), 149–161 (2009)
4. Collins, G.E.: A Method for Overlapping and Erasure of Lists. Communications of the ACM 3(12), 655–657 (1960)
5. Doligez, D., Leroy, X.: A Concurrent, Generational Garbage Collector for a Multithreaded Implementation of ML. In: POPL 1993: 20th Symposium on Principles of Programming Languages, pp. 113–123. ACM, New York (1993)
6. Ghemawat, S., Gobioff, H., Leung, S.T.: The Google file system. SIGOPS Oper. Syst. Rev. 37(5), 29–43 (2003)
7. Grelck, C., Scholz, S.B.: Towards an Efficient Functional Implementation of the NAS Benchmark FT. In: Malyshkin, V.E. (ed.) PaCT 2003. LNCS, vol. 2763, pp. 230–235. Springer, Heidelberg (2003)
8. Grelck, C.: Shared memory multiprocessor support for functional array processing in SAC. Journal of Functional Programming 15(3), 353–401 (2005)
9. Grelck, C., Kreye, D., Scholz, S.B.: On Code Generation for Multi-Generator WITH-Loops in SAC. In: Koopman, P., Clack, C. (eds.) IFL 1999. LNCS, vol. 1868, pp. 77–94. Springer, Heidelberg (2000)
10. Grelck, C., Scholz, S.B.: Merging compositions of array skeletons in SAC. Journal of Parallel Computing 32(7+8), 507–522 (2006)
11. Grelck, C., Scholz, S.B.: SAC: A Functional Array Language for Efficient Multithreaded Execution. Int. Journal of Parallel Programming 34(4), 383–427 (2006)
12. Grelck, C., Scholz, S.B.: Efficient Heap Management for Declarative Data Parallel Programming on Multicores. In: 3rd Workshop on Declarative Aspects of Multicore Programming (DAMP 2008), San Francisco, USA, pp. 17–31. ACM Press, New York (2008)
13. Grelck, C., Trojahner, K.: Implicit Memory Management for SaC. In: Grelck, C., Huch, F. (eds.) IFL 2004, pp. 335–348 (2004); University of Kiel, Institute of Computer Science and Applied Mathematics technical report 0408
14. Jesshope, C.: A model for the design and programming of multi-cores. Advances in Parallel Computing, High Performance Computing and Grids in Action (16), 37–55 (2008)
15. Joisha, P.G.: A principled approach to nondeferred reference-counting garbage collection. In: 4th International Conference on Virtual Execution Environments (VEE 2008), pp. 131–140. ACM, New York (2008)
16. Marlow, S., Harris, T., James, R.P., Peyton Jones, S.: Parallel Generational-Copying Garbage Collection with a Block-Structured Heap. In: ISMM 2008: 7th International Symposium on Memory Management, pp. 11–20. ACM, New York (2008)
17. Scholz, S.B.: Single Assignment C: Efficient Support for High-Level Array Operations in a Functional Setting. J. Functional Programming 13(6), 1005–1059 (2003)
18. Shvachko, K., Kuang, H., Radia, S., Chansler, R.: The Hadoop distributed file system. In: 26th Symposium on Massive Storage Systems and Technologies (MSST 2010). IEEE Press, Incline Village, USA (May 2010)

Composing Reactive GUIs in F# Using WebSharper

Joel Bjornson, Anton Tayanovskyy, and Adam Granicz

IntelliFactory
http://www.intellifactory.com

Abstract. We present a generic library for constructing composable and interactive user interfaces in a declarative style. The paper introduces *flowlets*, an extension of *formlets*[3,2] providing interactivity. Real-world examples are given using the current implementation that compiles flowlets defined in F# to JavaScript with WebSharper[1].

Keywords: functional reactive programming, GUI, F#, flowlets, formlets.

1 Introduction

One of the remaining challenges for functional programming is to tackle the construction of graphical user interfaces with demonstrable advantages over the mainstream object-oriented techniques such as reduced code size and improved guarantees for correctness. The challenge is to make user interfaces compositional and amenable to equational reasoning. There are two aspects:

- *Compositionality.* Functional programming naturally favors a combinatory design. Ideally, widgets should be closed under composition.
- *Purity.* Side effects permeate mainstream GUI (graphical user interface) programming as a model for expressing change, yet side-effectful widgets are difficult to reason about equationally.

There is a growing number of projects that use functional programming to answer the GUI challenge [1,10,12,13]. We focus on *formlets* [3,2], which give a practical and easy to understand abstraction for compositional data-collecting forms. While the original implementation targeted the CGI environment and generated HTML forms, the concept of formlets is by no means limited to that environment.

In this paper we introduce flowlets, our extension of formlets relying on functional reactive programming (FRP [7]) to deal with change. Flowlets are practical to use as they reuse arbitrary mainstream object-oriented widget toolkits for rendering. They are pure, compositional, and expressive enough to address dynamic validation and other interactive scenarios one expects from a modern

---

[1] http://www.websharper.com

J. Hage, M.T. Morazán (Eds.): IFL 2010, LNCS 6647, pp. 203–216, 2011.
© Springer-Verlag Berlin Heidelberg 2011

GUI. We describe our generic F#[2] implementation of flowlets and discuss a specific instantiation targeting the browser environment with WebSharper[3], our F# to JavaScript compiler.

2   Design

Flowlets strive to provide a GUI abstraction that is practical, easy to reason about, and compositional. A flowlet is a capability to display an editor of a certain value and react to the user's edits of that value. For example, a flowlet of type `string flowlet` renders to a text box and notifies the program of all intermediate `string` values of the box as the user types in or edits the text.

Flowlet values are designed to be immutable to promote ease of use. Purity ensures that composing simpler flowlets into complex ones is always safe.

To be of practical use in applications, flowlets are designed to run in a rich GUI environment like the desktop or the web browser. Flowlets reuse existing widget toolkits for rendering, which poses a challenge: most toolkits assume mutation. Flowlets are therefore not themselves widgets, but can be rendered to the widgets of the underlying toolkit. They can be thought of as widget factories.

Flowlets support two different kinds of composition: static and dynamic.

2.1   Static Composition

The applicative functor operators, borrowed from formlets [2], provide the primary means of flowlet composition:

```
val pure  : 'a -> 'a flowlet
val ⊗ : ('a -> 'b) flowlet -> 'a flowlet -> 'b flowlet
```

Here is an example of composing a `textBox` flowlet and an `intBox` flowlet into a flowlet for collecting a user record:

```
let user =
    pure (fun name age -> { Name = name; Age = age })
    ⊗ textBox
    ⊗ intBox
```

Visually, flowlets obtained in this manner typically render to a table, with one row for every constituent flowlet (except the `pure` flowlets which are invisible). Logically, the lambda function defines how to combine the values gathered from constituent flowlets. Every time the state of one of the nested flowlets is updated, the changes are pushed to the composed flowlet, updating its state. The operator ⊗ is left-associative.

---

[2] `http://fsharp.net`
[3] `http://www.websharper.com`

2.2   Dynamic Composition

The applicative functor composition of flowlets is based on the design of form-lets [3]. While fairly expressive, these combinators cannot construct flowlets that interactively depend on the state of other flowlets. The following example demonstrates a flowlet for collecting contact information that presents the user with a choice between entering a phone or an email, and then renders a phone or an email flowlet depending on the choice made:

```
let contactFlowlet = do
    contactType <- contactTypeFlowlet
    match contactType with
    | Phone -> phoneFlowlet
    | Email -> emailFlowlet
```

In order to express these additional interactive aspects, flowlets support a bind function:

```
val * : 'a flowlet -> ('a -> 'b flowlet) -> 'b flowlet
```

The operators * and **pure** provide flowlets with a monadic interface[11] . The fact that flowlets support a monadic interface, and not just that of applicative functors, makes them strictly more expressive than formlets.

Proving that the laws of applicative functors and monads are obeyed requires a formal definition of the semantics of flowlets, and is not addressed in this introductory paper.

2.3   Representation

Flowlets are represented as factories of (mutable) widgets. When rendered, they provide the following elements:

- *state*, a value of type 'a that changes over time as the user interacts with the interface.
- *body*, a time-varying list of native widgets that are presented to the user. This list can vary over time because of the dynamic nature of the **bind** combinator.

Every flowlet also provides a layout, a specification of how to visually render the body to a native widget. The default layout uses a vertical table that displays the native widget list with one widget per row and automatically updates when the body changes.

The implementation details including the representations of time-varying values, the efficient propagation of body updates and the practical issues of validation, and form resetting are the subject of the next section.

3   Flowlet Architecture

We now present the generic flowlet architecture. Our implementation is available as an F# library reusable with multiple rendering backends. We obtained this implementation by generalizing WebSharper flowlets, which are now our primary backend, targeting the AJAX environment with WebSharper.

Flowlets are essentially factories of `form` values parametrized by the type of the logical state and the type of the native widgets:

```
type ('body, 'a) flowlet =
    {
        layout  : layout
        build   : unit -> ('body, 'a) form
    }
```

Flowlet composition and the basic combinators described in Section 3.1 are defined in terms of the generic flowlet type with two type parameters. For concrete instances of flowlets, the type of `body` is fixed.

Flowlets construct `form` values that are triples of `state`, `body`, and `reset` components, which are used by flowlet combinators to observe the user's actions, implement validation and form resetting:

```
type ('body, 'a) form =
    {
        state   : 'a result stream
        body    : 'body edit stream
        reset   : unit -> unit
    }
```

Our design makes flowlets lazy in the sense that the form construction is delayed until rendering. This allows flowlets to be pure even when `body` widgets are stateful objects. In particular, definitions such as $f \otimes g \otimes g$ where g is used twice are valid because the uses of g generate fresh widgets.

The `body` element represents a time-varying list of native widgets. To make updates efficient, the form communicates list changes as `edit` values instead of complete lists. The `edit` type is described in Section 3.3.

The `layout` element is a layout manager that defines how to render the `body` stream into a single widget. Among other things, this permits nested flowlets to be rendered using their own layout.

We assume the availability of a push-based FRP implementation that defines a `stream` type: a typed channel of notifications. Streams are used in order to model the time varying nature of the logical and the visual state of flowlet instantiations. The operations required for composing the stream components of forms are defined in Section 3.4.

The `result` wrapper around the `state` values allows the state stream to carry validation messages.

3.1   Composition

The primitive combinators are *pure*, ⊗ and ⋆. The first two, *pure* and ⊗, provide means of static composition, making flowlets support the applicative functor interface [2], while ⋆ introduces dynamic dependencies:

- A flowlet `pure x` has a constant logical state equal to `x`, and its `body` is a constant, empty list of widgets.
- A flowlet $f \otimes g$ is obtained by applying the $\otimes_s$ operation on the `state` streams of `f` and `g` and concatenating their `body` lists. The concatenation has to be done in terms of edits. Assuming there is a merge operation that takes two streams and produces a stream that fires events from both, this is definable as:

  $$\text{merge}_s\ (\text{map}_s\ \texttt{Left f.body})\ (\text{map}_s\ \texttt{Right f.body})$$

  The remaining component, `reset`, propagates the `reset` call to both flowlets.
- A flowlet $x \star f$ starts by rendering `x`, and then, every time the value of `x` changes, constructs and appends a new flowlet dynamically. In order to remove old components, the body stream yields a `Replace` operation, indicating that the previous visual components of the *right branch* are to be deleted. The ⋆ operation is implemented using the $\star_s$ on streams.

From these, one can derive a `map`:

```
val map : ('a -> 'b) -> ('body, 'a) flowlet -> ('body, 'b) flowlet
```

In addition to mapping over the logical state of a flowlet, we might also apply a transformation function to the body. `mapBody` serves this purpose:

```
val mapBody : ('body -> 'body) ->
              ('body, 'a) flowlet -> ('body, 'a) flowlet
```

Another common scenario is to map over the `result` values, allowing the function to access the validation state:

```
val mapResult : ('a result -> 'b result) ->
                ('body, 'a) flowlet -> ('body, 'b) flowlet
```

A special case of this scenario is validation. A validator restricts the admissible values of a flowlet. It does so by putting it into a failing state (an error `result` value) whenever the current logical value is invalid. As an example, a text box flowlet could be enhanced to only permit strings consisting of digits. The signature for a general validation function is:

```
val validate : ('a -> bool) -> string ->
               ('b, 'a) flowlet -> ('b, 'a) flowlet
```

This function maps over a flowlet to produce a validating flowlet. The first argument is a predicate for determining whether a value is valid or not and the second argument specifies the error message to be associated with failing results.

For example, a text box flowlet enhanced with integer validation could be transformed into a flowlet that produces values of type integer rather than string:

```
let intBox =
    map int (validate isInt "Only integers allowed" textBox)
```

Another interesting combinator that can be derived from the primitives is sequence. A list of flowlets carrying values of type 'a can be turned into a flowlet carrying values of type 'a list, displaying the flowlets simultaneously:

```
val sequence : ('b, 'a) flowlet list -> ('b, 'a list) flowlet
```

3.2   Layout

Flowlets are rendered to a widget by the layout function. The relevant definitions include:

```
type 'b layout = 'b edit stream -> 'b option
val withLayout : 'b layout -> ('b, 'a) flowlet -> ('b, 'a) flowlet
val horizontal : 'b layout
val vertical   : 'b layout
```

Note that repetitive use of withLayout will *override* the layout, so that:

```
withLayout x (withLayout y f) = withLayout x f
```

A layout is thus a function from a time-varying widget list represented as a stream of edit operations to a single widget. Composed flowlets such as $f_1 \otimes f_2$ always try to apply the layout functions of their components. If a layout of a flowlet succeeds and returns Some x, the container treats this flowlet as a single widget x. Otherwise, it treats it as a list of its component widgets.

This design allows composed flowlets to render uniformly by default, while also permitting nested custom layouts. Consider:

```
pure (fun a b c -> ...)
⊗ textBox
⊗ textBox
⊗ textBox
```

As the default layout always returns None, the body streams of the inner textbox flowlets will be merged without applying any layout functions. This delegates rendering to the layout manager of the outer flowlet and will be rendered to a table with one row per textBox by default. We can modify this

behavior to render the first two `textBox` flowlets horizontally on the same row
by specifying a custom layout manager:

```
withLayout horizontal (
    pure (fun a b c -> ...)
    ⊗ textBox
    ⊗ textBox
)
⊗ textBox
```

Since `body` is exposed on `form` values, flowlet combinators by default have the
ability to observe the list structure implied by the `body`, which is often useful. In
other cases, it makes sense to hide this structure by reducing the list to a single
widget. The function `applyLayout` does this by applying the layout of a flowlet
for every `form` it constructs:

```
val applyLayout : 'a flowlet -> 'a flowlet
```

A common way to implement a layout is by using a mutating container of native
widgets and then lifting it to a layout with the `newLayout` function provided by
the flowlets library:

```
type 'a container =
    {
        body   : 'a
        insert : int -> 'a -> unit
        remove : 'a list -> unit
    }
```

```
val newLayout : (unit -> 'a container) -> 'a layout
```

The container is a widget (body) along with functions for mutating its list of
inner widgets by either inserting or removing elements. The insert function accepts an additional integer argument for specifying the position of the element
to be inserted. The implementation of `newLayout` consumes the stream of edits and translates them to the mutation operations on the container. Using the
`newLayout` function for constructing layouts relieves the user from the burden
of having to deal with streams and edit operations explicitly.

3.3   Rendering

Receiving notifications with the complete list of widgets would force the rendering engine to redraw the entire form at every update. This is inefficient and
not always feasible. A better strategy is to only update the changing part of the
form.

To encode updates we use a tree representation of the body list, where the list is obtained by in-order traversal and a derivative `edit` representation of the changes:

```
type 'a tree =
    | Empty
    | Leaf of 'a
    | Fork of ('a tree) * ('a tree)

type 'a edit =
    | Replace of 'a tree
    | Left of 'a edit
    | Right of 'a edit
```

For example, the body component of a primitive flowlet, such as a single input box, is represented by a tree consisting of a `Leaf` node. A flowlet composed using $\otimes$ is represented by a `Fork` that separates the bodies of both arguments into two branches.

The `edit` data structure encodes how to modify any tree by replacing a subtree. A function for applying an edit operation to a tree is easy to define:

```
val apply : 'a edit -> 'a tree -> 'a tree
```

Encoding body components as streams of edit operations allows to efficiently observe and react to the changes of a flowlet between two points in time. No information is lost since the state of the tree at any point in time can be restored by integrating over the sequence of edits.

3.4   Streams

We have been assuming the existence of a stream type. Streams represent time-varying values of a given type implemented as push-based event channels. The stream contract is a function that subscribes an event handler:

```
type 'a stream : ('a option -> unit) -> unit
```

The value `None` notifies the handler about the termination of the stream. The following stream combinators are required by the flowlet implementation:

```
val never_s : unit -> 'a stream
val pure_s  : 'a -> 'a stream
val ⊗_s : ('a -> 'b) stream -> 'a stream -> 'b stream
val ⋆_s : 'a stream -> ('a -> 'b stream) -> 'b stream
val merge_s : 'a stream -> 'a stream -> 'a stream
val ⊕_s : 'a stream -> 'a stream -> 'a stream
```

These definitions provide an empty stream, the monad and applicative functor operators, stream interleaving, and concatenation:

- **never** yields an empty stream immediately completing without any values.
- **pure** x lifts x into a stream that, when subscribed to, invokes the handler with x once and then completes.
- $f \otimes_s s$ is the applicative functor operator, applying a stream of functions f to a stream of values s.
- $s \star_s f$ yields values from the latest stream produced by applying f to the values of s.
- **merge** a b combines the streams by interleaving the values from both streams.
- $x \oplus_s y$ yields values from x until it completes, followed by the subsequent values from y.

The implementation of streams is outside of the scope of this paper.

4   WebSharper Flowlets

4.1   Underlying Technology

F#[4] is a succinct, strongly-typed functional and object-oriented language for the .NET platform from Microsoft Research, Cambridge. Since 2009, F# is being supported by Microsoft as a first-class language on par with C# and Visual Basic. Starting as a port of OCaml [9] for the .NET, F# has evolved into a successful language in its own right. It incorporates traditional functional (closures, tail call elimination, Hindley-Milner type inference) and object-oriented (interfaces, subtyping, polymorphism) features as well as some innovations (units of measure, active patterns, asynchronous workflows).

The choice of F# is motivated by our conviction that it occupies a unique spot among functional languages, enjoying unparalleled industrial backing, tool support, library abundance, and runtime implementation quality. It fits perfectly with our vision of making functional programming widely adopted by industrial users.

IntelliFactory WebSharper is a web application development platform centered around an F# to JavaScript compiler. It enables the development of complete web applications in F# and compile them to interacting server-side (.NET) and client-side (JavaScript/HTML) components. WebSharper's main strength is its support for a broad set of .NET libraries in the JavaScript environment and a growing collection of JavaScript libraries available from F# in a type-safe manner.

Representation. WebSharper comes with a default instantiation for flowlets based on DOM nodes. The F# code base is translated to JavaScript using the WebSharper compiler and is executed in the browser. It specializes generic flowlets by fixing the type of the body component:

---

[4] http://www.fsharp.net

```
type Body =
    {
        Element: Element
        Label: Element option
    }
type Flowlet<'T> = Base.Flowlet<Body, 'T>
```

Values of type `Body` contain two fields; an `Element`, corresponding to the form, and an optional value holding label information. The reason we chose to augment body components with a label field, rather than embedding it in the element directly, is that it better enables table-based layouts with aligned labels. `Element` values are simple wrappers around DOM nodes, providing additional utility members that support common operations and accommodate for browser incompatibilities.

4.2 Controls

The WebSharper flowlet library defines basic flowlets corresponding to HTML form elements such as:

- text fields,
- buttons,
- text areas,
- select boxes,
- and radio buttons.

There are also extension libraries, providing flowlet interfaces for controls from third-party JavaScript technologies such as $jQueryUI$[5] and YUI[6]. These libraries contain more advanced controls including widgets such as calendars, tab sets, and tree views.

4.3 Layout Managers

Default layout managers are provided to render flowlets in a vertical or horizontal layout in a single visual block, and also in multiple blocks that follow each other in a sequence.

Layouts are defined using the `newLayout` (described in Section 3.2) function from the base library. For example, to implement the vertical layout manager, a function for constructing containers consisting of a table element is defined. The insert function constructs new table rows containing the label and the element of the provided body component. The rows are inserted at the specified row index. The DOM node identity of an element is used to keep track of existing rows. The container function responsible for removing elements finds and deletes rows based on the identity of the requested element.

The ability to insert new rows at an arbitrary index in the table container is crucial for rendering nested dynamically composed flowlets.

---

[5] http://jqueryui.com/
[6] http://developer.yahoo.com/yui/

4.4   Combinators

Specializing the type of body components enables the definition of additional combinators for common aspects of web-form creation. Examples include:

- adding labels,
- adding validation feedback,
- and extending flowlets with submit and reset buttons.

As an example, the `WithLabel` function lets the user enhance a flowlet with a label. It may be defined in terms the more general function `MapBody` (described in Section 3.1):

```
let WithLabel label =
    MapBody (fun body -> {body with Label = label})
```

As with formlets, more complex combinators are easily constructed by composing basic ones. To illustrate, the following function enhances a flowlet by combining a set of primitive combinators.

```
type ContactInfo  = | Email of string | ...

let ToEmail (inputString: Flowlet<string>)
    inputString
    |> Validator.IsEmail "A valid email address is required"
    |> Flowlet.Map Email
    |> Enhance.WithValidationIcon
    |> Enhance.WithTextLabel "Email"
```

The function accepts a string flowlet and returns a flowlet of the custom type `ContactInfo` extended with email validation. It also enhances the flowlet with a text label. The definition makes use of the F# *pipe operator* (`|>`) to increase readability by avoiding parentheses. The operator is defined as:

```
let (|>) x f = f x
```

Another example of a WebSharper flowlet combinator is the function `Many`. It transforms a flowlet of type `T` into a flowlet of type list of `T`, by enhancing it with an interface for inputting multiple values:

```
Many : Flowlet<'T> -> Flowlet<List<'T>>
```

The following flowlet definition combines `Many` with `ToEmail` from above, to define a flowlet for inputting a list of email addresses:

```
let Emails =
    Controls.Input ""
    |> ToEmail
    |> Enhance.Many
    |> Enhance.WithSubmitAndResetButtons
```

The **Many** combinator highlights the dynamic capabilities of flowlets. Figure 1 shows a screenshot of the rendered flowlet. The end user can add or delete emails dynamically by using the interface **Many** provides when rendered.

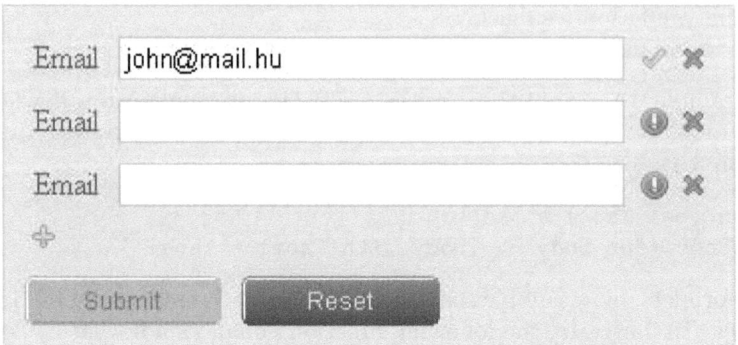

Fig. 1. Flowlet for inputting email addresses using *Many*

5 Related Work

Formlets [3,2] provide a direct inspiration for flowlets. Flowlets borrow the idea of type-safe compositional forms and the use of the applicative functor operators. Flowlets go further by providing additional dynamism and abstracting away from the HTML/CGI environment context in which formlets were originally developed.

Another relevant project is the iData/iTasks [12] system implemented in Clean. iData implements automatic derivation of HTML and AJAX editors for arbitrary data types, which is possible with Clean's generic programming facility. The scope of iTasks is much wider: they provide a distributed workflow system that coordinates the actions of many users employing iData to interact with them. We plan to implement the type-generic aspects of editor construction with WebSharper flowlets in the future.

Fudgets [1] provide an alternative early example of a functional programming approach to UI construction. This Haskell library composes UIs from stream processor elements, hiding the dataflow, mutation, and the X Window System details from the user. A denotational semantics for fudgets has been developed [14] by embedding them into π-calculus.

Several projects explore FRP systems with Haskell. Notably FranTk [13], a Tcl/Tk-based UI system supported by FRAN [7,6,8], a Haskell FRP library which models both real-time behaviors and discrete events. As FRAN is tailored to real-time reactivity and animations, its efficient implementation poses several challenges. Some of these were addressed in YAMPA [5], which uses *arrows* to statically prevent some of the space leaks common in such real-time dataflow systems. These ideas are not directly applicable in the context of WebSharper flowlets.

In the closer world of call-by-value languages, FrTime [4] uses Scheme to implement a dynamically updateable push-based dataflow graph and is capable of modeling animations. Flapjax [10], a related project, implements a similar system directly in JavaScript. WebSharper flowlets can be easily instantiated to work with Flapjax as the underlying FRP implementation.

6 Conclusions

In this paper we presented flowlets – a practical abstraction for dynamic user interfaces for collecting data. Flowlets support the same compositional operators as formlets [2]. In addition, flowlets extend formlets by providing a monadic interface to express dynamic dependencies.

We described the implementation of an F# library of generic flowlets and their combinators parametrized by the underlying widget and event stream implementations. By supplying a general mechanism for defining and plugging in custom layouts, the task of rendering flowlets is separated from the task of designing them. We also demonstrate how flowlets can be rendered efficiently by representing changes in their visual state as a stream of edit operations.

We also described a concrete implementation of flowlets based on WebSharper, a web application development platform for F# with a tool set that, among others, can compile F# code into JavaScript. WebSharper flowlets run in the browser and use DOM nodes for rendering. Flowlets provide a rich set of combinators to accommodate for common scenarios in web form construction; examples include dynamic validation feedback, multi-step forms, or enhancing with form labels, submit, and reset buttons.

Our experience with WebSharper flowlets suggests that flowlets dramatically simplify the task of building dynamic user interfaces by abstracting away the imperative structure of the underlying graphical components. The major direction for future work on flowlets is formalizing the semantics, in particular finding a formalism for flowlet equivalence and proving monad and applicative laws with respect to this equivalence notion. On the practical side, we also intend to continue improving our flowlet library and porting it to more programming environments and widget toolkits.

References

1. Carlsson, M., Hallgren, T.: FUDGETS: a Graphical User Interface in a Lazy Functional Language. In: FPCA 1993: Proceedings of the Conference on Functional Programming Languages and Computer Architecture, pp. 321–330. ACM, New York (1993)
2. Cooper, E., Lindley, S., Wadler, P., Yallop, J.: An Idioms Guide to Formlets. Technical report, University of Edinburgh (2008)
3. Cooper, E., Lindley, S., Wadler, P., Yallop, J.: The Essence of Form Abstraction. In: Sixth Asian Symposium on Programming Languages and Systems (2008)

4. Cooper, G., Krishnamurthi, S.: Embedding Dynamic Dataflow in a Call-by-Value Language. In: Sestoft, P. (ed.) ESOP 2006. LNCS, vol. 3924, pp. 294–308. Springer, Heidelberg (2006)
5. Courtney, A., Nilsson, H., Peterson, J.: The Yampa Arcade. In: Haskell 2003: Proceedings of the 2003 ACM SIGPLAN workshop on Haskell, pp. 7–18. ACM, New York (2003)
6. Elliott, C., Hudak, P.: Functional Reactive Animation. In: ICFP 1997: Proceedings of the Second ACM SIGPLAN International Conference on Functional Programming, pp. 263–273. ACM, New York (1997)
7. Hudak, P.: Functional Reactive Programming. In: Swierstra, S. (ed.) ESOP 1999. LNCS, vol. 1576, pp. 67–67. Springer, Heidelberg (1999)
8. Hudak, P., Courtney, A., Nilsson, H., Peterson, J.: Arrows, Robots, and Functional Reactive Programming. In: Jeuring, J., Jones, S. (eds.) AFP 2002. LNCS, vol. 2638, pp. 1949–1949. Springer, Heidelberg (2003)
9. Leroy, X.: The OCaml Programming Language (1998), http://caml.inria.fr
10. Meyerovich, L.A., Guha, A., Baskin, J., Cooper, G.H., Greenberg, M., Bromfield, A., Krishnamurthi, S.: Flapjax: a Programming Language for Ajax Applications. In: OOPSLA 2009: Proceeding of the 24th ACM SIGPLAN Conference on Object-Oriented Programming Systems, Languages and Applications, pp. 1–20. ACM, New York (2009)
11. Moggi, E.: Notions of Computation and Monads. Information and Computation 93(1), 55–92 (1991); Selections from 1989 IEEE Symposium on Logic in Computer Science
12. Plasmeijer, R., Achten, P.: The Implementation of iData. In: Butterfield, A., Grelck, C., Huch, F. (eds.) IFL 2005. LNCS, vol. 4015, pp. 106–123. Springer, Heidelberg (2006)
13. Sage, M.: FranTk - a Declarative GUI Language for Haskell. In: ICFP 2000: Proceedings of the Fifth ACM SIGPLAN International Conference on Functional Programming, pp. 106–117. ACM, New York (2000)
14. Taylor, C.J.: Formalising and Reasoning About Fudgets. Technical Report NOTTCS-TR-98-4, University of Nottingham (1998)

Author Index